Fried in a Hubcap:

Tales from the 70's

To Melessa —
So happy
to meet you.
Enjoy the
read.
♡ Sukoshi

Sukoshi Rice

This is a mostly true story, taken from memory. What I remember is not necessarily exactly what happened, just how I remember it. If you were there and you remember it differently, I look forward to reading your stories. If I offended anyone, sorry. I tried to say what I thought as kindly as possible. Well, honestly, anyway.

Copyright © 2018 Sukoshi Rice

ISBN-13: 978-1-970038-00-2

Ageless Hipster Press
PO Box 1602
Murphy, NC 28906
USA
Find us on Facebook:
Fried in a Hubcap: Tales from the 70's

DEDICATION

For Rasta and Pablo, the reasons for everything

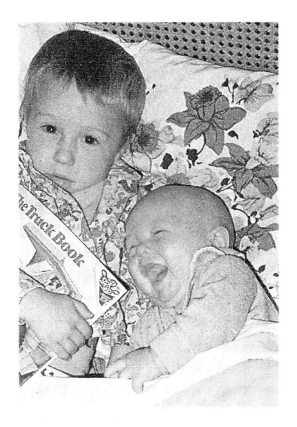

and for the One who makes everything possible.

CONTENTS

The Book of Doug

Geneva, Switzerland:
1966, 17, and on my own

Oh my God, they were gorgeous.

When the two most glamorous people I'd ever seen crunched to a stop right in front of me in their ridiculously luxurious, low-slung red convertible, I was ready for whatever came next. I'd just been sitting there waiting for something to happen, since things had to change. That was all I knew, and it turned out to be enough.

If I had known anything about praying, besides the terrifying nightly prayer "if I should die before I wake," I'd have said my prayers were answered, but I didn't. The only time I'd ever heard about people praying for something, our Catholic neighbors in Long Island had scraped together every penny to send the mother and their crippled infant son to Lourdes for a miracle. It hadn't worked, and my parents, who weren't big believers in miracles, even though they should have been, talked about it. My dad had lived through the Bataan Death March and years as a Prisoner of War in the Philippines. My mom had gone from poor girl in Alabama to fashion model in New York City. On the scale of human lives, those are both pretty miraculous. But the only exposure I'd had to answered prayer was hearing about that

1

one that hadn't worked. Maybe it was just chance, but I don't believe in anything accidental anymore. Now I see it as pure Grace that the world's swankiest red Lamborghini came to pick me up.

Here I was outside Geneva, Switzerland, where my dad Bert and his friend Geoff had arranged a summer job for me in a very high-end stable near Geoff's home. Geoff was a business friend of Bert's, portly, English, wealthy and snobby. My parents had two distinct kinds of friends, either adventurous and amazing or entitled and stuffy. Geoff was in the latter camp; I knew he'd be good if I got in a fix but I didn't want to see any more of him or his wife than I had to and still be polite. I had just left my own parents for the summer. I sure didn't want to pick up a surrogate set, especially ones who might be way less fun than my own, who would have been great to know as friends. My older brother Rocky was working a summer temp. job in Geneva, on the outskirts of the city, and Geoff was a phone call away, so I wasn't totally alone. But at the moment, I felt like it. It was only for a couple of months, until I went back to school in Boston, but I felt like it was going to be a long summer.

I had arrived from New York the night before and was picked up at the Geneva airport by Geoff, his wife, and my brother. We went out for an elegant dinner at a candlelit patio restaurant where I tried my first and last dish of osso buco, a stew of red wine and vegetables and oxtails, or veal tails. I'm an adventurous eater, but something about that meal didn't appeal. I was still two years out from being grossed out by a huge steak and becoming a vegetarian, so maybe it was jet lag, or that combined with such polite conversation. When we left the restaurant and drove to the stable, which looked pretty much like the stable at home, Geoff got out to make sure someone knew I was coming. Then they left, and my solo adventure began.

My room was huge and bare, with a single bed made for me, a table, chair, and a lamp. If the bed hadn't been made, I'm not sure what I would have done. Except for summer camp, where I resorted to a sleeping bag, I had never made my own bed. I'm not bragging about this at all; it's just how I was raised. Undoubtedly my parents thought this was a great advantage. My dad had grown up with servants; even when they went "broke" during the Depression, they had a maid, at least. My mom had grown up "poor as church mice" as she would have put it. After her father died when she was a young teen, her mom raised six children, and sent them all to college, on her wits, government chits, and sweet potatoes. My mom probably felt so happy to be able to have maids and nannies, but it was disabling for us, the kids. We didn't make our beds, clean our rooms, do our own laundry or help with household chores. I loved going off to school in the morning with my room all askew and coming home to find it all neat and put together. It took me years to figure out how *that* happened! No matter if parents think they are *always* going to be rich and their kids are *never* going to have to make their own way in the world, there are no guarantees. I look at my life, and the beds I've made!

My room above the stable was bare but clean; it would do. I could hear the horses snuffling around below, a comforting sound that allowed me to fall into a deep and exhausted sleep.

The next morning I cautiously crept downstairs toward the sound of voices. Four or five stable guys and one older woman stood in the kitchen, all speaking Basque, a language linguistically unrelated to any other European language. Everyone who worked there was Basque! My high school French was going to be worth just about squat here. Even my high school Spanish would be useless.

The woman asked me in very elementary French (like mine) what I wanted for breakfast and I told her toast, yogurt, fruit, cereal, milk, anything like that. She handed me a big thick slice of delicious homemade bread covered with

3

equally yummy fresh butter. Then she took a shallow metal pan off a high shelf and poured me a glass of thick, clotty, room temperature milk. Hmmmmmmm. I'd been thinking of nice cold milk from the fridge, or cold yogurt with the fruit in the bottom, but I was hungry and thirsty, so I went for it without a peep. It wasn't what I was used to; I didn't know what to expect, but I knew to roll with it and not say anything. It was a survival technique that was essential when living with my dad's PTSD. Keep your head down and your mouth shut was a good rule of thumb.

Then one of the guys nudged me and said it was time to clean the stalls.

Clean the stalls? Pardonnez-moi, but there must be some mistake! Clearly, or as clearly as we could all express ourselves in our French-as-a-second-language, that was what was expected of me. Here I was thinking I had been hired to be a riding instructor for the whole summer but I had just found out what I had instead was a job as a stable girl, cleaning stalls. I'd been teaching riding for a few years even though I was only seventeen, so thinking I'd been hired for that wasn't so far-fetched. Instead of being welcomed as the outside talent, I was going to be shoveling shit with the Basque stable boys.

This was *not* what my dad thought, or promised. He didn't speak French, or Basque. They could have told him anything! This was so not going to work: I could feel it, but at the moment I didn't see an option, so I followed my Basque mentor, aka the guy who was going to show me how to shovel the shit, out to the stalls.

I love horses, and these were top of the line: clean, shiny, expensive and well-cared-for. The smell of the stable was of hay and that soft yummy smell of horses, not of old manure since the stalls were close to immaculate, being cleaned not once but twice a day. Still, a 1000 lb. horse eliminates quite a bit. All that has to be removed, and fresh bedding brought in, requiring pitchforks, shovels, wheelbarrows and muscle. It's way outside my area of expertise or interest, but I gave it a shot.

One of the guys showed me on the first stall, cleaning the whole thing for me, so I batted my eyes and he "showed" me on one more. Then he wised up and left, and I cleaned two by myself. By then it was 10 or 11 in the morning and I still had six stalls to clean. Hmmm. This was not good, and required some contemplation in the sun before I continued.

I hadn't saved every penny of my clothes allowance for four years for *this!* Nearly every day of high school I had worn the same tan corduroy skirt, squirreling away my money so I could go to Europe when I graduated. I wasn't sure what I thought I would find in Europe, or what I expected, but I sure (as shit?) didn't think I'd find it at the end of a shovel. And so I went outside to rest and reconnoiter.

It's quite possible that some girls would have cried at this point, especially seventeen year old girls like me who'd had a predictable and easy life so far. But crying was not in my vocabulary. When my dad was in prison camp he learned very quickly that weakness meant death, and he translated that into a parenting program to keep his children safe. The few times I cried, I got hit. In his trauma infused thinking, crying could get me killed. I could say it wasn't in my nature to cry, but it might be in everyone's nature. Just some of us have it trained out of us.

I had only been sitting there in the sun for a couple of minutes when that elegant convertible came crunching to a halt on the gravel right in front of me. Out climbed a couple so glamorous and gorgeous, all I could do was stare. He was huge, with long red hair and a red moustache that twirled up at the ends. His leather coat was trimmed with fur, and he roared when he laughed.

She was light and beautiful. Her laugh was gentle and musical, and she floated across the gravel.

5

"Darling," she purred to him in some language I had never heard, "take her for a ride. She looks lonely."

I don't know what she really said to him, but turning to me she said, in heavily accented English, "Go. Go for a ride!" and urged me toward the car. It didn't take much urging. Behind me were six stalls that needed cleaning and the promise of more clotty milk. In front of me stood this gorgeous man and his sports car with leopard skin seats. I climbed in.

He didn't say a word; he just cranked that car out until we were flying. Around the stable were narrow lanes bordered by fences and hedges. As our speed picked up, I fearfully envisioned running into a herd of sheep, or someone opening a gate and losing an arm. But those fears couldn't stick. We were going too fast.

At something around 100 mph, he was roaring with laughter again, moustache flying in the wind. Somewhere around there, maybe 130 or so, I started laughing, too. What else was there to do? I couldn't hold tight or stay scared. It was way too much fun. I imagine this is what a roller coaster does to some people, when it just blows the scared right out of you.

When we got back to the stable, I went straight upstairs, put all my stuff back in my new travel suitcase, and moved into the city. I was *not* going to spend my summer cleaning stalls. My brother was staying in a lovely old building just a short walk from the famous Jet d'Eau, the huge fountain on Lake Geneva. I got a room right down the hall from him. He worked all day and slept at night; I slept late every day and played at night, so we had dinners together, the one intersection in our busy schedules.

I had saved enough clothes allowance to spend the rest of the summer sleeping late, meeting young people from all over the world and having fun. All my money would be spent by the end of summer, but that was ok. I wanted to have fun, not perfect my skills with a wheelbarrow. In the afternoons I'd walk down to the Jet d'Eau and sit around talking to the other young travelers there, making plans for the evening, either to meet up there or at a club. Sometimes I'd walk alone, just looking in store windows, especially bakeries. I didn't care about clothes, but was fascinated by how Swiss bakers turned loaves of bread into works of art. One window was full of huge curved loaves covered with bread stars, an inspiration for years later, when I became a baker.

Geneva is a beautiful city, very clean and basically safe. Or so I thought until I accepted a dinner date with a young Swedish businessman. He looked *exactly* like the guys my dad taught me were safe and desirable: short hair, suit and tie, plenty of money, smooth and worldly. What my dad didn't teach me was what to do when, instead of driving me home after a lovely dinner, this smooth handsome guy drove to a deserted place on the outskirts of town and started kissing me and then holding me down in his car. There were no lights on anywhere; I didn't know where I was. Where would I run to? And fight? He was bigger and stronger than me.

I guess I could have fought him for a while, if that was something I thought of. I'd never had to physically fight with anyone; it was not my natural response, and I was afraid if I did, he might beat me up. I tried begging, but that didn't work. In fact, it seemed to excite him more, my begging him to stop. I shut my eyes and hoped that was the worst of it, and it was. He might not have called it rape, since I didn't try to fight or run, but it was.

I didn't think about it much, or feel the trauma of it until 52 years later, when I was telling a friend about it while we were talking about the "Me, too" movement. She asked, "How old were you?" and I said, "17." When I saw the sadness on her face, I felt for the first time how sad and fucked up that was. It's the kind of thing, in my family, I would have been blamed for: my skirt was too short, I was too friendly, I would have been somehow in the wrong. And so I blew it off and never told anyone. It's not like I wasn't sleeping with boys I met; I was, but it was by choice, a mutual choice. I knew the difference pretty easily. One was fun and one was horrible.

One of the worst responses to this story came from another woman, who suggested that rape was too strong a word for what happened. This is a *woman* saying that I shouldn't call it rape. Maybe call it "sex I didn't want to have but I didn't get beaten up so it was really ok?" I guess that sounds better.

The morning after that, I left for Paris. It never occurred to me to go to the police. I didn't even know his last name, and I was just a young hippie chick and he was a businessman. Who would they believe? I wanted to get out of town. It was easy to travel: I bought a train ticket for Paris and off I went. There was another week before I was due to fly home with my brother, and I didn't want to be in Geneva like a sitting duck. The Swedish guy had called for another date before I even left my pensione for the train! I had to move. Going to Paris seemed like a wonderful alternative to telling him no and managing to avoid him for the next week. Besides, I'd never been to Paris.

A high school friend from Chappaqua was studying at the Sorbonne for the summer and she told me I could stay in the dorm with her. Along the Seine, on the quai, hippies from every country in the world, it seemed, gathered to drink cheap wine, eat if they could afford it, and smoke hash if they had it. That's what I did for a few days while my friend went to class.

I hung out long enough to meet some Finnish guys, drink a little too much red wine and eat baguettes, those long skinny crunchy loaves of white bread that cost about a dime, in those days. The idea was to eat enough bread to soak up some of the wine and not get too dizzy and whacked out drinking. I had never been a drinker, so I overestimated my tolerance by a good measure. When it was time to go back to my friend's dorm, one of the Finnish guys, the handsome blond-haired blue-eyed one, said he'd walk me there. By then I'd been talking with him and his equally gorgeous best friend for hours, and I already knew he spoke thirteen languages and was fun and sweet; I figured I'd be safer with him than walking alone, drunk, even though it wasn't far. It was all fun and games until he kissed me goodbye at the front door of the dorm and the world began to spin.

To my credit, I didn't throw up until I got to the bathroom. Those American student girls, the friend from home and a few others, could not have been nicer. They put me to bed, and wisely left me there 'til the next afternoon, when they came home from class and I was human again.

I wanted to take them out as thanks, since I was leaving the next day, so three of us walked to a little café they knew nearby. It was my friend Nancy from home and her best friend and me. Paris was all brand new and I had hardly seen any of it, besides hippie life at the quai and student life at the dorm. Three young Arab guys at the café started talking to us. They were cute and friendly, wanted to show us Paris, and had a car. We were in.

You might think after the mess in Geneva, I'd be more nervous around men and boys, but I wasn't. The Finnish guy from the day before was a total hippie, probably with torn old blue jeans, and he was so nice. As to the Arab guys, I didn't think twice because there were three of us girls and it felt like it would be fine, especially since the other two girls, smart Sorbonne students, were so enthusiastically agreeable to it.

We got into an old Deux Chevaux and took off to see the sights. After riding around all squished up together and having one of those laughing can't really speak the language conversations for a while, I had to pee. There was no getting around it, and I think the guys really didn't know what to do about it. In Paris there were pissoirs on the streets where men could take a piss, but what was a girl to do? After much debate, we went to where they lived, a small apartment building on a quiet and not very well lit street. Two of the guys stayed out with the car; one walked us in. I'm not sure if the other girls had to pee, but we were for sure sticking together.

We had to put a coin in a little slot to even get the light to go on in the hallway, and then we walked up a flight of stairs to the bathroom. I know from comparing my memories to what I have written in old journals that memory can be tricky and not trustworthy, but here's what I remember:

I opened the door into a room about eight by ten feet. When I turned on the light, which I didn't have to pay to turn on since we paid downstairs, I was in a completely bare room with a hole in the middle of the floor. No sink, no toilet, nada. There were piles of human shit all over the room. Not *all* over, but a bunch of them. What the hell, I had to pee, so I got as close to the hole as I could, picking my way carefully along, squatted carefully and relieved myself. When I came out in the hallway where the other two girls were waiting, I told them what was in there. In one voice they said, "I'll hold it," and we were off to the Sorbonne and our nice clean beds and lovely clean indoor toilets.

That was the absolute nastiest bathroom I'd ever seen or heard of. It was an eye opener, a warning of more to come in years of travel. People live like this, with one horrible nasty roomful of poop and pee for a whole apartment building? I've been to lots of bathrooms in lots of countries since then, but that was the <u>worst</u> I've *ever* seen or had to use, and in the "City of Lights," too.

As far as I was concerned, Paris was a success! I got drunk for the first time, got kissed by a handsome Finnish hippie, spent my nights at the Sorbonne and got away from Geneva and the Swedish guy. The next morning I caught the train back to Geneva just in time to pack and fly home with my brother. He was headed back to Brown and I was starting at Boston U. I hadn't ever considered whether or not I really wanted to go to college. I had never considered an option, such as working. Everyone I knew and was friends with was going to college, so I did, too.

The Book of Glenn

Boston in the Sixties-1966

The West Coast was jumpin' with "love-ins" and acid consciousness expanding in every direction. The Doors, Country Joe and the Fish, Jefferson Airplane, Haight Ashbury: it was all happening. Meanwhile, three thousand miles away, I drove down tree-lined Bay State Road in Boston with my mom and dad to my assigned dormitory housing in an old converted brownstone. I was going to college!

Station wagons were parked up and down the street, full of suitcases and rugs and lamps. I had new skirt and sweater sets, having read with my mother, and accepted as law, the Boston University guideline that "all female students are to be properly attired in skirts, not pants." Just like high school where we had to wear skirts unless the temperature was below ten degrees, the same rule applied in Boston, which was even colder.

You might find that hard to believe now, and the rule did change the first month I was there. When it did, I went straight downtown with my new roommate Margie, and we bought the tightest, most flared black and silver striped bell bottoms we could find. With black turtlenecks, we were stylin'. As if I knew what stylin' was, being from Chappaqua and arriving in the big city for the first time.

Well, not exactly the first time. From the time I was fifteen I started going in to NYC alone on the train, and coming home on the last one at night. I told my parents I was going to a museum, but what I really did was hang around Washington Square Park and meet beatniks. This older guy Bill gave me drugs and a free trip to the public health clinic. It's painful to think about what a messed up kid I must have been to have left my comfortable, upper-middle-class home in Chappaqua to go to Washington Square Park and meet up with this thirty-something-year-old semi-homeless beatnik bum, smoke pot and have sex in someone's apartment in the East Village. In my defense, he was an interesting artist: I used to have a self-portrait he did in pastels, kind of van Gogh-ish, very gaunt and haunted.

And my trip to public health, while not something I am even borderline proud of, stands in my memory because I'd just never seen people like this. There was one woman ranting about her VD, saying she got it from the dirty toilets on Second Avenue. I didn't have anything; I didn't have to go back. I was supremely grateful for that.

Why I didn't have higher self-esteem is still a mystery to me. The only thing I can figure is my dad was trying to hold me to such ridiculously high standards that the only "power" I had was proving him wrong. Knowing my own nature, this is the only explanation that makes any sense..

When a policeman came to my parents' house because one of my high school "friends" told the cops I had gone to the city and come back with pot, I was sitting up in my room doing my homework or talking on the phone. It was seriously not something I was expecting. I never liked the girl who told the police about me, because she was "worried about me and told for my own good." I especially didn't like her after that.

My father came up the stairs to get me. He almost *never* came up to the third floor, where my brother Rocky and I had our bedrooms. When he did, it was not good. This time his blue eyes were blazing, also a bad sign. "There's a policeman downstairs who told me you have been smoking marijuana. I know that's not true because if you had, I could see it in your eyes, but you'd better come talk to him."

It didn't take much; there wasn't even a good cop/bad cop routine. It was just this one cop, and my dad, Bert. I folded in seconds and immediately spilled out Bill's first and last names because the policeman scared me a little and my dad scared me a lot.

Seriously, what the hell was a middle-class teenage girl from Chappaqua doing hanging out in Washington Square Park all day with beatniks and drug addicts? What were my parents thinking when I got home at midnight from a day at the museum? What kind of museum stays open that late? (None.) Once I became a mother, someone had to tell me it was my job to check on where my sons were going and what movie they were going to see and how they were getting there and home. I didn't know the first thing about parenting.

When I look back, my parents were unnaturally strict about some things and totally lax about others. Mostly my dad was crazy strict and my mom just didn't want to deal with the minutia of raising children. They must have thought I knew how to navigate, because I didn't get much guidance. I know people who did, whose parents actually sat down and talked with them. But I don't remember much of that unless it was my mom, Gaham, telling stories from her life when my dad was away and she was drinking alone. They were good stories, for the most part, but they didn't help me figure out anything about life, except that my mom had had a pretty fun life before she got married. She had moved to New York City from Alabama to be a fashion model like her older sister who was already there. They drank and partied and worked. My mom lived with two gay guys and even tried smoking weed, which she didn't care for. She and her sister drank lots of champagne and dated all manner of fabulous men.

One of my favorite vignettes of her life was when she and her sister Lizzie ordered a bottle of champagne, because they both had a free afternoon. Those were the days when liquor stores delivered. After the first bottle, they had another delivered, and all through the afternoon they sat and drank and laughed and had bottle after bottle delivered. Until she was in her mid-90's, Gaham had a pretty healthy tolerance for alcohol and I guess, from this story, that Lizzie did, too.

Gaham liked her edgy life and was to the end of it free of prejudice about things like being gay or drinking and smoking. She pretended to be the girlfriend when one of the gay guys' moms was visiting. All that came to a screeching halt when she married Bert, who was homophobic and as we already know, not fond of marijuana. He was the much loved son of Jewish immigrants who had made a lot of money, then lost most of it in the Depression. He was charming and witty, a smart ass and a control freak. My mother's dry wit and soft Southern charm withered under his criticism.

Here I am, rolling into my 70th trip around the sun, and I'm just beginning to understand why I've had so much trouble having a healthy relationship. My brothers, too. What did we know but fighting and undermining, criticism and covert warfare? My biggest fascinations with men have been focused on guys who thought they hung the moon, even guys who have been critical of me. The nice, supportive men I've been with didn't give me a big enough run for my money and I usually left them for some asshole who was more challenging.

As a teenager, I intuitively knew what was going to be trouble, like staying out until 3 a.m., but I saved most of that for when my dad was out of town, whenever possible. I had my own car, I had a horse at a nearby stable, I had my

18

clothes allowance, and my friends loved to stay at my house and talk to my mom. She was cool because you could come to our house, when Bert was away, and get stoned or drunk and talk to her and she'd be fine with it. When one of our friends would come and get really stoned, she'd say, "Freddy will be really hungry when he gets up from his nap," and actually start putting food together for him. In that way, she was so sweet.

You could talk to Gaham about anything, and she was home most of the time, when she wasn't at the Garden Club or doing good deeds. She was everyone's favorite mom, not very motherly, but lots of fun and so understanding, unless you were one of her children or, more specifically, me. A couple of times I confided in her and later heard her mockingly sharing my story with her snobby friends from the Garden Club. Add difficulty in trusting women's friendship to the pile.

Bert, on the other hand, was a challenge. He had big expectations for all of us, so when he went to Hong Kong for three months every fall, it was party time. When he was gone, things got pretty ridiculously lax, but when he came home, oh baby! Then we had to straighten our asses out in a hurry: no more friends getting stoned and sleeping all over the place. No more impromptu anything.

My parents drank daily and often to excess, and when my mom was alone with me, and drinking, she would tell me about Bert's affairs and how she couldn't get a divorce because he wouldn't support us if she left him. She could confide in me, because she knew I was good for it. Who was I going to tell that my dad didn't love us enough to support us, which was my interpretation?

When he was home, he was my great supporter, even though I was never good enough, never living up to the greatness he saw in me. The pressure to be better and better, to live up to his crazy and unrealistic expectations, made me nuts. He simultaneously adored and berated me, to the point

19

that it was not uncommon for me to leave the family dinner table to go throw up. He was unrelenting. It was supposed to encourage me to live up to my potential, but what it did was make me anxious and angry and rebellious and confused, resenting and loving him as much as he adored and berated me.

Good God, no wonder I had eating issues and threw up lots of days and couldn't wait to get away from their crazy asses! I loved them both, but they were seriously driving me insane with all their own unresolved shit.

I craved love and security, but like most girls from alcoholic and unbalanced families, I didn't know the first thing about how to create that. I didn't know anything about being kind and loving with someone. All I saw between my parents was spitefulness and obligation. I don't remember friendliness, good will or kindness between them. What I do remember is an ongoing battle of wills; for years, all my relationships were about getting what I wanted, getting my seemingly endless needs met. One day I even said out loud, "oh no, 'relationship' must mean you have to relate to the other person! They must have needs, too!" And I laughed. Ha ha. I was about sixty when I figured that much out. So I went looking for love in all the wrong places, and admittedly, when I wasn't about to kill myself over how bad I felt or how many drugs I'd taken, I had some good times, too.

My parents were both big on how we were supposed to act and supposed to be. There was an unspoken code of how "good" people, aka "socially acceptable people," act. There wasn't much emphasis on *being* ok or feeling well with yourself, but there was plenty on appearing that way. On the late train coming home I'd run into one of my parents' best friends, drunk as a skunk. There was no way he could drive, so I'd take him home. He was a nice guy and never gave me any bullshit about how people were supposed to be; of course, he didn't have much of a pedestal to climb on. I had the feeling he got plenty of lectures at home, too, knowing his wife as I did. Alcohol was the fuel that allowed the adults in my world to tell the truth, have fun and be themselves. All my parents friends drank; I saw most of them shit-faced drunk at least a time or two. My mother fell down sometimes, or burned the dinner. I'm sure they did too, in the privacy of their own homes.

So Boston, and going to college, was a real break for me. Europe had been fun, but now I was going to actually be living somewhere away from my parents, not just visiting. That first day my sophomore advisor, HS, showed up in my dorm room. My parents had just left on the four hour drive back to Chappaqua and in comes this gorgeous girl, with long silky black hair to her waist, asking me if I want to go out and get high! As sophomore advisors are supposed to do, she pretty much set the tone for my college career.

The student union was the center of social life. On one side was food, a huge cafeteria style place open from early morning to late at night. On the other was the library, which I rarely frequented unless a class required it. I was there to escape the suburbs and gather life experience, not to learn anything specific. The idea of learning was integrated, not a separate intellectual activity. Surely this is part of why my college career foundered and I dropped out. The more obvious reason is all the drugs I was taking.

We all ate at the Union and hung out people-watching between classes. It's where I met most of the guys I dated, and where a construction worker actually let me run his bulldozer as he was clearing some space out front. Talk about OSHA and FEMA and every other safety organization! In 1966, we were on less of a safety rampage and it probably was funny to him, this cute eighteen year old girl wanting to drive the bulldozer. It's actually how I met my first college boyfriend Alan, who was beautiful, New York City sophisticated, and knew quite a bit about designer drugs. He told me when he saw me driving that bulldozer he thought, "I have got to meet this chick!"

Alan and I spent the first six months or so of our freshman year together. He came from a wealthy family and was just the best, sweet and smart and gorgeous. I had visions of a life together, picket fence and all. I fell crazy in love with him in first real love innocence. We smoked DMT regularly, a wild kind of hallucinogenic drug that made LSD look like a walk in the park, when I finally took that. We would smoke and listen to Al Kooper and the Blues Project, "I Can't Keep from Crying Sometimes." I'd watch a net of patterns cover the room in time with the music. I don't know what we really had going on besides that, and sex, and beauty. Most of our time together was spent getting high and having sex, and it wasn't enough for him. We were just kids taking drugs, so when he found someone new, someone older and more stable, whom he eventually married, I was heartbroken. A few years later he died in a tragic accident, diving into shallow water and breaking his neck. By then it had been years since I had seen him and the news made me sad for him, his wife, and all our mutual friends, but I had pretty much spent my heartbreak over him years before.

Occasionally I had dinner with a three hundred fifty pound college senior who lived in the single room on our floor. Every afternoon she ate a loaf of white bread and a pound of Velveeta cheese and drank a quart of apple juice, then locked herself in the shower and sobbed. Then she hardly ate any dinner. People wondered how she could be so huge when she "ate like a bird."

I'd pound on the bathroom door while she wailed and yell at her for using up all the hot water. It might have seemed cruel, but I was the only one who paid any attention to her crying at all, and it was the only way I could think of to get her to stop. When I was growing up I got hit if I cried, so she was getting off easy.

My dad's years in Japanese prison camp during WWII had enforced this belief that crying could get you killed. Of course in prison camp it was true, but it terrified him when I cried because to him it meant I was putting myself in danger. I still rarely cry even if I feel like it. If I really feel like I have to, I can put on "Out of Africa," and watch the scene where Meryl finds out that Denys (aka Robert Redford) has crashed his plane and died. That does the trick. Hope that wasn't a spoiler for anyone, but if you haven't seen a thirty year old movie by now, you're probably not going to.

Of my three roommates, two were normal, cheerful American girls. And then there was Margie, a teen model from upstate NY. It was the Twiggy era, which fit Margie to a T. She wore cute little mini-dresses and tights, boots, false eyelashes and fake hair called falls, gigantic ponytails you clipped into your hair. Margie and I had obviously both grown up with maids; our end of the huge room was a warren of never made beds with clothes piled everywhere. I at least wore clean clothes, but Margie would get up in the morning, all plain and unadorned. She'd wash her face and brush her teeth, reach under her bed, pull out a dress, sniff the armpits, and if it passed, shake it out and put it on. She'd layer on the makeup, mostly eye makeup, with thick false eyelashes, comb back her short hair, which she almost never washed, and stick a long fall on, but only after she shook out the dust bunnies. The effect was ravishing. The boys went wild, I kid you not.

Margie and I would be great friends for awhile, then not. We were both freaky characters, and we didn't fit in with most of the girls in the dorm, middle class Jewish girls who sat in the Common Room every afternoon and watched soap operas. She and I didn't sit in the Common Room the entire year, unless we had a mandatory house meeting. There was a house boss who lived on the ground floor and we were on the third floor. Every available spot was bedrooms. There were five of us on the top floor with one bathroom. I didn't remember it ever being a problem until years later when I was trying to pare things down after my mother's death and found letters I had written home, telling my parents how hard dorm life was because I couldn't study for all the noise and comings and goings.

Funny thing is that in my memory, I was the one coming and going, but I was also trying like hell to pass biology, which was like taking a class taught in classical Russian. I studied, I got weekly tutoring, and I managed to squeak by with a D. Obviously it was a forbidden subject for me, or as a Great Master told me years later, "It was obviously not information meant for you."

Although all of the girls in the dorm were supposed to be in by a certain time, I still felt freer than I had at home where I basically ran wild. No one at home offered guidance or advice, just punishment when I crossed the invisible line. That line shifted with moods, with alcohol intake (more lenient) or lack of it (bitchy and serious!) There was a certain security in knowing the rules, where the line was, and how far I could bend it.

In Boston I found two things: more drugs and lots more people like me. I was free in Chappaqua, except there wasn't much to do. Now there was music in the cafes at night and liberation in the air. The effect was electric; it didn't take me long to find my tribe.

There were girls my age, young women of 18 or so, who had lives so different from mine. One of them was Connie, a beautiful young woman from Los Angeles with a highly developed intellect and sense of self. I had learned to avoid emotional intimacy while Connie felt empowered to examine and contemplate life. If my inner center was a riot of noise and deflection, hers was a pool of quiet observation. She was short, with long red hair and large, dramatic kohl-rimmed eyes. Her best friend was Amy, teeny like Connie, around five feet tall, and also quite an intellect. I wasn't used to seriousness and focus; I felt threatened by closeness and intimacy, by people wanting to really know me. But I liked and looked up to them both, so one night I accepted their invitation to go over to Harvard and meet the

Maharishi. This was 1966, before he became famous as the Beatles' Guru.

We entered a room that held about thirty people, although it wasn't full. There was a small group of gentle, long-haired, long-skirted young women, and a contingent of smart-ass, smart-as-hell young Harvard guys. The Maharishi came in, a teeny little man no bigger than Connie and Amy, with long graying hair and beard. He sat on a chair with a tiger skin on it. His demeanor was extremely friendly and giggly.

I don't remember what he said, but I do remember those Harvard boys asking him rude questions, challenging everything from his authenticity to his spiritual knowledge. Every single question was answered with kindness, good humor and certainty. He never defended himself or tried to make those boys look bad. His humility and sense of play won the day for me. I wanted what he was having.

So I signed up for the secret mantra initiation. I still remember the mantra, sort of, but we were never to tell because it was a special mantra just for each of us. Of course I didn't get it directly from the Maharishi, but from one of his devotees, a guy named Jerry who had been trained to initiate people to Transcendental Meditation. There were a few of us at his apartment that night, and we each got our mantra, for $35 apiece.

I tried my best to use that mantra, and occasionally it would bring me to a really wonderful peaceful state, but usually I fell asleep. I preferred smoking weed. It was just so much *easier*, and didn't require the first iota of discipline, a gene I seemed to be lacking.

After Alan broke up with me, I started dating JP, an Irish New Yorker in his mid- thirties who told me he was hiding from the New York Mafia. His story was that he had been *in* the Mafia, but wouldn't carry a real gun. Somehow he ran afoul of them and came to hide out with his friends Ricky and DJ in Cambridge. JP introduced me to a whole new world, which was pretty easy for a street-wise Brooklyn rat to do with a girl from Chappaqua. Growing up in the country, my exposure to clubs that stayed open all night and the music and musicians that fuelled them was non-existent. JP had been a music promoter, before becoming a refugee from the Mafia, so he knew lots of people in the business.

While this whole new world wasn't necessarily one I wanted to live in, parts of it fascinated me. I've always been a sucker for adventure, and for the men who would introduce me to something new, so when he announced, with great delight, that he had somebody he wanted me to meet in the city that night, I was all for it. We were going to see Tiny Tim, who JP said, was "really a trip." I'll say!

This was before Tiny got well known by appearing on the Ed Sullivan show, so we went to some scuzzy club in midtown Manhattan and watched his act. He was a huge human raven, with long stringy greasy looking black hair hanging in his face, a long beaklike nose and long skinny fingers on his teeny ukulele. It was definitely an effect he had worked on. When JP introduced us, Tiny extended a soft wet fish of a hand and trilled, "Oh Miss Koshie!"

He was to repeat that several times as we drove him up to his mom's apartment in the Bronx, where he still lived at the age of forty five or so. JP had a Porsche, so Tiny and I were crushed together in the front seat. Every turn brought on another trill, "Oh Miss Koshie!" alternating with, "Oh, Mr. Jimmy!"

What I remember from that predawn breakfast was that Tiny admired my scarf. I liked it too. My high school boyfriend had given it to me right off his neck. It was cream wool, hand knitted. Tiny fingered it and trilled over it until I said, "Here, you want to see it?" It went around his neck and never graced mine again. When I tried to get it back, he had gone deaf.

"Oh Miss Koshie!" He was such a weird scammy hustler. He had a free breakfast and a free ride home to the Bronx, and he still hustled me out of my scarf. JP laughed his ass off about it. "Yeah, that's Tiny."

"Yeah, thanks, asshole."

JP and I were together for a few months, and after we had broken up, he asked me to marry him! I was still only eighteen, and that was about the last thing on my mind. Had I known he would be the last one who ever formally officially asked, I might have paused as I pushed him out the door to get dressed for a date with someone else. I knew I didn't want to get married to him. I'd wanted to marry Alan, but we were like two kids playing. JP was a grown man, and he was seriously asking.

JP died years ago after running two of the hottest, most popular clubs in New York City. He never outgrew his love of young girls, from what I heard, but cancer won.

My professors at college were in the middle of the consciousness revolution along with the rest of us. I was in what was considered an advanced liberal arts school of Boston U., so it attracted more eclectic students and professors.

My favorite professor called me in to his office after class one day. I had an instant flashback to my dad: I was usually in trouble if I got singled out like this. This time the professor just wanted to ask me if I had ever taken mescaline! I hadn't, and he had, and had no context for the beauty of his experience, so he wanted to tell *me* about it. *Me!* Telling his eighteen year old freshman student about his trip must have seemed like a reasonable idea at the moment.

I tried my hand at protesting. Vietnam was the issue of the day and every caring and aware young person was appalled and protesting. I was against the Vietnam War on general principles, but don't remember concerning myself with much of what went on in the world. I was just happy to be out of the confined homogeneous world of upper middle class white Chappaqua. What was going on in the rest of the world didn't seem to concern me very much or often. I was skittering across the surface and taking too many drugs, but I knew it was an issue I ought to stand up for (against) so I gave it my best shot. In early 1967, I went to a Radical Women's Meeting in Cambridge.

We were sitting in a circle introducing ourselves when the woman next to me, a lesbian in black leather, slid her hand up my thigh and said, "I think you'll make a great radical chickie."

A great radical chickie? I was up and out of there, uncomfortable and confused. I have never been good at confrontation. There's no way I was going to stand up for myself in a roomful of hipster women I'd never met before. I thought I was there to help save the world, and instead, it was my little black leather miniskirt. The only logical move was to stop protesting, at least with this group. Before it even got off the ground, my career as a radical woman was done for.

Still, I tried again at a demonstration by the SDS (Students for a Democratic Society) about dorm conditions at BU. My dorm conditions had been great, but apparently the big new dorms had some issues. A bunch of kids came out swinging dead rats the size of kittens. I had never seen anything like it. We were supposed to march around with these dead rats so that conditions would improve. I thought hiring a good attorney and taking legal action would work better, and the rats were disgusting, so I didn't stay. But it worked. I heard later that the University sent a representative down to make some promises because they didn't want people to see the rats and know they had been negligent, but I was way down Commonwealth Ave. by then, maybe driving JP's Porsche. He lent it to me all the time and drove my little beater, just to be sweet.

JP and I were sitting in his car parked on Commonwealth one afternoon when someone pulled in to parallel park in the spot in front of us. JP leaned over to me, "If he so much as touches the bumper, Baby, bang your head into the dashboard."

I looked at him like he was surely insane.

"Insurance," was his one word explanation. "It's what I live on."

It was a world I had never experienced before, and while it was fun for a while, it definitely wasn't what I wanted to marry into.

Somewhere after JP, I met Glenn. It was probably at the Student Union where I would hang out with my new little dog, Arthur. Arthur was a rescue from the local pound, the cutest and smartest of dogs. Glenn had just given his own dog away because he didn't have time for him, and stopped to play with Arthur. The rest was kismet.

We were immediately together. Neither of us raised any questions about it for years, like what we wanted our lives to be like, whether we wanted children, country or city, that sort of thing. We fell into bed and when we got up a few days later, we were a couple.

When Glenn asked me to move to Brooklyn with him in a few months after he graduated law school, it was clear. Since all I was doing with college was taking drugs and wasting my parents' money, it seemed like not only a good idea, but the most obvious path ahead. I wanted to be with him; we were getting along great and had fun and loved being together.

A new life awaited me in Brooklyn. For one thing, I had to get a job. Glenn had a job. Along with almost all our male friends, he was teaching in an inner city school, a draft deferred job. Our friends were all college graduates. Without a college degree, things would have been more difficult. The

29

Vietnam War was raging but there were a few jobs that deferred you; teaching at an inner city school was one.

Of course, there were other draft deferments besides teaching, like being the sole support of your family, or physical conditions, or being a homosexual or a drug addict. The things guys did to get deferred could have killed them. *Every* young male was subject to the draft, and even if they nearly killed themselves with speed or acid or not sleeping or whatever, it often didn't work.

Guys sometimes didn't sleep or eat or bathe for a week before their intake interviews. They swore they were gay. They took acid and wore dresses. They did anything and everything they could think of, including crossing the border into Canada, sometimes leaving their homes and families for years. One of my friends, a gorgeous guy with long blond hair and big blue eyes, went to his intake interview in a pretty floral dress, kind of a flouncy little frock, after taking speed and acid for a week or two. They asked him if he was homosexual and his answer was, "Bring me a chicken and I'll fuck it." Even though lots of ploys didn't work, I think he got his deferment.

My concerns about the war were so localized: I worried about guys being drafted and what they had to do to avoid it. I don't remember worrying about the people of Vietnam. I wasn't a news watcher and it was all so abstract and so far away.

Then on December 1, 1969, the Selective Service instituted the lottery. The Draft Lottery. Every birthday had a number attached to it, chosen at random. If yours was chosen between #1 and #100, you were pretty sure of going. But if your number was 100 to 200, you could breathe a little easier. The higher the number, the less chance of being sent to Vietnam. Some of the guys I knew who had become teachers kept doing it, but others stopped if their numbers were high enough and they felt safe to give that up and get on with their lives.

I had it easy. I just needed a job because we needed two incomes, small as they were, to live in Brooklyn in our own place. Well, it wasn't really our own place, at first. We found an awesome duplex that we shared with our friend Freddy, who left a candle burning one night while he took his girlfriend back to Manhattan and the place burned down. Glenn, Arthur the dog and I stood on the sidewalk while the firemen hosed and chopped, and when they were finished, the fire was out and the place was unlivable.

After a brief stint with Glenn's Grandma Betty, who refused to learn my name because Glenn and I weren't married, we found a big studio overlooking Prospect Park, with room just for us. And I looked for a job.

The first one I found was answering the phone for a fundraising company. I'm good at talking on the phone, but hardly anyone ever called, so I wandered the building meeting the neighbors. Lucky for me, Marshall McLuhan's publisher Jerry Agel and his graphic designer Quentin Fiore were right down the hall. *The Medium is the Message* had just come out, and they were hot. One day we were talking about the new politics of protest, which I thought of as a derailment of the beauty of the acid/consciousness movement. Quentin told me protest expressed the "poetics of despair," a phrase I liked well enough to save in my journal for fifty years.

How did I get to wander around when I was supposed to be answering the phone? Easy. My job was 9 to 5, but no one else came in until 11 a.m. Pretty soon I was sliding in about 10:45, since there was nothing to do there anyway. The devil does indeed find work for idle hands. I started going out to lunch with a married man I knew from Chappaqua. It all started innocently enough when I asked if he could help me get a better job, and he suggested we talk about it over lunch. When he picked me up in a nice stretch limo, I admit that impressed me.

He was fun. Pretty soon we were having two and three hour lunches complete with smoking pot and doing what came naturally. Glenn, a proponent of open marriage, never asked me anything about it. I was confused, guilty, and having fun all at the same time.

One word about married men: don't. It's unfair for everyone, most of all his wife. If you are married to someone who philosophically supports it, as I came to be, it should be smooth. But it wasn't. It didn't feel right, but it was so tempting and fun that I did it anyway. I wouldn't have done it but for the expensive lunches, the limos and most of all, the dangled promise of a great new job. OMG you'd think I was born yesterday.

My hours didn't suit my employer, but by the time they fired me, I was already headed down 57th Street to my new job, selling shoes at Henri Bendel, the most exclusive boutique department store in the city. Selling shoes? I went through all that to get a job selling shoes?

Of course there was a whole long story about the job he was *going* to get me with the up and coming designer Betsey Johnson. But first I had to learn all about different styles of shoes, which landed me at Bendel's in one of the most fun jobs I ever had. Our boss, a very effete man in his late 50's or so, didn't care what we did as long as we sold shoes.

I'd go in the stockroom and snort some speed with Billy, the guy who stocked the shelves, then come out and be the top seller, day after day. My boss kindly took me aside and said, "You are the best advertisement for drugs I've ever met." Uhh, thanks, I guess.

The shoe manager was a Southern gal who had come to New York to be a model, but soon realized she couldn't stand strange men handling her body, so she turned to selling shoes. She knew how to cheat a time card and walk out with a free new pair of shoes. In the hustle and bustle of New York, she and her husband were a breath of fresh air. In their dining room was the wooden table they had brought with them from Tennessee, and visitors were encouraged to carve their names into its surface.

She taught me all her tricks of the trade, shoe-wise. Glenn sometimes picked me up at their place, and then we'd go over to Max's Kansas City to meet friends for dinner. I knew it was supposed to be a totally happening place, but all I ever did there was eat my dinner while my friends watched for celebrities. I saw plenty of those at work.

Bendel's was fun. I saw famous actresses and models and got lots of new shoes, but the subway was the subway and a job is a job. When Glenn offered me a way out of working, I jumped at it.

One day during that first year he said, "If we're going to travel, either you have to keep working or we get married." We had talked about travel, something we both wanted to do. That was an easy call for me, as I very conveniently overlooked the ramifications of choice B.

Unlike Grandma Betty, my parents didn't really care if we got married or not. They were big believers in living together for a year or two before marriage, just to be sure. Having been raised religiously Baptist (my mom) and conservatively Jewish (my dad) they did not subscribe to dogma, except their own. I told them our plan, but told my mother I wouldn't get married in the 60's; once we got to 1970, we were home free. On January 31, 1970 we had a small and beautiful wedding at the house in Chappaqua. I had to take three Valiums to go through with it, but I did it.

My parents -- and God rest their souls on this and everything else -- had given me a horrible model of what marriage meant. Theirs was one of unaddressed anger, silent treatments, workaholism, infidelity and alcoholism. I had never seen, and never did see, any sign of affection between them, not the first hug or kiss or even really a warm smile.

Nada. Their relationship often seemed to have one purpose: to undermine each other. No wonder I took Valium; it wasn't looking good from my perspective.

Of course I *liked* Glenn a lot, but marrying him? My favorite wedding picture is this one -- with Lenny! I didn't know a good reason to get married, but travel seemed like one. As it turned out, it wasn't -- a miscalculation that hurt him, his family and mine. It was not a good enough reason to get married, as most people reading this probably already know. But I didn't.

My Brooklyn Life of Leisure

Glenn and I were getting married! I didn't have to work anymore! The second sentence excited me much more than the first.

I enrolled in pottery school at the Brooklyn Museum of Art. It was heaven, walking to school every morning along Prospect Park and hanging out all day with Artists. I never got very good at throwing pots, but I did have a good time. And did I mention: I didn't have to go to work!

One morning I was walking along the park when some construction guys started whistling and catcalling me. I immediately turned one of my feet in and dragged it in a limp and they stopped right away. It was hard work to walk like that, but I did it until I was well past them. When I told the chubby German woman in class about it, she puffed out her sizeable chest and asked, "Vy vould you do dat? I *luff* ven dey vistle at me!"

I didn't love when they whistled at me. I hated that kind of attention but I was pretty amazed that changing my walk stopped it. I still had the same face and body, but I somehow knew that would back them off. I felt sad about it, thinking of all the pretty girls who might not be thought of as attractive because they had a limp. At the same time, I was glad it worked for me.

That German potter went on to open a sweet little pottery shop in the East Village. On Christmas Eve Glenn and I went in and did all our Christmas shopping between 10pm and midnight in her shop and the one next door. It was snowing; all the shops had hot cider and mulled wine, and it remains my favorite Christmas present buying experience ever.

About this time, I started getting obscene phone calls. Now that we all have caller ID, they rarely happen anymore, but they used to be such a common occurrence that one of my friends would say, "Hang on, let me get a cigarette," at the first sign.

I was getting these calls during the day, when Glenn was at work. The guy would breathe hard and say scary stuff like, "I'm watching you. I see you going to the park every day with your little dog," which I did. This went on at random hours for several weeks. Glenn said not to answer the phone when I was home alone, but I have had a love affair with the phone since I learned to dial and I just couldn't resist.

One day the caller was describing my routine in such detail that I called Glenn's school in a complete hysterical panic. His little students all called me Miss Miniskirt, and Miss Miniskirt had hit her wall. Glenn came home to be with me until I could get it together again but I couldn't; I went back to school with him and sat outside on the wall until the school day ended.

The next time the guy called, he said something really odd, a specific little turn of phrase, and all of a sudden I knew who it was. This guy we knew was in dental school and was an absolute master of excess. He and his girlfriend had sex about ten times a day. I'm serious. He was never satisfied, and she always looked exhausted. I knew it was him and said his name, and he never called again.

He was so excessive he ended up in the hospital at least once from overeating, where he physically damaged himself with so much food. First he ate a whole pizza and then a seafood linguine dinner. I know the last thing he ate that night was an entire Entenmann's Blackout Cake, a chocolate cake so rich and potentially lethal they no longer make it. He's probably single-handedly responsible for that.

And then, as if the obscene phone calls weren't bad enough, one night one of Glenn's friends decided he had to kill me.

That was Buzzy, and the extenuating circumstance was the heavy use of PCP. We were all about it. It was elephant tranquilizer or something similar, sprayed onto parsley and dried. We smoked it, and danced or had sex, or in this case, got in a car to go to a party in Boston and almost got killed.

Well, only one of us almost got killed, and it was me.

Glenn was driving and Freddy and Jeffrey were in the front with him in Jeffrey's giant Pontiac convertible. Glenn was always the wheel man. He was the best driver, and he loved it. In the back seat I sat between Buzzy and Lenny. The pipe was going around and around as we drove. This is how totally crazy we were, because the driver was smoking, too. We had just had this PCP for a couple of weeks, and we thought we were pretty on top of things, invincible. We were flyin'.

Buzzy was saying some weird things, making crazy noises and saying his head was going to explode. In most circumstances, that would be a definite red flag, and I was trying to talk him down over the music. Lenny was getting bits and pieces of this very crazy conversation that was going on, and little by little realizing the extent of just how serious Buzzy was. He told Glenn we had to stop at the next place. He remembers a gas station, I remember a rest area, but no matter. We were all so high I'm not sure how clearly I remember some of it.

I just know that once we stopped, all of a sudden everyone was getting out of the car but me and Buzzy. It was a two-door and as I went to climb out, he pulled me back. Lenny must have thought I was getting out on Buzzy's side and closed his door. Buzzy leapt forward, locked the doors and held me in the back. Then he put his hands around my throat and told me he had to kill me. He had to, it was what he had to do.

It was obvious he had gone crazy. His eyes were wild, and his hands were, as I said, around my throat, so I didn't want to get him any crazier. "No, you don't, you really don't. It will be just fine, you'll see," I tried telling him in my gentlest voice, which is hard to manage when someone is holding you by the throat.

"Yes, I do, I have to," he told me as his hands tightened.

Meanwhile, the rest of the guys were walking away from the car when Lenny realized something bad was happening. He said to Glenn, "Hey Buzzy's in the car alone with Sukoshi and they're not getting out."

I was starting to panic, because I couldn't get loose or get a breath, when Lenny started pounding on the window, yelling "Hey, what's going on in there?" and Buzzy snapped to and realized what he was doing. He unlocked his side door and started running.

They got me out of the car, crying and shaking. On the way home I sat in the front seat between Glenn and Freddy. Freddy drove so Glenn could hold me the whole way home, or Glenn drove and Freddy held me all the way home. I remember someone held me, and how totally pin-drop silent it got.

Someone else sat in the back seat with Buzzy. Glenn was the one who had caught him running and talked him down enough to get him back to the car. Later on, when he found out that Buzzy had wanted to kill me, he said, "I wish I had let the son of a bitch run out in the road and get killed," or something like that, which was not like Glenn at all.

I never saw Buzzy again and I never wanted to. The inside of that car was quiet like a tomb all the way back to Brooklyn. Trip to Boston: aborted. Pipe going round and round: ditto. That was truly one toke over the line. As Lenny says now, that was the first time we realized there could be consequences to all this unlimited drug experimenting we were doing. It was a sobering thought, I suppose. I mean, you'd think after something like that, we'd get serious about not being stoned all the time, but that didn't actually happen.

A word about drugs:
There's so much propaganda about drugs. I grew up in a house where alcohol was the drug of choice. In some houses it is perfectionism. In some houses I hear people are actually ok with being how they are and letting each other be. Mine was not one of them.

My personal drug use started when I had an accident on my horse. He reared under a beam that caught me across the front of my riding helmet, and then he plunged forward, snapping my head back. A week later, when I still had serious pain, my mom took me to the doctor. I was fourteen.

After taking x-rays and not seeing anything obvious, and this being light years away from massage therapy, chiropractic or God forbid acupuncture, the doc prescribed speed, Dexamyl I think it was, to make me feel better, and Valium to calm me down in case I started to feel too much better. No one seemed to think it odd to give a kid drugs like these. I reached my goal weight in no time flat!

I loved that doctor. I could tell him anything. When I started having sex not too long after I got started on the drugs, he prescribed birth control pills to avoid accidents. He was so open minded that his wife shot him to death when she caught him practicing on one of his patients. It wasn't me; I was just a kid.

Back to The Perils of PCP:

PCP was some crazy shit. It made people like my husband Glenn, who never had a thought for inner consciousness, start talking to God. It made people dance funny and act crazy. I guess it was fun. Until it wasn't. Like the old macrobiotic aphorism, "Everything taken to its extreme becomes its opposite."

One time we were going to meet some friends down in the East Village to go to the movies, and we smoked it in the car to enhance our experience of whatever was to come. It was a cold, windy winter night—New York City cold--and I hate being high and getting cold. I get colder than anyone I've ever seen when I get high, and that night I was really high.

I stood there and the wind was blowing and I was freezing and then the wind was blowing *through* me and all my molecules were being blown out of me and down Second Avenue in this blue stream that I could see. I started to cry. "My molecules are blowing away," I told them all, which, predictably, everyone thought was hilarious.

Our friend Dennis made up a little song which he began to chant accompanied by the snapping of his fingers. It went like this:

Sukoshi freaked out and we couldn't go to the mooooooovies.

Sukoshi freaked out and we couldn't go to the mooooooovies.

And on and on, over and over. I was trying to be a good sport but I was still freaked out and it really wasn't that funny, but I didn't want to let them know I was freaked out anymore because Dennis would clearly make *another* song out of it. Finally I laughed, too, and so we all knew I wasn't going to die of missing molecules, but dinner and a movie were off for that night.

Dennis was the world's freest spirit in a three piece suit, gone from this world way too soon for the many, many

40

people who loved him. One day on his lunch hour from being an attorney, he took me down to the basement of Grand Central station to listen to the way sound travelled on the arches. He would whisper something at the base of one arch and thirty feet away I could hear it, putting my ear against the base of the arch all the way across the room. I haven't found that spot in Grand Central again, and I'm afraid it might have been what is now food stalls from all over the world.

Dennis made us all laugh until we cried or peed our pants. The night we were meeting for movie night might have been before the Buzzy debacle. I hope so. I think it was right at the beginning of the PCP craze, when that choice of drug seemed reasonable for an evening out.

The morning of our wedding, I woke up and, as I said, took three valiums, which also seemed totally normal to me. I was doing something scary that I didn't really feel great about because it seemed like it was what I was supposed to do, and I didn't have anybody to talk to about it. We didn't get into feelings in my family, and if either of my parents ever asked me if this was what I really wanted to do, I don't remember it. As it turned out, I profoundly misunderstood and overlooked what the real deal was in getting married, causing heartbreak and disappointment on all sides. It broke Glenn's heart and his family's, especially his dad's, who loved me. My family was sad about it, too, but they were used to me by then.

Here's how I knew I had not read the fine print: a year later we were sitting on the beach in Batu Ferringhi, Penang, Malaysia, one of the most gorgeous places I have ever seen, or it was then. We always went out to the beach in the late afternoon to swim and visit with the friends we were meeting there, fellow travelers from all over the world. Our new friend Marissa, a beautiful Canadian woman, was traveling with a man she only liked, who adored her in a heartsick way. She was trying to figure love out: what makes it work, what makes it torture? So she asked us, "Why did you two get married? I mean, how did you know you were meant to be together?"

I answered right off the bat, "So we could travel," and saw a look of such heartbreak on Glenn's face I knew for a fact I had just paid attention to the words without listening to the music. Or vice versa. Glenn must have assumed we would get married anyway, so offered it as a means of travel and adventure. I assumed no such thing.

I didn't know, going in, that getting married would be so lucrative. Since he was Jewish, we got cash gifts from his family that supported us easily for a year of travel, since it's apparently a Jewish custom to give cash. From the same friend of my parents I used to drive home from the train in Chappaqua, we got a freighter trip around the world. The freighter was due to leave in February. It didn't, but it is the reason we got married when we did, so we'd be on board when it sailed, which eventually took months.

But I'm getting ahead of myself.

Looking back, it's easy to think the Valium use might have been a red flag for anyone who was paying attention, but no one in my family paid attention to stuff like that. My mother, who in my mind would traditionally have counseled me on needing to be tranquilized to get married, was busy decorating, which she was great at. She had white flowers and swags all over the living room, which had been the dining room of the original inn that our house had been in the 1700's.

That house was haunted. It had been an inn for many years. I was the only one who saw the ghosts, wafting across the living room. Paying attention to them, letting my eyes follow them, unsettled my family, so I tried to ignore them. I did have sex with one. I was only about twelve or so, and I remember waking myself up by moving in the bed, having sex with this white faceless form. I could feel my arms around "his" body, my hands resting on "his" back. It was pleasant and fun (we all know how that is) and not scary at all until later, when I thought about it. At the time, it felt really natural, which is pretty spooky, especially considering I was only twelve and had no experience of what sex was like.

Bad molesty things that happened to me at an early age probably opened some psychic cracks and set me up for this visit, which thankfully never happened again. When people tell me they don't believe in ghosts, I just roll my eyes.

In our New York City life, Glenn and I were both gone to work or school from morning to evening. Twice a week, on days there was no school, I drove up to Chappaqua to ride my horse at a nearby stable and visit my mom and little brother. Glenn went out with different friends at night and so did I sometimes. It's also when I started taking yoga classes on 21st St. in Manhattan at the Sivananda Yoga Ashram.

I'm pretty sure I started taking yoga because of my Aunt Florence, a soon-to-be hippie-yogini (as soon as her straight-laced military husband, Uncle John, passed away.) They lived in San Miguel de Allende, had been there since the late 1940's, and when they met, they shared the horrible passion of going out on safari, or whatever you call it in Central America, and killing wild animals. Sometime along in there, Florence discovered yoga. She even went to the ashram in India where my Guru resides, years before I was involved there; she admitted she always kept a bottle of vodka under her pillow, my kind of yogi. She was passionate about the benefits of yoga, so I figured I'd give it a whirl. I was twenty one and healthy and flexible. I thought.

During my first class, an eighty year old woman came in, graceful and flexible. At headstand time, while I nearly broke my neck, she went up straight and strong and stayed there about five minutes until we were told to stop. After class I asked about her and was told her first time there, she had to be carried in because she could no longer walk, but she loved it and kept practicing and now, four years later, she was in awesome shape. That was good enough for me. I started going every week, twice a week, and practicing for hours at home. I loved it. Yoga was the closest I'd ever come to getting really high without drugs. It gave me the feeling I'd looked for from drugs: centered, peaceful, content.

As to Aunt Florence and Uncle John: when he died he left the bulk of his millions to a military school in Alabama. He didn't want Florence to be one of those rich American women who get taken advantage of in Mexico, so he left her enough allowance to be comfortable, but not rich. She took that little bit of money and became, in her sixties, a backpacker. She wrote a book, traveled third class and slept in hostels and dorms. For her seventieth birthday, she climbed Mt. Kilimanjaro. The last thing she seemed to be in search of was another man!

But here I was, enmeshed with men. A marriage, an affair, and still not finding what I was looking for. I don't want to really give it away, but yeah, I do: what I was looking for was inside me the whole time and had nothing to do with anyone else. As a short version of a Rumi quote says, "I looked into my own heart and there I saw Him; He was there and nowhere else."

The married man I had the affair with once told me, "When it finally comes that you outgrow Glenn, leave him on your own and don't use someone else to do it." Even if he was right, he had no room to give relationship advice, especially advice that I didn't have the emotional maturity to either understand or follow.

Glenn and I would try to have a conversation that wasn't supposed to be an argument. When we were together sometimes, we'd talk and talk and talk. I found one of these "discussions" in my journal:

The first thing we talked about was natural life. The argument he always starts when I say I

*want to live naturally is, "It's natural for man to live
in cities because he is a social animal blah blah blah."
That's not what I mean at all, so I say "in nature" and
he immediately swings to the other extreme and
assumes I mean without any shelter or anything.*

*Sometimes I get so crazy at his unwillingness
to just listen instead of always challenging me. I
want him to listen with his heart.*

Glenn was a big proponent of "open relationships," an idea that went against the grain for me, by nature a serial monogamist. Since he was so into it, I was willing to try it out, but I really didn't believe in it, with the exception of the married guy who was going to get me a great job in the shoe biz. Glenn was having other girlfriends and it didn't bother me. I never saw them and had zero interest in what he did on his own. I wasn't interested and just honestly didn't care, weirdly enough. I never felt it as a threat to our relationship, or that it had anything to do with us or our being together.

I didn't believe in open relationships until a friend said I should meet a guy in the city and complications arose. My friend kept telling me that Paul and I would really like each other, and of course we did, a whole lot. I bemoaned the order of things, that I had just gotten married and *then* "fallen in love." I started going into the city (when you live in Brooklyn, Manhattan is "the city") every time I could, sometimes every day for a week. I'd go to Paul's apartment, smoke great Mexican weed, hang out, go for walks, and talk, talk, talk.

There was this part of me just aching to break loose, to stay with Paul and his artsy hipster flute playing friends who lived in the East Village and said, "OM" to their German Shepherd when they wanted him to chill. I fantasized leaving Glenn and staying with Paul, doing what I wasn't supposed to do at all, especially being a newlywed. And then this other part *still* wanted to be the good girl and do what would keep

45

my family and friends loving me. For a good girl, I did some pretty fucked up shit, but deep down, I was still trying to get love and approval or I would have told them all to leave me alone, I was staying with Paul.

Or would I?

Besides some obvious hot points, Paul's appeal might mainly have been that I *was* leaving and that, because of this, he wasn't really available. He was the perfect representation of the romantic fantasy boyfriend, which seemed to be my favorite kind. He was smart and fun and crazy good in bed. He had great weed and *I was leaving!* No matter what a tragedy I made that seem, in fact it enabled us to have this star-crossed lover quickie that required no depth or commitment. When we were alone together he was fabulous, but when we were with other people he was pretty obnoxious, like he had something to prove. He was part of the long line of non-committed relationships I both bemoaned and deftly created, and I don't really get it. It caused me such anguish to fall for guys who were unavailable for one reason or another, but it was safer and more appealing than guys who were available. In whatever form I found or created it, I kept running from intimacy.

"It'll be such a great trip, you have to take it," Paul kept telling me, but the freighter continued stalling, making it harder for me to imagine going when the time came. By that I mean, the freighter would get to a port and stay ten days instead of the three that were scheduled. It all depended on weather and deliveries, since freighters carry goods from port to port. I created an Oscar-worthy melodrama around whether or not I would take the trip, but in the end *of course* I went.

One day Paul and I were sitting by the lake in Central Park. My heart felt like it was going to break when he turned to me and said, "Wherever you are in the world, when you see the sun dancing on the waves like this, know that you and I and the sun make a triangle."

46

Here it is, over forty years later, and every time I see the sun dancing on the water....

He also said, "Remember there is only one moon and one sun, and wherever you are, we will make a triangle."

He was big on triangles. That was supposed to make it all ok.

My newly beloved boyfriend-on-the-side had just come back from a trip to Mexico with a trunk full (or gas tank full) of Acapulco Gold. In fact, the first time I went to his apartment, the old Mexican guy (he looked old to me then) who brought the weed to New York was staying there, waiting to sell enough to buy a plane ticket home. When it was time for us to leave on the freighter, Glenn and I got a bagful for our upcoming three months on the ocean, and instead of the lovely, fresh and potent weed Paul had been *giving* me for weeks, what he *sold* us was weak and tainted and gas soaked.

Glenn was not particularly upset about my having fallen in love, since I did get on the ship with him when the time came. And since he was the big proponent of open marriages, he didn't have a philosophical dog in that fight. But he was furious that I fell in love with a man so devoid of principles that he would send people off to sea with toxic unsmokeable weed!

Glenn never forgave the guy, I'm sure, and I never saw him again, but he became very well-known and moved to Hollywood. I Googled him a few years ago and looked at his awards and read about his family. Sometimes I wonder how many women in the world are making a triangle with him and the sun, dancing on the water?

I don't remember really caring much about the weed being bad, but I must have. I thought it was mainly Glenn who fussed and fumed about it, but this is from my journal:

I haven't been smoking because the grass just isn't that great, which pisses me off. Makes me realize that

I only knew a certain little bit of Paul, that part that combined with or reacted to the certain little bit of me he knew. For both of us I think it was the very best part.
I could be in love with him because he was the nicest person I had ever met, and I was so nice when I was with him that I could be in love with myself, too.

I am so glad that even then, at 21, I knew the goal was loving myself. Judging by the last nearly fifty years, it's still not easy to get here from there.

When two people love each other, they produce a magnetic field. D.H. Lawrence called it the star rising between two people. The first time I met Paul, he said, "It's not me, it's not you, it's in the space between us."

But as Keith Richards famously sang, *"Talk is cheap."*

So Glenn and I got married, and cash in hand, bags packed, apartment on a month to month, we waited. Time and tides wait for no man, I hear, but men and women do definitely wait for a freighter. We were set to leave in February, but in the world of freighters, schedules were very flexible. And so we waited. And waited. February moved to March, and then to April before the ship finally came to New York, and with my parents and a couple of friends there to see us off, we boarded.

Then it was just, gulp, the two of us. We stood on deck and watched as Manhattan, so impressive on land, became smaller and smaller, like kids' blocks stacked up on a flat surface, and we left all that behind.

There was a whole new smell to get used to, the mixture of diesel and salt air that defines freighter life. Our life, which had actually been two separate lives, with days spent working or at school, nights out several times a week with separate friends, became one life in a ten by ten cabin with only a boat to wander, and practically no one else to talk to. It wasn't twenty four hours before I started to wonder if this had been the smartest choice, the one that had seemed so fabulous and clever.

You know how with some people you just click, and you never run out of stuff to talk about and it's really easy and comfortable to be together? Well, Glenn and I weren't like that anymore. Maybe we had been, but by the time we had been together a couple of years we didn't really do that much together. Like lots of people that age, we got together because of physical attraction, but after a couple of years, that had worn down. I wanted more connection, only I didn't have the first clue how to create it except in bed. As I said, my early modeling of how to be married was pretty awful. In fact, many years later, my dad told me he liked the way I did relationships.

I said, "*Huh????*" At that point I was the Queen of the Escaped Relationship.

He said yeah, he liked the way I kept them to three years, so they never got boring and drove you crazy.

That was my dad, mind you, still married to my mom for sixty years at that point, telling me this in case I had any doubts how I got messed up in this arena. It may have been the same night he turned to me at dinner and said, "She never shuts the fuck up." Nice, right? That was pretty much their relationship by then.

From NYC we sailed to Baltimore, then through the Panama Canal, to LA, Tacoma, San Francisco and then out, for eighteen days across the Pacific to our first Asian port, Manila. We had plenty of time. On a freighter, there is just about nothing *but* time. There are no restaurants or bars, no gyms or climbing walls. There is the relentless chug chug chug of the diesel heart, and the slapping of waves.

49

I spent time contemplating my life. Here's what I had to report: *I'm not really too interested in working hard at a relationship, or anything else, for that matter.*
I can hardly believe I wrote that, but it does explain a lot.

Coming into port was always exciting. First of all, we were getting off the boat. Either we were meeting friends, or else we had a new completely unknown city to explore in the time allotted before we sailed again. Our "cabin boy" Tino made sure we knew the time constraints; we were his babies on this voyage.

This is the best way to travel. You have tons of time with no distractions. I managed to find a place on a teeny upper deck where I could sit and read or tan myself, but I don't remember if there was even a chair, or if I just lay on the deck? I think I took a blanket from the cabin up there. No deck chairs. Hell, no large decks but the main one, covered with cargo.

There were only four or five guest cabins, and the maximum guests were twelve on any trip. From New York to Los Angeles, we were the only ones. The Panama Canal was like a Disney ride. We crossed at midnight, in the pitch black dark. It was hot and there were jungle sounds and then I fell asleep. There was no air conditioning in the cabins in those days, but hopefully that has changed in the last fifty years.

Our cabin was roomy, with two extra-large single berths so we could sleep together when we wanted to. It seems as I read my journal from that time that we wanted to a lot more than I actually remember, since I remember us as being pretty distant and estranged, even though we were the only people we had to talk to! Not to mention that we were on our honeymoon, traditionally a romantic moment in time. But that was what I knew about relationships. I had watched my mom, who punished and controlled with her silences. I know I just told the story about her talking non-stop, but if she wanted something from you, or you had pissed her off, she just wouldn't talk to you. For days. Or weeks. It upset my dad something crazy.

He'd show up at my house, years later, and the first thing out of his mouth was generally, "Have you talked to your mother?"

"No," I'd tell him, "you know I don't talk to her."

"Well, she's not talking to me and I don't know what I've done."

I'd give him a pat on the shoulder and tell him, "Consider yourself lucky."

But he didn't.

When I think back on that freighter trip, I remember being guarded, having a whole lot of inner dialogue that I thought was secret, that I had to protect. I had this whole inner fantasy world going on about the lover I left behind in New York and the life I wasn't having that completely drowned out the life I was actually physically in. Just like my mother and father, I kept Glenn out with the silent treatment. The life in my mind was so much more satisfying than the one I was living. More dramatic, anyway. I've since learned that addiction to drama creates chemicals in our bodies just as potent as drugs people get addicted to. I get it. When we grow up in high stress families, we continue to create enough drama to feel alive until we learn a healthier way to live. I'm still working on it.

For crossing the ocean, Glenn and I had each brought a bunch of books to read. That, plus wandering and exploring the ship, was all we had to do. Back in New York I had practiced yoga every day for an hour and sometimes two, but here on the boat it was impossible to do since mostly all I knew were lying down postures. There was barely room to lie down anywhere flat, not to mention the constant rolling of the ship. Our trip was supposed to last several months, six weeks of which was the passage from Hong Kong to South Africa. We brought a lot of books.

51

Meals, which were huge, were served in the captain's dining room with the ship's officers at white table cloth settings. The crew ate below deck in some mess hall I never saw. Tino was horrified to find I was vegetarian (ish) so every port he got me fresh fruits and vegetables. Ensuring my health and happiness became his personal mission, a relationship I wholeheartedly approved.

From the back door, the docks, we got that view of how cities work. It's a whole world so few people experience. The ship carried big American cars and ball bearings and dogs and toilet paper to the Philippines. At every port, things got loaded and unloaded. We got off to go exploring once we found ground transportation. At each stop we had to get used to solid ground again.

In Baltimore and Los Angeles we had friends and relatives who met us, but in Tacoma and San Francisco we were on our own. Coming in to Tacoma, through the Juan de Fuca Straits, was stunningly beautiful. From out at sea, it was easy to imagine seeing it for the first time as an explorer hundreds of years ago. Until we got in close, all we could see was the contour of the land, all green with rolling hills.

By the time we got to San Francisco, we wanted to re-provision ourselves with hallucinogens to amuse us on the long crossing, so we headed out to Sausalito. I had a friend there, and tried to find him out at the Sausalito houseboats where he lived. No luck. Those West Coasters were *so* much hipper than we were, fresh off the boat. We poked around town a little, then decided just to ask someone who looked likely. We only had a few hours before the ship would sail again.

There was a gorgeous long haired blond guy talking to, or more accurately, listening to a very vivacious and animated young woman. She was like to never stop talking, so I very politely butted in, "Excuse me, but do you know where we could get some acid?" (We had to keep moving to get back to the ship in time.)

I was talking to him but she whirled around and said, "I've got something much better!"

When I asked her what it was, she said, "Jesus!"

I thought she was giving the name of a new drug, since drugs had all sorts of weird nicknames. I asked her, "What's that?" It turned out she was a "Jesus freak," already old hat in California, but new to me.

Acid in hand, it came up tails, it rhymed with sails, you know...

Eighteen days across the ocean went by in rhythmic bliss. If you cross the Pacific, spring is the time to go. It ended up being a blessing that the ship didn't come until April. Day after day the sun was out and the ocean was a giant lake. We never saw a wave or a whitecap, although the day we took the acid, dolphins followed us and played around the ship all day. I had gotten a little freaked out, but when Glenn looked out and saw the dolphins, everything felt ok again.

From my journal I report on our day:

Glenn took chairs up to the top deck. There seemed to be hundreds of dolphins, leaping and dancing around for the fun of it. The wind got stronger and stronger, the water got rougher and rougher. The boat was like a little toy for the air and water to play with. I began to understand how small I was.

For the first time, I was having an awareness of consciousness, or an awareness of the SELF:

I don't know who Sukoshi Rice is--she seems to change with each person I am with. I am tired of the person I am with Glenn and loved the person I was with Paul. Who would I be alone? I have a feeling I could really like it. At least I think I should give it a try. I want to be someone new; become myself.

Now that I've been "alone" for about thirty years, I can testify that it's no guarantee of anything. I still have weird patterns that show up in relationships, because I still have

53

relationships. Each feels like it might be the last, which was never the case in my younger years.

> *It's always easier to make a new start than to stick with where you are and make it work. But I'm not remotely interested in making it work. I'm not really tired of the boat or the ocean, just of myself.*

It's too bad as I read this that I had no experience of going deeper, of confronting issues, of working things out. I had never been taught or shown those skills, and it was many years later when I actually became aware of them.

Our cabin became our little home, a teeny little home where I wrestled with why I was there, with no one to talk to but Glenn. I was used to the distraction of all kinds of friends around. It changed when more passengers came on; suddenly we had to share the dining room. Any dream I had of having some people to talk to was squelched when I met our fellow passengers.

In Los Angeles we picked up a wealthy, snobby Filipino couple, much older than we were, who treated Tino like shit. He was also their cabin boy and it was not in their culture to be nice to "servants." We had a few conversations, but they were such dreadful snobs, even if they did give us good ideas of places we should visit outside Manila. The whole crossing they only deigned to speak with the Captain, besides us, the young white couple.

Then in San Francisco, we picked up a family of missionaries from Kansas, a red headed father and mother and their four pale little carrot topped children. As I gathered from our very brief single conversation, they were headed to the Philippines to put clothes on the natives

"Do you know," they asked me, horrified, "that people there go naked?"

"Do you know," I asked them, "how hot it is in the tropical jungles?"

There are cannibals in the jungles there. We laughed, considering the possibilities.

54

The Philippines

Manila was hot and sweaty; the smell of diesel was all over the port. Every metal railing we touched felt hot and greasy. We were going straight to the bus station to catch the next bus to the mountain resort town of Baguio, since everyone on the ship, especially Tino, had been telling us how beautiful it was. He talked about it like it was Fantasia; for him, it probably was.

Walking toward the Maritime Agency immigration office to get our passports stamped, we noticed a tall, well-dressed businessman getting out of the back of a Lincoln Continental. Surprisingly, he was Mr. Jose Francisco who was there *for us*! to make sure our time in Manila was easeful and stress-free! He was associated with the shipping line, a friend of the man who had gifted our freighter trip honeymoon. Mr. Francisco had also met my dad. It was customary then that he welcome and take care of us. He was charming, his English was impeccable, and we happily climbed into his lovely air-conditioned chauffeur-driven car to see the town.

First we stopped at the Yacht Club, then the Army Navy Club so Glenn could get the New York papers and find out how the Yankees were doing. It turned out the Manila Times had all the New York baseball scores anyway, but Mr. Francisco seemed to enjoy showing us all the upscale amenities Manila had to offer. After that, it was on to lunch at the Savoy Hotel.

I was raised comfortably, but this level of lavishness was beyond me. The buffet was impressive by any standards: mountains of shrimp and fresh fruits, roast pork, beans and rice, vegetables and salads all surrounded by ice carvings of swans and water buffalo and palm trees. It was an absolute orgy of conspicuous consumption, glorious, beautiful and ridiculously opulent. I ate everything I could hold (except the pork); it was so delicious.

When we left to catch the bus to Baguio, I noticed what was on the outside of the hotel: cardboard lean-to's lined the long wall surrounding the property. On the other side of the wall, what people at the Savoy spent on eating and sleeping in one night was more than the lean-to dwellers would see in a year, if ever.

When I Google the Savoy Hotel today, there is nothing like I remember. Now it is a huge concrete and glass box, part of an international hotel consortium. Back then, it was old and charming, with trees and gardens inside a surrounding wall. Now there would be no place to put a lean-to, since it's surrounded by four lane roads and concrete sidewalks.

I was so sheltered. I'd seen people beg before, but I'd never seen where those people lived. They sure didn't live in Chappaqua, and I had never seen lean-to's or anything like them in Brooklyn.

I asked Mr. Francisco, "Who helps those people? How do they live?"

He kindly but firmly turned me away, toward his waiting car. This was just the way it was. If you were lucky, you were eating the hotel buffet, and otherwise, you might live in a lean-to made of flattened boxes. This was my first inkling of *karma*. I had a lot to learn. Girl fresh off the boat.

The next lesson was about *balut*, pronounced bah-loot.

As we were getting on the bus to Baguio, Mr. Francisco handed me two large warm eggs he bought from a street vendor. "These are *balut*, a delicious snack for the trip," he told me with a twinkle in his eye. He also told me quite pointedly that they were for me, not Glenn. Duck eggs.

After we got on the road, I opened the first one and there was a little gelatinous, partially-cooked, mostly-formed baby duck. I think it even had teeny feathers. In my memory I see its little beak and beady little eye. Yikes, there had to be some mistake. I threw it out the window.

I opened the next one. These things are supposed to be good for fertility, which was not what we were after at the moment, so I gave that little half cooked duckling to a woman across the aisle, who slurped it right up. I was simultaneously grossed out and relieved to have been able to provide such a delicacy for someone who appreciated it so much.

Driving through the mountains, we saw a man in a loincloth with huge bandoliers strapped crisscrossing his chest. As we drove by, he was just disappearing down into the bushes on the side of the road. The jungle looked impenetrable, but he slid into it without a ripple. I thought about those stupid missionaries on the ship. Good luck getting pants on that dude!

The first night in Baguio, we stayed in a regular hotel with electricity. Turning to get into bed, I saw a three inch long bug climbing the wall, right behind our heads. Naturally this forced me to scream and sleep with the light on, which probably attracted more bugs, but I didn't care. The thought of going to sleep in the dark with something that size crawling up the wall behind me was terrifying.

We hung out on the village square and started meeting people. This is one cool thing about traveling: it's so easy to meet local folks and other travelers. Glenn became friends with the guy who owned the local radio station, so we got to go inside and see how that worked. On the recommendation of a friendly German backpacker, we moved to a lovely hostel right near the center of town. The huts were thatched, immaculately clean, and didn't have any electricity, hence fewer bugs at night. We met more people. Travelers on the road share stories: don't miss this, definitely skip that. We ate great street food, mostly fried rice dishes served on banana leaves cooked to varying degrees of spiciness.

And then there were mangoes. No one had ever told me about mangoes and I had never seen one before. They were so amazingly delicious, I ate them for breakfast, lunch and dinner, even sucking on the pit after I ate the fruit. No one told me that mangoes are related to my old arch-enemy, poison ivy, and that the poison is in the little hairs around the pit. Old hands at the mango game later told me all the tricks: wash your hands and mouth immediately after eating one and don't ever suck the pits. The sap is also just under the skin, so if you peel them and cut the fruit off the pit, you should be fine.

I wanted to see Banaue, and it was kind of on our way to catch the ship again at its next port at the north end of the island. Banaue is famous for its rice paddies, which are mind-bogglingly gorgeous. They made such an impression on me that five years later, when I first saw the valley I would eventually move to in the mountains of North Georgia, USA, I knew I was home. There was the same seemingly endless array of shades of green, from deep emerald to the softest pale baby lime. That's how the rice paddies were, shade after shade of green, in sensuous curving sculpture covering every mountainside.

Our hotel in Banaue was a giant youth hostel, and even though we were the *only* guests, they insisted I stay in the girls' dorm, with the forty nine other empty beds surrounding me, while my husband stayed in the boys', with its forty nine equally empty ones. In the middle of the night, Glenn decided to come stay with me and ease my troubled mind, even though the desk man assured us that the guerrillas had not been active lately and that there was a night watchman on guard.

In the early morning as we left to catch the dawn bus to the coast, we saw that night watchman, a twelve year old boy with a stick.

A few words about buses in that part of the world, back then: the leg room was very tight. It was ok for me. The prescription doc in New York had set me up with this new thing called Quaaludes that made everything easy. Hard wooden bus seat for ten hours? No problem. I just took a pill and except for almost getting a concussion when my head smacked into the seat in front of me, I was good. Ahh, but my poor long-legged husband, who was not a fan of the little white pills, was very uncomfortable. As I remember it, he bitched about it for the entire ten hour trip, which showed great fortitude. Glenn would have been a wonderful companion for a five-star tour of Europe, but travel on the cheap through Asia did not suit him. Besides any other considerations, his legs were too long.

Another thing was the bathroom situation. By now, present time, every bus just about anywhere has a bathroom in it, but back then we made stops. Every few hours we'd pull over and all the women would go into this corral with a wall around it. Down the center was a long trough and all the women straddled it and pissed, hiking their long wrap skirts a bit. I had on jeans. And underpants. All I'm saying is, dress for the occasion. And if you'd like to know how I managed that one, I'm sure it was very gracefully!

The bus careened around mountain passes with sheer drops of hundreds of feet. The daring young ticket taker hung on to the side bars, leaning way out over thin air. There were chickens and ducks and lots of people spitting betel juice. For those who think that is just a movie, it's not. It's a nut that stains people's mouths red and seems to rot their teeth, since all the old people I saw chewing it had red mouths and rotten teeth. You have to spit a lot when you have it in your mouth. Of all the things I've tried, that was never one.

By the time we caught up with the ship and sailed to our next port, a mining camp on a small island, I was feeling not so great. The edges of my mouth had little cracks and I felt funny. When we docked, we got off to go see the nurse. All these camps have their own clinics.

The nurse there handed me a packet of white pills, telling me, "This is the lightest case of mango allergy I have ever seen, but in case it gets worse, take one of these, every 12 hours."

The next morning I woke up and OMGodzilla!! My head felt the size of a watermelon, my hands were blown up like balloons and I was covered with watery blisters that itched like mad. It was about 98 degrees and we were in port, so nothing was moving but this one little teeny joke of a fan. I took a pill. Twelve hours later, seriously, I woke up and took another one.

Tino was completely freaking out that I wasn't coming to meals, so the second day he came to the cabin to see me. Aye Dios!!!!! He was so scared that this had happened on his watch, so upset for me, and probably terrified that it could be blamed on him. I told him not to worry and took another pill.

Gradually, over the next week, the pills became less effective. I would only sleep maybe four or five hours instead of twelve, but gradually the effects of the allergy lessened, too. The swelling receded, the blisters disappeared, we travelled north, the air cooled a little, and I have not eaten another mango since. I don't even eat mango ice cream, just in case.

Japan: An intro to travel on the cheap

Once we got to Japan, Glenn and I had had enough of freighter travel. Even though we had liked it so far, and our gift was supposed to be "around the world," if we stayed on board we would be *three months* en-route to South Africa, then a stop in England, then back to New York City. To see two more new cities we'd spend another four or five months on the ship. No thanks. We jumped ship in Japan, the most polite and safe place I could ever imagine.

When we landed in Japan, we were still the green New Yorkers who started our trip, even though we'd been traveling for months by then and had braved mango allergy, countless ports, tropical heat and acid at sea. That's LSD, not acid reflux. We were too young for that. Nothing had *changed* us, which was my idea of why I wanted to travel. Looking back, that was one fundamental difference we had that was never resolved: I wanted to learn a new way of being in the world, Glenn wanted to visit new places but go back to New York basically unchanged. He wanted to be a tourist and collect anecdotes and handicrafts. I wanted to experience things I hadn't even imagined yet. I know because

61

once I got started, I couldn't have imagined where life took me.

Our start in Japan was *not* going to be the great life changer. When we arrived in Osaka Station on the bullet train, we were met by business associates of my dad's, who delivered us to the home of family friends where we were going to stay. They all went out and left Glenn and me alone with nothing to do but watch TV. Boring! They were all Americans so we probably got some English language show, but it seemed like a shitty welcome to me, just dumping us in the living room and going out without us! But my dad would be there in the morning, and then we'd be included in everything.

Once Bert was in town, we were coddled and handled at every turn. Meals were all taken care of as managers arranged and corralled our every move, planning and pre-planning everything possible. When we said we wanted to tour the country, someone from the office got us rail tickets that were good for thirty days, to go anywhere. Having everything done for us was nice, but debilitating. Were these people ever going to turn us loose? As much as we had a good time with Bert, we were looking forward to his going back to New York so we'd finally be on our own.

After a couple of days, there was a big party for Bert with all his old friends, and I went out to the golf course with him the next day. The golf course was an island of Paradise in a very crowded country. The gnarled, wind-bent trees looked just like the trees in the paintings of Japan in our house. The caddies were short, stocky women, carrying two bags apiece. In my journal I note that it was a very hot day, so while the men were golfing I went down to the river and swam naked. That seems awfully brave for me, but I guess it's true since it's in the journal, and after I read about doing it, I remembered the furtive feeling of hanging my clothes on the reeds and cooling off in the clear water, hoping nobody could see me. After their golf game, we searched for our old house in Shukugawa, where I had spent my first four years, but we never could find it. Later on Bert figured out that our beautiful house surrounded by formal gardens was now a big condo building.

Golf is called a game, but especially there, it was a serious one. Membership in the course they were playing cost something astronomical, close to a million dollars. Surely they meant yen? But no. I could barely believe it, but it was where all business deals were done, so belonging to a prestigious club was essential to success.

We were still staying with our American hosts and before I left town, I thought maybe I ought to see a doctor because I hadn't had a period in quite awhile, maybe three or four months. Our hostess insisted on taking me to the hospital for a checkup and a pregnancy test.

When I was taken for my exam, by a nurse who spoke zero English, I first had the mandatory pee in the cup, and I could figure that out ok. Then I was told or pantomimed to undress and get on a table, lying on my back. Still standard. When I did, a curtain like contraption came down all around my bottom half that covered from the waist down, so I couldn't see the doctor or what was going on. I sort of liked the idea, even though it was weird. I didn't really want to see the doctor, or make eye contact with the guy who was pawing around in there. Turned out I wasn't pregnant, but nobody knew why I didn't get my period except maybe the stress of traveling.

Glenn was already hating on Asia by the end of our first few days. In a very crowded department store he told me, "They should drop another bomb on this country every few years to keep the population down."

I wanted to cry. For one thing, Japan was kind of my home country, even though I had left when I was four. Mainly, it was just a shitty thing to say, so instead of crying I gave him the same silent treatment I had learned from my mom, and got pissed off at him. I was not sure I wanted to be married to someone who said shit like that. Of course, I wasn't sure I wanted to be married to him for more reasons than that, but that was a really good one.

Around Bert and his friends, Glenn kept it together and acted like he was having a great time, so they all loved him and thought I had married very well. I was the only one who knew he was rapidly losing his sense of humor and sense of adventure and really just wanted to go back to New York and be with his friends. In fact, through the whole of our travels, all he really wanted was to go back to New York, except he wanted to stay with me more, I guess, because that's what he did. He also knew this was a great opportunity that he wouldn't probably get again, even though he pretty much hated most of it.

When Bert's stay in Japan ended, we were free to travel. We had train tickets and reservations. First we visited with my nanny, Takako, who raised me. During my first four years, she was my world. While my parents drank cocktails and entertained, she was with me six days and seven nights a week. My earliest memory is of climbing out of my crib to sleep with her on her futon on the floor. She bathed and brushed and dressed me daily. She'd named me Sukoshi, which means *little*, by saying that word when she first saw me, still a teeny preemie after a month in the Army hospital incubator. She's the one who held me and comforted me. She was really my mommy, and then when I was four, we moved to the States and left her behind. I had big issues over that, sleep walking and refusing to eat being the main ones.

All of that took a toll on me. Being in an Army Hospital incubator, I was touched only for feeding and changing, so I didn't bond with anyone the way babies do who are held a lot. And leaving Takako when I was four was devastating. I cried and had nightmares that woke up the whole family. I had trouble with my mom, who wanted to suddenly be my mom, when she never had really been. She wasn't much of a toucher or hugger, so loving touch was rare.

64

Check this out: my parents kept razor blades in their bottom drawer. First of all, who does that? And second of all, who still keeps them there after their four year old daughter finds them and starts cutting her hands? I was fascinated with them, with how I could cut my hands and not feel anything and then they would bleed. Not only did my parents not put the fucking things where I couldn't get them, I got a spanking for cutting my hands, especially after the first time. So yeah, I was seriously missing Takako, with her gentle, loving voice and touch.

I was nervous and also excited to see her again. Now she was a married woman with four kids, who turned out to be open and friendly and just great. Her husband was a Japanese man, a professor of German language at a University in Tokyo. She had probably been about 18 when she was first hired to take care of me. Glenn and I were made so comfortable in their little house. The whole family gave us the upstairs to sleep while they all slept downstairs.

They lived in the traditional Japanese fashion. In their small house, the dining room doubled as a bedroom. For meals, a small table was brought out and everyone sat around it on the floor. At night, the futons and comforters came out of their hiding places behind rice paper walls, and the family went to bed, putting it all away in the morning before breakfast. Our visit was both emotional and detached, since when we saw each other last I was a toddler and she a young woman. Most of what we had was what we remembered and imagined, but it was still very sweet. Also, her English was limited and my Japanese virtually non-existent, unlike when I left and it was four year old fluent.

When we left, we had one more scheduled visit with the daughter of a family friend, then we were on our own. Traveling by train, we went from town to town, to our reserved hostels. And then, in early August, 1970, we met Louie.

With his huge mass of blond curls, Louie would have stood out anywhere in Asia. Add in his gorgeous red-haired girlfriend Sandy, with a soundtrack from the blues harp he was usually blowing and her dancing along and you couldn't miss them. They were hitching around Japan for a few months, sleeping in a tent, picking up young adventurous Japanese here and there, as we had, even by train. Louie would play his harp to the immense delight of all the people we met, and the women went nuts over Sandy's hair, sometimes running out from their houses just to touch it. She was a real flaming redhead and a major attraction in the public baths.

Young Japanese kids wanted what we had. Japanese hippies and wanna-be hippies who met us sometimes hooked up for a few days, hitching rides with us, camping wherever we stopped. Louie found weed growing wild and it was a big hit with these guys. And of course with us. There was Homi, who confused the words Jewish and juicy. Biting into a peach he would ecstatically exclaim, "Oh this peach is so Jewish!" and look perplexed when we all laughed. The young Japanese guys wanted blue jeans and rock and roll, and they loved to smoke weed.

I know the day we all met because of my journal. I have dozens of them, some more detailed than others. This one tells everywhere we stayed, everything we ate, and what we paid for it all. Amazingly, Japan in those times was really cheap.

Lou and Sandy definitely loosened us up. We bought a cheap little pup tent, got a refund from the hostel, and started hitching everywhere we wanted to go, rather than traveling by train. Now there were five of us, with Homi for a while and then a new guy, Hideo, who stayed for the duration. Sometimes the first driver who stopped would wave down cars until someone else stopped and we were all taken care of. For a few days there were seven of us traveling together, and we were still taken care of in this way.

We were taken to people's homes. They fed us and filled their baths for us. The next morning they got us on the road again, not leaving until our next rides were a sure thing. On the night of August 14, 1970 there were seven of us sleeping in the town park of Aomori, where we had arrived around midnight. We had stacked all our bags under a gazebo since it was supposed to rain. We had been stacking our bags and backpacks against the walls of stores and leaving them for hours everywhere we went. They had never been touched.

At six in the morning, a man woke us up to return my duffle bag. I had the *only* bag with nothing valuable, no camera, just clothes. Several men had collected my clothes that the thief had strewn in haste, looking for something of value. These guys were bowing and apologizing profusely for the dishonor of a thief doing this. Nothing was missing. My clothes were jeans and tee shirts and underwear. It was the only time in Japan that anyone ever touched our stuff, but the amazing part was the profound apology on the part of the man who returned my bag. He told us it dishonored him and it dishonored his country to have someone steal from us when we were guests there.

Since we were camping out, we bathed at night in the public baths, the o-furo. Usually Sandy's red hair was quite the sensation on the women's side. Going to the o-furo was a wonderful reward at the end of the day. Most villages had one and except for the one luxury hotel we splurged on, the baths were always segregated, men on one side, women on the other, separated by a solid wall. All the women would lather up and rinse in the first room, then, squeaky clean, get in the super-hot communal tub to soak. In the small towns and farming areas, we saw women who were absolutely bent in half at the waist from all the farm work, probably work in the rice fields, bent over in an L-shape. Whenever Sandy let down her hair to wash it, there was pandemonium in the washroom. Everyone wanted to touch it. They had never seen the like. She was the most popular girl in town until she ended her soak, night after night, with a good dousing of cold water, which she managed to splash on whoever was close by. Sandy was pretty sure of her standing in the Universe.

The one time we all bathed together, men and women, the men held little washcloths over their genitals. I guess the women did, too. I just swam around. I was pretty much of a nudist in those days, or at least, I wasn't self-conscious about being naked. Of course, things were cuter then.

Everywhere we went people paid for us, our food, travel, sometimes free hotel rooms, sometimes bikes or water skiing. One night we were sleeping on a deserted beach when we heard the sound of hoof beats coming our way. Glenn got up because I was scared. *"Oh no, what now?"* was my first paranoid and unhappy thought, but it was a guy who had ridden his horse down to the beach to bring us a delicious, very Jewish melon from his garden.

Louie caught fish everywhere we stopped. That's his thing, fishing, along with playing the blues. You can find him these days on Facebook, Louiethefish Denolfo, and buy his beautiful carvings, sign up for some exotic fishing expeditions, and hear him play the blues. In Japan, trout are called nigi mas and we ate a bunch of them fresh from the streams. We explored a tiny island full of caves, originally used for meditation, but now seemingly more useful for dumping garbage. I took lots of solitary walks, a habit I had started in my teens and kept up wherever it seemed safe to do, which Japan definitely was.

On August 25, the five of us met up with three more travelers from Hawaii and converged on the home of Gerd, a German who was studying traditional Japanese pottery. He showed me the bowls he was throwing. With my six months at the Brooklyn Museum Art School, they looked perfect to me, but he said they were all to be destroyed, that he couldn't keep any for the first three years or so until he could really express the essence of the form. Years later I met a French guy in Paris who studied sitar in India for three years. After one year of sitting at the master's feet clapping out the beat, he was allowed to touch a sitar. Gerd's apprenticeship was like that.

We spent three days repapering the walls of Gerd's little traditional Japanese house. The outer walls, the wooden ones, were all open for the summer, and the inner walls, the paper ones, had lots of holes. But not once we got through with our repapering job! It was a cool project and had to be done properly so the walls would shed water, not collect it. Mostly I did the cooking for everyone, but the wall project was fun and relaxing to do all together.

Traveling in a group was a relief from the enforced intimacy of just me and Glenn together, and what a group! Lou was always a trip, ready for fun. Sandy was a real princess. According to my journal, I was always doing the cooking and cleaning up while she danced around being beautiful. Since I've been accused many times of being entitled and acting privileged, I am really happy to have this bit of proof. Glenn couldn't stand her, so she had to be pretty bad, because I know I can be spoiled and difficult and he could stand me most of the time. My final assessment of her was, "she was a good confidante and girlfriend, once I learned not to trust her to keep her mouth shut!"

I actually ran into her in Belize, years later. Suffice to say, she still looked beautiful and had been nude modeling in NYC while I was six months pregnant and beginning to waddle.

Oddly enough, I loved sleeping in a tent and slept great. Even better for me was sleeping with no tent at all, just in a sleeping bag under the stars. Glenn did not go for this at all. Hotel beat tent, and tent way beat no tent. He often spoke longingly of New York, while I rarely gave it a thought. He couldn't sleep in his clothes, or in a room with other people. He was moody and grumpy much of the time, even though he wanted to travel with these folks. I watched him and by the end of August I was sure I didn't want to spend the rest of my life with him, seeking a settled and predictable existence back in New York. I liked traveling, I liked foreign things and figuring stuff out, but he didn't. He liked things to be comfortable and familiar, which travel on the cheap through Asia definitely was not.

I weighed 115 lbs. in Osaka, but all we seemed to do was eat. My journal is full of meal descriptions. I complain about feeling fat. Lord, don't catch up with me today! We slept at temples and I wondered at the monks. They ate meat and drank beer. I don't know if they had sex or not. We always paid something like 100 yen to sleep there, which is very little, like thirty cents.

In early September, as we worked our way south, we picked up another friend, a guy named Albert from New York. Albert was kind of a trust-a-farian, a trust fund kid you'd picture in a bow tie, but I got along with him fine and he had a great music collection with him. I had had a terrible sore throat for a few days, our last days with Louie and Sandy before they went back to Hawaii, and now Glenn had it, so we spent some of our travel time resting. We sat around and listened to the likes of Bonnie and Delaney and friends, courtesy of Albert. Hardly torture.

We wanted to get to Bangkok via Taiwan and Hong Kong, and we liked the laid back pace of boat travel, so we decided to take a passenger ferry to Taiwan through the southern islands of Japan. It was about a week long trip that became known as the "Great Ball of Fire" segment of our journey. From Kagoshima on the main southernmost island of Japan, Kyushu, we island hopped first to Amami O Shima, then to Okinawa and ending in Taiwan.

Albert was an eccentric and intrepid traveler, but could be rude and imperious and piss people off. He was prone to misinterpret offers as someone trying to get something, rather than what we had experienced so far, that it was generally someone trying to give us something. Maybe he was just fresh out of New York. Sometimes he slowed us down by being an asshole, but by virtue of good tunes and interesting conversation, he was a reasonably good travel companion. Glenn and I needed someone else to talk to, and we both liked Albert and could hang out with him easily. Our route was trippy and off any tourist beat, and he was up for the adventure.

Looking through boxes of old stuff for this book, I found a postcard from Albert from 1975, sent to my parents' house in Chappaqua. I Googled him. I had no idea he was an heir to the extent he was, and is now famous as an art collector and philanthropist!

Before we even got on the boat ride, a family near the port put us up for the night. In the morning they gave their little daughter this breakfast: black coffee with sugar and two pieces of white bread with butter and sweetened condensed milk on it. I nearly gagged at it, and thought sadly about how the traditional Japanese breakfast of green tea and miso soup and noodles and boiled eggs was being replaced by this crap, and what it would do to the health of future generations.

We got on the first boat, which was none too comfortable in the cheap seats, bound for Amami O Shima. Landing in the port of Naze, we went first to the little stores surrounding the port. Every store had jars and jars and jars of snakes in liquid, plus snakeskin belts, bags and boots in all sizes and shapes. They were all the same brown color and stupid crazy us, nobody gave it a mention or said, "Gee, I wonder why there are so many of these fucking hideous nightmare-looking sea snakes in jars in every single store."

Wouldn't you think we'd wonder? Not one of us said one thing or even mentioned it except a casual, "Boy, they sure have a lot of ugly fucking snakes in jars here." Instead we bought some food and bottles of water and hitchhiked out to a beautiful and deserted cove where we spent the entire afternoon swimming in water that we later were told was home to the highest concentration in the world of the highly poisonous habu sea snake. The island was so overrun by habu that the mongoose had been introduced to kill them, given their reputation with cobras. Instead, the mongoose decimated the local population of Amami rabbits, an ancient breed that traced its lineage back hundreds of years, now hell bent on extinction.

We left the beach in the late afternoon and that evening ended up at the house of a funny little old man who took quite a shine to Glenn. He had the old fashioned o-furo, a single person Japanese bath with a metal bottom out on the wooden porch. He built a fire under the bath, and when it was hot, we stepped onto a heavy wooden lid and pushed it down to the bottom so we didn't burn our feet. Glenn was back there by himself and the old man wanted to wash his privates for him. I heard Glenn protesting, over and over, and pushing the guy away, but also trying to be his usual very polite self. Albert and I had already bathed and were sitting out front drinking tea and laughing, but when Glenn came out, he was upset. He wasn't used to old men hitting on him; I'm sure it had never happened before.

For someone who was willing to be so highly experimental in his sexual adventures, for someone who allowed his dog to be a participant (this was before me, believe me, but he told me about it) I was surprised he didn't just close his eyes and enjoy things. But he didn't. In fact, I believe it was the trauma of the old man that caused his on-coming malady, the "great ball of fire."

We took the boat the next day to Okinawa, which none of us liked. It was a border town, mongrel-feeling place of hookers and unfriendly lookers. There wasn't another boat for a couple of days, so we were stuck there in the kind of no man's land populated by MP's, soldiers who didn't want to be there, and locals who resented the hell out of them while simultaneously trying to take them for all they were worth. As soon as we could, we were on the next boat to Taiwan, where we were to stay with my dad's friend Mike Kawabata, a Japanese businessman who had lived there for many years.

On the boat over to Taiwan, Glenn said he didn't feel well and didn't want to eat, which was rare for him. He just wanted to lie down and rest, also very rare. There were lots of foreigners on the boat so Albert and I had fun talking and visiting since we were all traveling deck class, which meant we shared a big room where we unrolled our sleeping bags at night and sat around during the day, when we weren't up on deck. We had a couple of bathrooms and occasionally we helped Glenn over to one. Twenty four hours later, Glenn's left testicle had swollen to the size and shape of a small football, and was bright red. He could barely stand and was feverish and in bad pain.

I had contacted Mike from Okinawa to tell him when we'd be arriving; when he met the boat, we took Glenn straight to the hospital. He stayed for nine days while I saw the sights, ate tons of good food, and went to museums when I wasn't dutifully sitting by his bedside. I slept, badly, on a cot in his room but went out every day, meeting Albert or being taken out by some of Bert and Mike Kawabata's friends, who were all so nice to me.

They gave Glenn antibiotics and bed rest but the thing was still red and swollen and painful. Finally, on day nine, right there in the hospital room, I closed the door and we had sex and as soon as he came the swelling went down pretty much instantly and he was ok again.

Gee Doc, I don't know....

Taipei was weird and paranoid. The society was very rigid in those days as it was a police state. Some men told us their plan to invade the mainland, which I found imprudent to talk about, at best. In restaurants, people looked over their shoulders before they talked. Children had to wear their book bags over their right shoulders on the way to school, and on their left on the way home (or vice versa). They actually got stopped by police, or traffic police, if they were in violation of this. It wasn't a place we wanted to hang around, now that Glenn could walk again.

Besides wanting to leave, I could tell we had used up a huge coupon book of goodwill from our hosts. These guys, Mike Kawabata and a few others, had never mentioned the cost of the hospital stay, or the apartment where we were staying. They wined and dined us and took us all over the island, and I was getting the feeling they were looking forward to our departure even more than we were. We bought tickets on a passenger ship to Hong Kong for September 29, 1970.

On September 28th, we got up at 4 a.m. to celebrate both Glenn's and Confucius' birthdays. We went to a large courtyard of a very ornate temple with a few hundred people. It was very crowded. As the sun rose, from 5 a.m. to about 7, there were small boys in yellow robes dancing with feathers, and then there was a fucking sacrifice! No, not the small boys, but a goat and a huge bull got their throats slit in front of the crowd. Happy Birthday, Confucius. I hope you like meat! We went to a coffee shop instead.

The next day, September 29, we got on a five hundred passenger ship bound for Hong Kong. Funny thing was, there were only about a hundred people on the ship, and mostly it was foreigners, not Chinese people. We found out why when the typhoon hit.

We were sitting around a big table in the nearly empty dining room, holding on to the table to keep from being thrown to the floor as the ship pitched violently from side to side. There were about twelve of us foreign hippie types talking animatedly about this typhoon, which was on the local news, of course, in Chinese. I looked out the large dining room window, which was on the upper deck, to see a wave break *over* the side. That was quite enough for me! I went down to my berth to prepare to die.

To save money, Glenn was in a man's cabin with ten or twelve berths, and I was in a similar one for women. We

74

were in the bowels of the ship. Everyone knew the Titanic story. There was no hope, and the officers of the ship would not budge and let us move upstairs to the empty first class section. I lay down in my bunk and as the ship rose and then crashed down with the movement of a large wave, I heard a huge crack and felt the ship shudder. I knew this was "it" and passed out immediately so I would sleep through my imminent death by drowning.

In the morning I awoke to smooth seas and sunlight. We all met up in the dining room again, all still amazingly alive, and exchanged contact info. The only person I saw again, besides Glenn, was a guy named Portuguese Tony, who ended up being a heroin dealer in Hong Kong that I got to know too well.

We had an invitation to stay in my father's friend's country home in Hong Kong, a three bedroom modern house with a swimming pool, tennis court and sports car included. They only used the house for Sunday afternoon lunches and tennis. It was a great house, with a very mod sunken living room, a live-in groundskeeper, and a Mazda sports car which we were free to use. We had the run of the place all week. On Sundays, we ate a great big family lunch with them.

These people were one of the wealthiest families in Hong Kong (then and now). Glenn and I were treated to numerous family dinners where he was expected to keep up with the men as they toasted each other with Scotch. Thank God women were exempted. I can drink nearly anything, but not Scotch. Sometimes we'd go to one of their lavish apartments up on the Peak and play mahjong. Glenn was learning; I was hopeless. At midnight, someone would go out for noodles, and we'd eat huge bowls of noodles before calling it a night.

Sometimes Glenn and I would be on our own, walking around the city at night. On Saturdays there was always the clatter of mahjong tiles coming from open windows. There was trading in the alleys, of things that would have upset me if I saw it today. OK, puppies, which I knew were not destined to be pets. At least I never saw any humans being trafficked, which was surely happening, too.

No matter what time of day or night, there were always people up and about. At three in the morning it was not at all unusual to see little kids out on the sidewalk, eating big bowls of noodles, obviously with chopsticks that looked way too long for them, wearing flip flops and pajamas. Or clothes that looked like pajamas. My theory was that several families shared an apartment, and took turns sleeping inside. That was the only way I could explain little kids out there at 3 a.m. like the sidewalk was their living room. When I see the shows now about people living in cages there because that's all they can afford, my theory seems likely.

We stayed out at the weekend house for a month, playing tennis and being bums, really. I wish I could report we learned Cantonese *and* Mandarin, but no such luck. The only thing I remember learning was how to chop with a cleaver.

On Sundays, the cooks arrived first with mountains of food. I would stand entranced in the doorway of the kitchen while they chopped with lightning speed and absolute precision. There would be ducks and chickens and probably fish or beef and a table full of vegetables to turn into the ten or so distinctive dishes required when eight or ten family members arrived for Sunday lunch. I learned by watching, since I was never invited into the kitchen.

The hallmark of good Chinese food is absolute freshness. Our hostess, Rosalind, told me one time she and her husband were in Paris, staying at the Ritz and having dinner at Maxim's, one of Paris' most celebrated five star restaurants. When the maitre'd came over to their table, he unctuously inquired about their enjoyment of the meal. "Is everything to your liking, Monsieur et Madame?"

"No," responded Rosalind. "The chicken is not fresh enough."

They were used to the freshest and best. In seafood restaurants, it was fairly common to pick your dinner out from the tank where it was swimming around with its friends.

Besides learning to appreciate the freshness of food, I learned that when you are a passenger in a little Mazda sports car and the driver makes the wrong turn on a crowded road and is in the incoming lane, since they drive on the left, it's a good idea to put your head down, get down in the floorboard and pray. Or pass out. I did one of those, coming home from town late one night. I don't really know how Glenn got us out of it, since we were on a major road with a tall divider and cars were coming right at us, and of course I can't ask him since he's no longer with us.

You might think I was incredibly calm. I was, but I had help. When we ran into Portuguese Tony in town, he gave me a little envelope of heroin, which I liked way too much. "The first one's free" was very effective marketing. I became, for a few weeks, a good customer. And when I put it down, I could just walk away from it, so I must have just used it occasionally. I knew better than to use it every day.

Glenn never did really have the stomach for opiates. In my journal I note that "Glenn threw up several times -- once in the sink as I was washing the dishes." That's the power of being stoned, that I didn't even register how disgusting that was.

A word about heroin here: I liked the way heroin made all my inner pain disappear. I liked the smoothness of days with it. What I didn't like was how bad I felt without it. In fact, I felt so bad I figured it was something not to do again. But of course, I did. It was so available, so easy.

Albert was in and out of our lives, visiting us out at the country house in Repulse Bay before leaving for Saigon. We mainly went out with our hosts, went to the racetrack, ate in a zillion restaurants. Even I knew the races were fixed. In one afternoon, a horse broke its leg and was shot right there,

77

a horse left the gate riderless, and one fell in the middle of the race. Years and years later, one of my dad's business associates, the richest one, not our host, was indicted for fixing the races at Happy Valley Racecourse. He was the one who always seemed scary to me, inscrutable in a hard and cold way. I'm sure he was a very dangerous man.

We went to the floating restaurant in Aberdeen, but being on such a flamboyant boat, eating tons of gorgeous seafood, surrounded by all these poor fisher families on sampans with their skinny kids eating rice with their hands was flat depressing to me. I just couldn't get used to that part of Asia, that such extremes existed side by side with seeming acceptance on all parts. Our rich hosts never seemed to notice; it was just part of life. I had never seen so many poor people. Of course I ate, and the food was amazing, but going on the restaurant and leaving, we were surrounded by people so much less fortunate it felt wrong.

And somewhere along in there, I met Ernie, a half Portuguese, half Chinese guy who might have been a friend of Portuguese Tony. Or anyone else for that matter; he knew half the city. He was an intriguing blend, kind of typical in a way of the polyglot, mixed-race Asian world he grew up in. His beautiful features were more Khmer than Chinese. He looked just like the pictures I'd seen from the Temples at Angkor Wat in Cambodia, his favorite place. He studied, bought and collected artifacts from every temple he could get to, spoke a bunch of languages and was married to a much older blond Russian prostitute with a crippled leg. If I wanted to scramble up my honeymoon, I sure was doing an excellent job of it.

At first Ernie and his friend Jeanne were friends with both me and Glenn. Jeanne was a twenty seven year old frustrated English school teacher who spent her two years teaching in the "Colony" by getting high, masturbating (she told me) and filling her apartment full of freaks. There was Frank, the forty year old bleached blond gay guy who danced in an ice skating show at Expo, and Girly, the three foot seven inch Filipina midget who was twenty eight and looked fourteen. Jeanne sort of had the hots for everyone and anyone, but nothing seemed to come her way, and she and Ernie were just friends.

He was very guarded, but as we got to know him, he let his walls down little by little. As I noted in my journal, "He is opening up and giving up his pretenses, one by one, and becoming more human and less mysterious." Glenn and I became more estranged, more distant, and Ernie and I became lovers, first secretly, and then not so secretly. It was a time of tension and horrible conversations about splitting up or not, and sometimes pretending none of it was happening, like when Glenn, Ernie and I all went out for dinner.

Really, if you were married and had a lover, would you agree to all go out to dinner? It was like going out for dinner and a big hairy gorilla comes and sits on the table and you keep passing the dishes around it, trying not to notice its big ass there. It was such bullshit not to just talk about what was going on, but I was well trained in the dubious art of pretending everything was ok, and Glenn and Ernie didn't want to touch the monkey, either. So we talked about things like the racetrack and world events and the food and not the fact that I was married to Glenn and sleeping with Ernie, or what, if anything, that might mean to the future of our marriage. Besides being second rate conversation, it was uncomfortable. There was a feeling of holding my breath, of my stomach being tight, of dreading the moment when someone would say the obvious and we'd have to tell the truth.

That must have come from childhood, when telling the truth got me slapped or the silent treatment. When I was about twelve, my mother uncharacteristically touched my hair and told me, "You have such beautiful hair," to which I responded, "Don't be jealous." Why would I say that, anyway? My dad knocked me across the room, yelling, "Don't talk to your mother like that!"

What made it such a horrible lifelong issue to just tell the truth, as if pretending was going to make things ok and get me what I wanted? I sure have created a lot of tension with that game plan.

The deal finally was that Glenn would go to Bangkok and I would meet him there in a week. I was happy to have the week without him, with Ernie, who told me he was going to Bangkok in a week, too. Aye yi yi!

Our relationship seemed to have reversed again. After a month of coldness and contempt, Glenn was suddenly mad for me, to touch me, to look at me, to talk to me. It seemed the only thing he wanted to see or know about in all of Southeast Asia was me, and while I had my doubts about the survival of our relationship, he was thrilled that in a week we would be back together again.

After Glenn left for Bangkok, Bert's friend Buddy Myers invited me to dinner. Buddy had started his own little company Marlboro Textiles that made shirts. Just after he registered the name, the US passed a law that cigarettes couldn't be advertised on TV anymore. Marlboro cigarettes wanted to make hats and t-shirts with their logo, but since he held the patent on "Marlboro Textiles," they couldn't. He sold his little company to Marlboro cigarettes for Fifteen Million Dollars, a huge sum in the early 70's, when being a millionaire was rare and noteworthy.

He invited me out to dinner and ordered a steak for me. "But Buddy," I told him, "I don't eat steak."

"You will if I get it for you," he told me.

Even though I told him no, he insisted. I had salad and a potato while he sat there absolutely incredulous that I didn't touch the steak on my plate. Buddy got so much money it confused him and he thought he was in charge of the Universe.

Welcome to Penang

Bangkok

When I got to Bangkok I met Glenn at the Atlanta, aka the Hippy Hotel, full of hippy foreigners, while Ernie went to stay at Ming's downtown Chinese hotel where he always stayed. He had stuff to do, so we decided to just keep in touch over the next few days and see how things played out with me and Glenn.

The Hippy Hotel was at the end of a small dead end street with almost no traffic. People came there to recharge and take refuge. It was like a safe house. Room doors were pretty much open up on the second floor where we were, because people wandered in and out playing music and sharing drugs and road stories.

There was someone who had just arrived from Ecuador with cocaine. I had never tried cocaine before and it was absolutely pure. For years afterwards I tried to match that experience of starry luminous walls and euphoria, but it led me down some darker paths, unwittingly substituting heroin for cocaine since at least it gave a buzz. This batch *might* have come from one of the Air America guys who hung out there. They were big American cowboys, and even

81

though they were supposed to be there upholding some kind of law and order, (puh-leeze!) they loved hanging out and getting high. So they were fun, in a wary, borderline kind of way.

All through my journals from the Asia days I talk about coke, and about feeling so badly when I don't have it, and then when I get some I feel so much better. I even wonder why I've got the sniffles, which dry right up when I get a little "coke" again. Wake up, little Susie! That wasn't coke, that was heroin. Was I that dopey (literally) or was I just trying to kid myself???

I use it back and forth, all through the Asian adventures, but especially when we go up to Laos and it is $1 a gram for pure heroin. As if I would know pure from not pure, but it was pretty potent. I'd do a teeny bit, snort it, and then sit for hours and stare at nothing. We wondered why Glenn threw up so much, but he never was able to stomach opiates. I could. I finally quit using it when we ran out in Chieng Mai, in northern Thailand and I became as mean as a snake, actually spitting at Glenn. Yeah, glamorous.

And here's the craziest part: I didn't even know I was doing heroin until I sat here writing this book nearly fifty years later and started reading my old journals. Coke? Throwing up? Runny nose? Feeling sick? Getting mean? These are not coke problems, they are heroin after effects. Boy am I glad and lucky I didn't die or become a true to life junkie. I think I didn't do it long enough, and thank God I ran out.

The first day I was in Bangkok, Glenn told me we should avoid the prostitute he'd been hanging out with since she'd threatened to kill or beat me if she saw me. She obviously thought he was her ticket to the US. He obviously hadn't found anything *too* inspiring to do there, but look who's talking, Mrs. Having another Affair on Her Honeymoon. As honeymoons go, ours was pretty weird. I wanted to go off on an adventure with Ernie, and wanted Glenn to go off on what I conceived of as a consciousness-raising mission for him. I wanted something to happen to him, some spark to get lit that would make me want to be with him and feel inspired as I once had been. He had been such a free thinker and seemed so ahead of the game in New York, but now he was kind of lost and uninterested and negative. Asia was not his optimal playing field.

I wanted a way to connect, and I admit I didn't really know how except to try to change *him*. As obvious as it is now that this approach never works, I tried it for many years. All Glenn wanted to do was go back to New York, and I was so hungry for the travel experience, even if it was uncomfortable and dirty at times. We were having a hard time connecting except when we were stoned, which we managed to be most of the time. I wanted him to fall in love with Asia and traveling, but he never did. I'm sure he wanted me to dream of a life in New York City as the wife of a successful attorney, but I never did that, either.

The Hippy Hotel was full of characters. My hands-down favorite was Heinrich, who was unlike anyone I'd ever met. He was so unbounded. A year or so before, he had been travelling from Austria through Japan and met the cast of "Hair" in Tokyo. When he found out that none of the cast members had ever smoked weed, he took it upon himself to remedy that sad situation, his theology being you couldn't sing and dance a musical about hippies without at least trying a little weed. In an altruistic gesture, he traveled to Korea, purchased a kilo and brought it back into the country. I suppose you'd call it smuggling, only he just carried it in. There was so little focus on weed in 1970, especially in Japan.

Somehow the Japanese Mafia, aka the Yakuza, got involved. Maybe they thought this blond Afro'ed guy was cutting into their business, but suddenly there were both

83

gangsters and police looking for him. He became the focus of a countrywide manhunt.

Through his new friends in the cast, he met Patty, the baby-faced and uber-entitled daughter of an Italian Mafia boss and a Japanese woman. To her credit, when things got hot, Patty got Heinrich out of there. He had to run, and her ass was basically grass if they found out she was the one who got him away. So he took her with him, on her first non-luxury tour of the world.

They traveled by thumb and cheap boats, island to island. They didn't have enough money for more than the sub-economy class, which is pretty damn sub. You get a place on the floor to unroll a sleeping bag and there's a toilet, maybe a sink for all the passengers on that level. It was a great way to meet interesting travelers and trade information about places to go -- and places to avoid -- but a tough intro into economy travel for a princess. At first, this was high adventure for Patty; after a while, she got really tired of being poor.

Eventually the two of them made their way to Bangkok and the Hippy Hotel, which is where we met. Somewhere along the way they had picked up a fifteen-year-old sweet-faced American boy running away from his family in Singapore or Hong Kong; the three of them lived in the room down the hall. It fell on Heinrich to support them because Patty had saved his life. As he put it, he would take care of her as long as she needed because he owed her that. He told me that he didn't love her or basically even like her most of the time, but he owed her his life. The kid was sweet but really an extra mouth to feed when they basically had nothing. The kid and Patty buddied up, sometimes making fun of Heinrich behind his back, or giving him shit, while Heinrich tried to figure out ways to take care of them.

He would disappear for a few days with just the clothes he was wearing, leaving at night with only a tooth brush and a passport. When he came back, he had money. I can guess at how he got it, but I don't really know since I didn't ask. Or if I did, he didn't tell. Knowing him it was probably mildly illegal, but never violent. He was definitely not that kind of guy.

At some point the kid's brother showed up, tracking him down along the hippie trail, telling him their mother was just sick with worry. He went home to his family, probably happy to after a few weeks of shared cheap rooms and short rations. Heinrich stood by Patty and took care of her until the end, which came a little later when she turned him in to the police to save herself. That made her even harder to like than she already was. Impossible, actually.

On my own little adventure, Ernie offered me possibilities I wouldn't find anywhere else. Since I wanted to see the sights Westerners didn't get to see, he was the perfect guide. And bless his soul, Glenn held to his philosophical belief that marriage should be open for both people to do whatever they were called to do, and never complained or issued any ultimatums. They wouldn't have done him any good anyway, which I'm sure he knew.

So while Glenn headed north to Chiang Mai and the Elephant Festival, I went south with Ernie to Pattaya, which at the time was a small, one-street village where you could ride horses on the beach and eat delicious food off banana leaves. Young boys went up and down the beach selling food and crafts made by their families. They were on foot, smiling and cute and friendly. It was a very low tech place, well before the trend toward harassing tourists to buy your stuff. Or maybe it was like that for me because I was with an Asian guy.

We stayed in a little one story hotel right on the beach for a night, but we still wanted something quieter and more off-the-path. There was something Ernie wanted to show me about "his" Thailand that we needed to get further out for, so he asked around and got us a ride with a fisherman to an

85

island, out from Pattaya Beach. It may have been Ko Lan, Ko Phai or Ko Krok, a small island where the fisherman lived in a little village.

This was way before tourism hit that part of Thailand, and I was probably the first non-Asian who stayed on the island. I may have been the first non-Asian some of the people there, especially the children, had ever seen. A village family took us in and offered us food and a place to sleep for something like a dollar a day.

It was immediately obvious that this would *not* be happening if I were with Glenn. The whole thing would not be possible: Glenn would never go for it. I craved this adventure, which I never would have been able to envision or imagine. Trying to express it to Glenn would have sounded like, "I want to go out in a fishing boat to a tiny village on a remote island and sleep in a family's home on the floor under a mosquito net." I didn't know that was what I wanted, because I couldn't imagine it, and Glenn would have said a complete and final NO. As an added bonus, Ernie was really beautiful, capable, and lots of fun.

Our bed was a straw mat about 1/8" thick on a wooden floor under a mosquito net. The first night I rolled from bone to bone, but by the second night, I slept.

Our food was the same food the family ate, only they fed us first, then ate what was left. I didn't realize that the first night. Ernie kept telling me not to eat all the protein, whatever it was (I remember something soft and white, some kind of fish, I hope.) God, how tiresome I can be; nobody can tell me what to do without an explanation. So I ate all I wanted and then when I realized I was eating *their* protein, too, I felt sorry and a little embarrassed and never did that again. To atone, I went to the store the next day, which was a window in a hut, and bought them some stuff they probably never bought for themselves, like sardines and candy.

Bathing the village way was new for me, too. I learned to take a total bath in a sarong and put on a fresh one, letting the wet, washed cloth fall to the ground to be hung and dried for tomorrow. Here's how it works:

Tie your sarong across your chest, for women, squat and pour water over your head from the gourd in the pail you have filled from the communal water tank. Squatting lets the sarong hold the water like a little bathtub for your bottom parts. You wash with soap and rinse in your little tub, scooping water without ever getting soap into it. This takes a little care and education, but children can do it, so I did, too.

Then you tie your new sarong on as you let the wet one drop. Since it's usually in the 90's temperature wise, there's no problem of catching cold or needing a towel for your hair. Everything dries. And then you sweat again, which is why most of us bathed in the evening, so our skin would get cool and stay that way 'til morning. Pouring cool water over skin so hot it almost sizzles is an amazing feeling. It not only cools your body after another hot, tropical day, but eases your mind, too. Everything feels comfortable and ok, with just a bucket of water.

But the bathroom thing, how was that supposed to work? Except when I was taking a bath in the family enclosure, I was surrounded by little kids. I mean twenty or thirty of them. How was I supposed to shit? I asked Ernie and he laughed and said, just go down the beach. But he looked kind of like the villagers, so the children didn't follow him everywhere, as they did me.

It was at least the third day there when the kids all went back to school or something. We must have arrived on a weekend or holiday when they were all free. I was ecstatic and ran to the beach and walked and walked even though there was no one in sight anywhere, then found a nice quiet and seemingly hidden spot to relieve myself. When I got up and turned around, there was a fisherman, ten feet away, watching me. He had probably been doing the same, farther back in the bushes where I was kind of scared to go. What a lucky day for him!

He made the universal signal: thumb and fingers of one hand make a circle, index finger of other hand goes in and out of circle. Translates across the globe as "let's fuck."

OMG the kids and constipation were better than this; I took off running for the village and he didn't run after me. I'd want to ask on what planet does this look erotic, but since it happened again when I was camping in a remote area in Spain, and this time with a Guardia in uniform, I'd have to say Planet Earth.

Meanwhile, the seas calmed enough for the trip back to the mainland. We'd hitch rides up to Northern Thailand toward Chiang Mai and the mountains. In those days there were areas known as no-man's-lands. There was a big one, about six miles deep, along the border of Malaysia and Thailand where our California friend Craig got stuck one night. He was hitching rides up to Bangkok and fell asleep on a bench somewhere. When he woke up, he was surrounded by bandits with machetes and maybe a gun or two. They were going to rob him, but all he had was a toothbrush and a passport, and when he pulled his pockets out and showed they were empty, those bandits took a liking to him instead. They fed him, gave him a safe place to sleep and in the morning walked him to the other side. Ernie and I inadvertently ended up in a no-man's-land. It's not like these things were marked on a map, and anyway, we didn't have a map. We were just headed north.

On a very wide smooth road through the jungle, a jeep came along. It was the only vehicle we had seen for about an hour, and night was coming on. In the tropics, it's bright day and then it's night. I was nervously asking Ernie stuff like, "do you think anyone's going to come along?" and "where do you think we are?" as if he were a prophet and not some guy I had joined up with for an adventure. The jeep had two guys in the front and six in the back with machine guns. Oh boy.

They came to a screeching halt and the man in the front, the passenger and obviously the boss, yelled to us, "Come on up here with me." What to do? He seemed friendly enough and we didn't appear to have a choice, so we climbed in. We didn't have much stuff with us, just a little bag each. That's because in the tropics, you don't need much at all, just a few light clothes and a light cloth, like a sarong, to cover you at night and keep the mosquitoes off. Most of my stuff was stored in the big storeroom at the Hippy Hotel, another kind amenity.

The guy turned out to be really nice. He was the gangster head of the area. It was obvious he wasn't an elected official because he didn't have all that stuffy shit and medals going on. He also spoke perfect English. The first thing he asked me, when he found out I was from America was, "Does your father know where you are?" He was very concerned. I told him yes, my father knew I was in Thailand, and he would be very happy to know that there was a father in Thailand who looked after me. I told him there were fathers all over the world who looked after me, which was basically true, again thank God.

We pulled up to his house, a big sprawling affair in the jungle, where he invited us in for a drink, it being too late by then for food. I really never drank, but I knew the taste of a few things I liked. One of them was Drambuie and amazingly enough, he brought out a bottle. Yes, I would love a little drink, I told him enthusiastically. When I brought the glass to my lips and tasted the first sip, I almost gagged. He had filled this Drambuie bottle, which did look a little worn, with local Tiger whisky, a slightly refined form of gasoline. We got it down. We had to. Then they took us to the guesthouse where we slept like babies.

Next day his guards drove us out to the main road where we again stuck out our thumbs. As we neared Bangkok we were picked up by some Americans who were on their way to the ancient pottery kilns of Sukhothai. They had been before, many times, as had Ernie. Did we want to come along? For sure! I was astounded, mind-blown to find shards and pieces that were four, five or maybe six hundred years old.

At the end of the day, headed toward Bangkok, we stopped in a roadside diner. We had been in the hot sun all day. Nobody was hungry, but while they had ice cold drinks, I ordered some food because I knew I was supposed to eat. That's how disconnected I was. My food relationship has never gotten straightened out, like eating when I'm not hungry because I'm supposed to, or think I am. Now I'm seventy and it's way better than my old anorexic/bulimic days, but I still get disconnected, eating things that don't work, or too much or too little. It's the most basic life skill, eating when we are hungry, and it gets so tangled up in so many people.

These were the adventures I wanted to have, and I didn't even know about them until I was on them. Where in my imagination would I find that island off Thailand's coast, or that gangster boss in the jungle? Meanwhile, Glenn was awaiting me in Penang, so when we got back to Bangkok I hopped a bus or train and off I went. Ernie drifted back to Hong Kong and his life there, never to be seen by me again.

Penang

Penang is a beautiful island in Malaysia right near the border with Thailand, in the very north of the country. The main city, Georgetown, where you come and go on the ferry, is across the bay from the town of Butterworth. We eventually rented a house in the village of Batu Ferringhi, right near Tanjung Bungah, on the north coast of the island. I loved those names!

Glenn met me in Georgetown and the very first thing he wanted to show me, after we stowed our stuff in a hotel, was the opium den. He'd been going there every night, smoking opium with the emaciated Chinese guys who frequented it, and he thought he'd found the very thing that could impress me, which he had.

Right in the middle of Georgetown was a grotty looking big Army tent kind of structure. We went in through a flap door to a dark, silent space with four wooden beds in two rows down a center aisle. The man at the door indicated two of the beds. We took them and lay on our sides in the "smoke-de-pipe" position which he mimed for me, and Glenn paid for a gram of opium, which was six pipes, three for each of us. This is pretty astounding to consider as modern day Malaysia has some of the most draconian drug laws on the planet, and this was right there near the port.

It was something like $2. The man working the flames opened the packet of opium and put one sixth of it on his little skewer which he turned over the flame to soften it. When it was just right, he put it in Glenn's pipe, since I wanted a visual on how this was done. The rest of the sections of opium he heated the same way, putting it in each of our pipes in turn. The smoke was almost sickeningly sweet. After three pipes each, we were done and went out to walk along the port to a place to have drinks and dinner.

Since Glenn had been there a few days, he picked the restaurant we'd go to. I was feeling fine, actually not feeling much different than before, maybe a little calmer. I had never smoked opium before and didn't know what to expect, but I expected to feel more *something*. More stoned, more loopy, more something. Instead, I felt calm and quiet.

Glenn meanwhile definitely felt something because as we sat there having drinks, he got up, staggered over to the railing of the balcony and vomited over the side. Nobody yelled, so I guess he didn't get anyone, but it got me fit-to-be-tied laughing. He puked a few more times, something that generally makes me response-puke immediately but this time just made me laugh more, so maybe there was something to this opium smoking, after all.

I never have gotten sick on opiates. It's just body chemistry. They don't make me feel sick, they make me feel normal, or what I imagine as normal: calm and serene, as if they are the missing component of my chemical makeup.

The next day we went out to the beach town of Batu Ferringhi, because we heard some Australian girls had rooms to let in their house. They did, and who should be staying there but Heinrich and Patty, just in from Bangkok. The energy in the house was just a little intense, since one of the girls was getting set to smuggle twenty kilos of hash into Australia. She had been fasting for four days, so her eyes were brilliantly clear blue and she was skinny enough to have the extra forty pounds wrapped around her thin frame look normal.

Beach living was supposed to be fun and relaxing, not crazed and intense, so we found a house of our own, a large wooden three room house right by the center of town with a little back area for bathing and the outhouse. There was enough room for Heinrich and Patty, so they moved in with us. That was kind of weird as she and I weren't friendly. Glenn didn't pay much attention to her, and Heinrich just tried to keep her happy, a Herculean, never-ending task. I resented her treating him like one of the servants she had been brought up with, but it wasn't my dog fight. Heinrich and I could talk and hang for hours. Glenn and Heinrich got along fine. Patty we all just did our best with.

Down the street we met an Aussie guy, Jim, and his Spanish girlfriend Meira with huge dark eyes. They lived in a simple little beachside house with a local couple, Sammy the fisherman and his adorable and chubby second wife, Jenga. Jenga was way younger than Sammy and she cooked for him, and for all of us, every night. She served me the first stingray (manta ray?) I had ever eaten, in a curry. Everything she made was over-the-top delicious.

One day some of us decided to take some hallucinogen, and Sammy wanted to take some, too. Sammy just loved it. All evening he would call out, "Jenga! Come out here and see the colors." Jenga would run out and look, but to her, everything looked the same as usual.

A few minutes later something would catch his eye and again he would yell out, "Jenga, Jenga come look, come see the colors," and obediently she would run out and see nothing different from her usual beautiful Paradise.

On the final try she got impatient. She was trying to fix dinner, after all, and didn't have time for all this foolishness. When Sammy called her to come look at the colors, she stuck her hand on her hip and wagged her finger in his face, "You look at de colors, Sammy. You de one dat took de ting."

In her sweet accent, hand on her hip feigning anger, we all fell over laughing. Jenga was sweet like sugar. She didn't even know how to be not sweet.

More than anything she wanted a baby. She and Sammy had been trying, but so far, nothing took. She asked me to work on her or do something to help her, so I did what I knew at the time, which wasn't much. I did know enough to tell her she would probably conceive in the next few months, since I knew you had to think positively to get energy to move. I told her what was probably a cross between a lie and magical thinking, that she would probably get pregnant soon. My thinking was: what could it hurt? I knew worrying that it would never happen would constrict her energy, so I went with the idea that believing it would might open it up and let it happen.

The beach in Batu Ferringhi was gorgeous. We were there morning and evening, walking, hanging out. It was a lovely and quiet time for us where I did lots of drawings and wrote long letters home to my family and friends. We met new friends from all over the world. There was a Canadian couple where he was desperately in love with her, and she wasn't. There was an American girl following a guy from California because she was desperately in love with him, and he wasn't. There was nothing really to *do*, besides the occasional trip to a waterfall or to town, so there was plenty of time for introspection. It was the kind of place you could stay for a long time, if it weren't for extending visas and getting kinda bored after a while.

This was when, as I mentioned before, Marissa, the Canadian woman, asked us why we had gotten married. And without a second's hesitation, my response was, "We got married so we could travel." Then, when I saw Glenn's face, I knew I had way oversimplified.

It was obvious that Glenn and I were different. I was dreamy and artsy and interested in learning things about Chinese medicine from the herb doc down the street, while Glenn always bought the newspapers when he went to town and liked to keep up with and talk about world events, especially sports and politics.

And then Heinrich got this idea about getting forty kilos of hash and taking it to Australia. The Australian girl we first stayed with had been successful and gotten through safely. He'd been thinking of it ever since: tired of living hand-to-mouth, he wanted to do one big score and relax for a while. It seemed like a reasonable next move at the time to all pack up and head toward Kathmandu. But first, Glenn and I wanted to see Singapore, and then fly to Hong Kong. My father, Bert, was arriving in Hong Kong in a couple of weeks and we wanted to see him when we could. Flights between Hong Kong and Bangkok were less than $100, so that part was easy. We arranged to meet Heinrich and Patty in Calcutta in a month or so and make our way to Kathmandu together..

Everything was easy. We'd hitchhike down to Singapore, just to see it, and then go back to Bangkok, get our stored belongings and fly out of there. Since we were going to stay with Bert's friends, as usual, and be wined and dined, one more low budget adventure would be a perfect prelude to the high class city life of Hong Kong.

Singapore and back

It was kind of amazing that Glenn would agree to hitchhike down to Singapore. Of course we had hitched around Japan, but that was with Louie, an intrepid guide if ever there was one, and it was in Japan, the cleanest and safest of places. Just the two of us traveling down the length of Malaysia, I was amazed he'd go for it, but he did.

Our first ride was on the back of a newspaper truck, and we spread out sleeping bags on the tops of stacks and stacks of bound newspapers, bound for Kuala Lumpur, and hung on as best we could. Kuala Lumpur is a huge city, with the largest airport in Southeast Asia, but we didn't see much of it since the truck let us off on the outskirts of town, in front of a small apartment building where an Indian guy and a Malay guy were sitting out on the step, talking. We ended up spending the night there; the Indian guy was the night watchman and he had one of those beds made of rope and knots. The guys all decided I should have the bed, and they'd hang out and drink and tell lies. That was the most torturous

95

excuse for a bed I've ever spent the night on, and I was glad to get up and on our way in the morning.

One of the best lessons I got from Ernie was to always stay in Chinatown, or in Chinese hotels, to get the cheapest, cleanest deals. Glenn and I got a room in a Chinese hotel that overlooked a market, and early the next morning, market sounds woke me up. I looked out the window to see a man with the huge headless corpse of an enormous snake wrapped round and round him, carrying it in to the market.

Singapore was like Hong Kong without the rich friends who treated us to every last thing, so after just a day or so, we got on the train and headed back toward Bangkok, the Hippy Hotel, and the plane to Hong Kong. Somewhere along in there, we took the local train instead of the express, and it seemed to stop in every town and village. A fat Thai Grandma told me she loved me and that we should come to her house, and so we did.

The Nasomchai family of Bandon took us in like long lost family. We slept, we ate, we washed our clothes, nasty from just a few dusty sweaty days of travel. Our bed was on the second floor, right over the wooden platform that served as the grandma's bed. All night long she seemed to roll her fat body around, cutting huge farts. She was a great beauty and seemed to enjoy her life immensely. I was really glad we had taken a few days off with them, just because she said she loved me.

Glenn and I had created a project of buying souvenirs, presumably to sell in New York. We went to a special village to buy leather "shadow puppets" that we stored in my mom's shed in Chappaqua that got eaten by rodents. I bought Buddhas, which are now totally illegal to take out of the country and may have been then, too. Most of what I bought is gone, and has been for years, but for a time, it brought Glenn and me together and gave us something we could do as a project instead of talking about our marriage. That was getting pretty fucking tiresome!

Hong Kong, traveler's Paradise

We got to Hong Kong a few days before Bert was due to arrive and were staying with his friends the Kitamura's in their two bedroom apartment. Kit, the husband, was a retired Kamikaze pilot in business with Bert. Mitzi, his retired airline hostess wife, stayed home now, so she was there most of the time with very little to do since they had a housekeeper.

George Harrison's brand new "All Things Must Pass," had just come out, and we had brought an ample supply of Thai sticks, so all day long we smoked this amazing weed and played music and sang and danced. I did, anyway.

Mitzi watched me dancing around and laughing, and she wanted what I was having, so after a day or two she said, "I want to smoke marijuana."

"Ok," I agreed. What could happen? Just a little weed, right?

Forgetting, or just overlooking the fact that I was used to smoking this stuff for the last three months sitting on the beaches of everywhere, I rolled a nice fat joint and she took a

97

couple of hits, Glenn and I showing her how to do it. On the third one I thought, "Uhhh, that might be enough!"

The lag time was smooth. It usually is. And then it hit. OMG, she ran to her room, slammed and locked the door. I heard her throwing up, surely from nerves, and then she began to scream, "I'm going to die! I'm going to die!"

"Open your door, Mitzi, please. I promise you're not going to die!" I pleaded outside her door for an hour or so as she screamed inside. Finally I gave up, and waited for hell to pay. The housekeeper/cook was cowering in the background, surely wondering what the hell was going on with these crazy foreigners, which included the Japanese.

When her former Kamikaze pilot husband came home, I expected him to get all kinds of pissed off, but when she told him, he started laughing. He actually thought it was really funny. The reason he was still alive was that when his mission had come to fly with his squadron to sink an American ship, his mechanic had found a problem with his plane, so he had been grounded. Everyone else on the mission died. Small wonder he didn't take things very seriously.

Mitzi calmed down and eventually we all had dinner together and all was pretty much forgiven until the next day, when Kit had a business meeting with Bert and told him the story. As funny as Kit found it, Bert didn't. We had "dishonored him with his friends." I got a major earful about how I always associated with the worst people, and how these were nice people and I had done this bad thing.

I could have told him that the night before, his nice honorable friend had shown me and Glenn a porn film of a blonde girl getting fucked by a German Shepherd, and I mean a dog, not some Aryan storm trooper in lederhosen. I would have told him but it didn't seem the moment, and didn't appear it would advance my case.

After that, although I don't remember anything linking the two events of smoking pot and moving, Glenn and I moved back to Bert's other friend's house in Repulse Bay, the country house that came with the car and the gardener and the tennis court.

One thing happened that was really weird on that trip to Hong Kong, and that was seeing Ernie's mom. She was the manager of the most exclusive clothing store in Hong Kong where my dad had my mom's silk clothes made for her. Bert and I went in there, and this was months after Ernie and I had been hanging out. I hadn't seen him since we parted in Bangkok, and I got the feeling, since he had the pulse of Hong Kong pretty well down, he didn't want to run into me. Bert had no idea about all this, but Ernie's mom did and  also knew her son was married to a prostitute. My dad bought me some beautiful silk thing and she actually said, "That will be good for walking the streets in."

I just looked at her, like, whatever. When my dad and I left, he said, "Sheila was certainly weird today," and I said, "Whatever." Or whatever we said for whatever, back then.
And then this twenty year old Australian girl named Judy, red headed, very pretty and sexy, showed up from Bangkok. She had the hots for Glenn and was after him, no two ways about it.

Glenn just wanted me, but as soon as we moved back to the house in the country, I was back in relationship with that brown powder and nothing and nobody else really mattered to me. I actually told Glenn to go sleep with Judy and leave me alone, since after a while she had moved into the house with us.

And just to totally foul the nest, along came my father, who got the craziest crush on Judy. He started taking her out with him, buying her all kinds of expensive clothes and jewelry, and even took her to a business dinner with all his Chinese colleagues. These were big league guys, and they all had mistresses, sometimes several. They would *never* have brought those girls to a business dinner. It was *so* not done.

So Bert made a fool of himself to Judy, to his associates and to me. He was so embarrassed by the time he left for New York that he wouldn't even look at me when he said goodbye, and for the first time in our lives we didn't talk for months.

Judy continued her appeals to Glenn, who gave in pretty easily, considering my considerable lack of interest. At least I knew she hadn't slept with my father because she told me she hadn't, and since she was sleeping with my husband, she really had no reason to lie. Now *that* would have been a story. Yuck!

Years later my mom was looking at some pictures I had from then and immediately prickled when she saw the pictures of Judy.

"Who's that?" she wanted to know. She had remarkable antennae.

"Oh that was our Australian friend Judy who had a crush on Glenn and followed him around for a while hoping he'd leave me," I told her, to her very immediate and obvious relief.

Standing on a corner in Calcutta

I was only afraid in Calcutta once, right near the beginning of our stay. I was walking with Glenn, and Heinrich and Patty, who were going to buy hash in India and Nepal, fly to Australia with it and go to jail after getting in safely and living off their sales for several months. Well, Heinrich did. Patty turned him in to save herself when she got caught smoking a joint with a friend. According to Heinrich's first letter from prison, she told the police, "If you let me go, I'll tell you where you can find a guy with five kilos of hash (or whatever was left at the time)" and they did and she did. He spent three years in prison and she went back to Japan, presumably to continue her life as an entitled princess.

As I peedoodled along, looking at stuff and thinkin' about other stuff, I realized the three of them were way ahead and suddenly I was surrounded by grubby little street urchins, ten or twelve of them. They all started grabbing my arms and hands shouting, "Baksheesh! Baksheesh!" That translates as "money" or more exactly, "Give me your money."

First I panicked and froze, since there was a whole dirty little pack of them hanging onto me, and I'm not really all that great with bunches of kids at the best of times. Then I turned it on them: "No, *YOU* Baksheesh *ME*!" ha, ha, ha, "You baksheesh me!"

I might've had some change or something I gave them and then we all started laughing and I relaxed and they walked along with me for a while until I caught up to my pack. When I did, the kids just melted off and disappeared. Nothing bothered me much in Calcutta again, besides bedbugs in one hotel room. In a town where the list of what can bother you is pretty endless -- corpses in the train station were a problem for Glenn -- I fell into the Calcutta groove and had a good time.

But India was more than a good time; it was the place of transition for me, where I became aware of a whole different way of being in life. It was where I was introduced to the energetic aspect of life, of the power of what we could sense or feel, even if we couldn't see or name it. I don't remember lots of activities besides eating in restaurants and walking around buying trinkets to send home to New York. I loved the food; I still do. I loved that corn flakes tasted like corn instead of cardboard, and I loved that we could eat in the nicest restaurants in town because they were so cheap. We were business class hippies.

I walked around alone, *a lot*. I don't know what Glenn and the others were doing, but I took long walks alone and nobody bothered me. My interaction with the kids had left me relaxed and non-defensive so I just got left alone. I had experiences that completely changed my life even if they didn't seem like much on the outside. The first was with that bunch of beggar kids. They had *nothing*. Their clothes were rags. They lived on the street, washed at a public faucet and got their food by begging or by the soup wagon that came around once a day. And still, they were laughing and smiling and joking around and cute as they could be. And looking back on it, I realize once I started goofing around with them, they were super friendly. Also, the skill with which they melted into the surroundings and disappeared was something like the man disappearing into the dense jungle in the Philippines. It was artful.

I thought about the kids I knew at home. Hell, I thought about the kid I had been. Even with every single creature comfort, with every toy I ever wanted, I could be a pouty thing, always wanting more. It didn't make me a bad person, or make spoiled rich kids inherently bad, it's just that we all equated happiness with getting what we wanted, with *stuff*. And here, right in front of me, were these kids who were happy with what we would call nothing. One thing they did have was each other.

Later on, when Glenn and I were parting, because, come on, you already knew that was going to happen, right? He was telling me about all the things he wanted that would make him happy. They included, but were not limited to, a penthouse in New York City and a country home with a pool and a tennis court. My reply was, "Happiness doesn't come from what you have. Happiness comes from inside you."

He looked at me like I was a tree huggin' sap and said, "Don't be ridiculous. Happiness comes from what you have." That was probably our deciding moment, in case I still had a doubt.

He ended up having all that and more, but I don't think he was ever really happy. He wouldn't talk to me, so I couldn't ask him.

The most life changing, Inner Life affirming experience happened when I was again walking alone in Calcutta and saw a man begging on a street corner. At first, I couldn't tell if it was a man or a woman, since the physical body was so grotesquely deformed, with legs bent and bowed and arms wrapped in a weird configuration. Later I figured it had to be a man, since he had on pants and no Indian woman would have gone out and stood on the corner in pants in 1970.

A word about beggars: it was once and may still be a practice for beggar parents to maim their own children, a form of job security, a sad lineage that would possibly disqualify them from any other life but one of begging, but that would more or less guarantee their survival in that profession. We cringe and cry and think it's so horrible, but I can only imagine it is a whole lot worse to see your children starve to death. Gratefully, I never had to know.

As I stood across the street looking at this being, standing there with his twisted limbs all contorted, I felt a huge wave of pity for him. "Oh that poor being!" was radiating out from me, and in that instant, I heard the words inside me, "You have *NO IDEA* who I am."

He stared across the street into my eyes and the power of his stare froze me on the spot. Rays of silver light like cords shot from his eyes into my body, right in my stomach area. I *saw* them and felt them enter my torso with a physically powerful impact, with a soft thud like a nerf fist might do.

I had never seen, heard of, or experienced anything like this in my life. I was standing all the way across a street, and I felt those silver cords enter my body and saw them with my own eyes. After a minute or two, I was able to turn away, stunned. My entire understanding of "reality" had just shifted in a way that *nothing* I had done before could even come close to. I did not, indeed, have any idea who he was. All I could see was a poor Indian beggar; all my judgment was on the form. To this day I have to remind myself to look beyond the form; it's so easy to judge purely by what I see.

I don't remember talking to Glenn about this experience. I didn't have the words to convey it, and he didn't have the ears to hear it. He would probably have said I was just stoned, or I was making it up, so I didn't bother. Surely he'd question the fact that the man spoke to me in English, but of course, the man didn't speak to me at all in the physical. Spirit appears to have an instant translation program.

We didn't do India on pennies a day, as many young travelers did. Glenn liked the white tablecloth restaurants where the rich people ate and honestly, I did, too. The food was great and we always felt they were cleaner, although as far as sanitation and water quality went, that was all questionable. But they *looked* cleaner, and that was the best we could do.

Glenn was never a hippie at all, even though he liked to smoke dope with the best of them. He read international newspapers all the time and kept up with world events. He also fairly consistently mentioned his burning desire to get the fuck out of Asia and go back to his friends and family in New York City, and start his career as an attorney.

I liked India well enough. Beggars didn't bother me; I could sit with them and chill, which would never in 1000 years have occurred to Glenn. Behind all the chaos and noise of Calcutta, I saw an ancient pattern of stillness. The time I noticed it the most was when we took the rickshaw ride to Howrah Station to catch the train out of town, heading north to Kathmandu with Heinrich and Patty.

Riding in a rickshaw is weird for Westerners. We're definitely not used to other humans being our beasts of burden, but I rode in them in Thailand and India. They were a common form of taxi, and riding in one, you gave someone the opportunity to earn their living, which was pretty close to the bone for rickshaw drivers. Now I hear they've mostly been replaced by motorized tuk-tuks, but back then, they were mostly powered by human muscle.

Patty and Heinrich were up ahead of us, since only two could ride in a rickshaw, especially with all our luggage. Our Calcutta rickshaw driver may not have been any more skilled than any other, but I was amazed as I watched him weaving his way through the intense "rush hour" end-of-day city traffic. There were cars, trucks and buses, some belching huge clouds of black exhaust. There were cows and bullocks crossing the roads, stopping in the street, holding up traffic.

There were taxis screaming around the corners to brake suddenly, horns blaring. And filling in every single bit of space that was left were the pedestrians, seemingly by the thousands wherever I looked. It was overwhelming.

The rickshaw has two long poles out the front that the man stands between and holds, just like a horse pulling a cart. As he swung around corners or moved through traffic, the ends of the poles missed peoples' heads and the corner lamp posts by inches or less. Motorized vehicles came within fractions of an inch of us, yet nothing ever hit or touched. In all that cacophony, suddenly all I saw was stillness under it all, that all this movement was a Divine Weave and all these beings amazingly knew their parts to keep everything moving smoothly, not colliding.

These days, the closest I've gotten to that experience is driving in Southern California traffic, where everyone goes 90 mph, inches away from each other. The last time I did it, I was acutely aware that if I entertained a thought ("this is really fucked up and dangerous" occurred to me) I would throw a wrench into the weave and someone could have an accident. I said affirmations out loud that whole three hour drive and haven't tried it since!

By the time we got into Calcutta's Howrah Station, I had had a big mind shift from the amazing rickshaw ride, so I said I'd sit with the luggage while Glenn went to buy our tickets. I was sitting there awhile with our bags and all the beggars when I noticed the cleanup squad looking for corpses. I don't *remember* seeing any, but when Glenn returned with our tickets after his heroic efforts, he had. Seeing dead bodies being collected freaked him out. It was kind of at the top of the list of things that freaked him out in India, especially.

He tried so hard to get someone in that station to be efficient, and it pissed him off so thoroughly that nobody was. There were always more people in starched spotless uniforms than could possibly be needed for the job, yet they

106

still didn't manage to get much done. He was always so frustrated by it, but I didn't even notice it. And it wasn't just the hash; he smoked just as much as I did. It was surrender to what was instead of struggling against what wasn't. And the hash.

I felt ok, expansive, at One with Mother India, and then a man punched me in the chest as we walked through a seething sea of humans to our train. It was so impersonal and fast, by the time I turned my head to see who had done it, all I saw were hundreds of identical white-shirted backs, swarming the other way. Looking back at this now, in light of all the sexual abuse crime that has been reported in India in the last few years, it seems less random than it did then.

Patty, Heinrich, Glenn and I traveled First Class with a compartment to ourselves. I remember at stops, people sticking their arms through the windows, either begging or trying to sell us some food items. One man stuck his stump of an arm through the window and Glenn yelled at him, "Get that thing out of here!" And right after that came the man to clean our cabin.

As befitted his station in life as what was then known as an "untouchable," he had to keep his head lower than ours. He came in kind of inching along on his bottom, walking more with his hands than certainly on his feet or even his knees. He wouldn't meet my eye. Glenn yelled at him too, to get the fuck out of there, before I explained that he was our sweeper. Then he just glowered at the poor guy until he left, which didn't take long.

In a way I was comfortable with Glenn's outlook since it was more familiar to me than all these new experiences. At the same time, I didn't like the feeling of agreeing with him when he faulted Indians for being Indian in India, or Asians in general being Asians in Asia. Of course they did fucked up shit, but who doesn't? It's just that our own cultural messes were familiar enough to go unnoticed, while theirs stood out to us like sore thumbs and were easy to ridicule.

107

I only experienced those silver rays one other time although I did hear about them from other people who had seen them pass from our dying Tai Chi Master to his lead student. A couple of years after the Calcutta adventure, I was standing on the balcony of a hotel room in Tangiers, looking out over the main square, watching all the packets and cash being passed from hand to hand under café tables. A young man, probably my age, looked up at me and the silver cords that went from his body to mine almost pulled me off the balcony. Wouldn't you know that my boyfriend chose that very moment to walk out on the balcony, talking to me? That handsome young stranger and I looked at each other for another moment, then turned away. The connection was completely broken.

The next day, we got on a train back to Paris, and who should get in our car but that same young guy. We could barely look at each other. We were so shy and I think amazed or bewildered by whatever it was that had passed between us. We never talked directly, but I remember singing "Maggie May" on that ride. I couldn't look at him directly because I didn't know what I would do if there were some powerful something and I was sitting there with my boyfriend, but when I sneaked looks at him, he was purposefully not looking at me, too.

The Smuggle

It was Glenn's idea from the start. He'd give me that look, then say, "Our friends will think we're punks if we come back from India with nothing!"

I honestly never gave much thought to whether those friends in New York thought we were punks or not, since we were the ones trekking around in Asia and they were the ones sitting in the same apartments in Brooklyn, smoking PCP. I was so tired of Glenn by then, even though we were only on our honeymoon and hadn't even been gone a year. This was his big concern, his friends back in New York thinking he was a punk for not bringing them some hash, so I said, "OK, let's do it." Maybe it would be one thing we could enjoy together on this trip through Asia, and besides, he wouldn't leave it alone.

He didn't like travelling right from the get go, at least not in Asia, where I was so comfortable that I didn't really ever notice how harsh the conditions could be. Except for the time we rented a room in India with four beds in it and one of them was totally infested with biting bugs, I didn't do any complaining about our accommodations. Everyone who knows me now and knows what a total princess I can be about being comfortable might find this surprising, but I slept in all kinds of funky places and learned to bathe in a bucket and lived in a sarong, and I was good with it all. Glenn wasn't -- didn't like it -- and talked constantly about how *great* it was going to be to get back to New York, a reality I was much less drawn to.

The whole idea of our doing a smuggle really started in Kathmandu, with Heinrich and Patty buying forty kgs. of hash to take to Australia. It seemed like a kind of fun project, buying the luggage and finding the guy who put in the false bottoms, then going shopping for new clothes with them and getting Heinrich's huge Afro to lie down enough for them to look like a typical couple of tourists. It was a stretch, especially knowing them, but we helped them get it all together.

And then, they were gone, and I didn't hear from him until a year or so later, from jail. He did three years and, from what I saw, was not the same person on the other side of it. His spirit was so broken, his beautiful free spirit. I never asked him what had happened to him there, but it was obviously terrible.

Anyway, we got about three or four kilos in Kathmandu. I let Glenn do all the bargaining. All I remember is the table in our hotel room covered, and I mean covered, with samples ranging from fist size down, of all these different kinds of hash. I would sit and smoke a bunch and then run to the bathroom, losing fluid and blood way more than was good. I was a rack of bones, feverish, crazed, and *always* smoking. I never gave it a thought until the day Glenn told me, "You've got to get out of this place or you're going to die here." He was probably right. When I got home, I weighed 96 lbs. and my own mother didn't recognize me.

Kathmandu was a dirty place. We got there the same week the very first jumbo jets full of tourists began to arrive. Before that, Nepal was the hidden kingdom, full of mystery and allure. After that it became a tourist mecca, where everything was for sale.

In May of 2018, I was talking to my friend Myfanwy who had just gotten back from ten days in Kathmandu at a tattoo convention with her husband, Chris. First she told me about the bottled water they had bought in the market, and how Chris was so thirsty he drank half of his before it even registered that the cap hadn't been sealed, or screwed on very tight. After fevers and convulsions all night, and losing fluids waaay too fast, he was able to pull himself together and keep tattooing, with frequent bathroom breaks. Yeah, that sounded pretty familiar to me. I don't know where I got it from, all that fluid loss, but the possibilities were many and varied.

"Did you go down to the river?" I asked her. "Did you see the vultures?"

She looked at me kind of blankly, wondering what I was talking about.

There were many visuals I had of Kathmandu: the marauding monkey bands surrounding the stupa at Swayambhu, stealing food from anyone trying to get by them; the corner in town where animals were slaughtered for meat, where the mud was always slick with blood; the green hash cakes for sale in the bakeries; the public fountain where people bathed together and shared germs a-plenty. But nothing stuck in my mind's eye more than the vultures down at the river, fighting over the carcasses of donkeys and goats.

Those vultures appeared to be about six feet tall, with a wingspan of maybe twelve feet. When I research it, this seems impossible: according to Wikipedia, the largest vulture is the cinereous vulture "a large raptorial bird also known as the black vulture, monk vulture, or Eurasian black vulture... It is one of the two largest Old World vultures, attaining a maximum size of 14 kg, (roughly 30 lbs), 1.2 m long (almost 4 ft) and 3.1 m (a bit over 10 ft) across the wings."

Okay, good enough. But why would or should anyone care about vultures? Besides the spectacle of huge birds of prey screaming and fighting over dead carcasses, I hadn't had much interest in vultures until I read about the plight of the Parsis, a small religious sect in India who believe that after death, in order to reach Heaven, the body had to be placed on a "Tower of Silence" to be consumed by vultures, liberating the soul.

But something happened in the 1990's: vultures began dying in unprecedented numbers. The Parsis had to reconfigure their ancient methods of disposing of bodies, because there just weren't enough vultures.

It turned out the culprit was an anti-inflammatory drug given to cattle. In a country where a huge percentage of the human population can't get their hands on the medications they need, I have trouble understanding how so many cows were given anti-inflammatories, but there you have it. Since 80% of Indians are Hindus and don't eat cows, the cows would just die, to be eaten by the vultures.

The vultures sickened and died, of kidney failure if you want to know, in huge numbers. In 1980 there were an estimated 80 million of them; today there are only several thousand.

Not just the Parsi people, but all of India has suffered from this loss. Without vultures to clean up carrion, there has been a huge spike in the numbers of rats and wild dogs, often carrying rabies. The estimated cost of the decline of vultures has been $26 BILLION a year in India alone. And all from wanting cows, that hardly anybody eats, to be pain free. That drug has since been outlawed and there is a vulture breeding project going on, but reestablishing a viable population is going to take a long time.

Of course, in 1971, none of this had happened yet. I'd just smoke some hash and go for a walk. Once or twice my meanderings led me sliding in the bloody mud down to the river, where I watched the vultures fighting over the bloated carcasses of animals lying on the riverbanks. It was a scene from Hell. Usually I went somewhere else, but I did see that and it was a scene of unrivaled carnage and violence. And now, according to Myfanwy, the carcasses just lie there, which is even worse, more dangerous to the water supply, and infinitely less interesting to watch.

So there we were in Kathmandu, planning the big smuggle back to our friends in New York. First Heinrich and Patty left, their bags all packed with their weight of hash. A few days later, we did. We wrapped the hash in tape, then taped it to our bodies. I forgot about my tape allergy until we got to Delhi. It was about 110 degrees, and I had this rash all around my torso, every place the tape touched. The night we arrived, it was close to midnight before we got into town from the airport. I was wearing a cotton dress I'd had made from prayer shawls in Kathmandu. Boy, was that a stupid idea. It was long sleeved and modest, but on it, in what I saw as a pretty red design on a bright yellow background, it said the name of the God Ram, over and over. As Glenn went ahead to find this hotel we'd been given the address for, men suddenly surrounded me, chanting "Ram, Ram, Ram, Ram." It was as if someone squeezed the buildings like sponges, and men appeared from every doorway, circling around me, all chanting "Ram, Ram, Ram, Ram."
I yelled for Glenn, who came running back and told the guys, now quite a large crew of them, to fuck off and leave me alone. From what I read about India in the last few years, things might go differently now. There is more violence. But in 1971 they did just that: they fucked off and left me alone.
We stayed in a hotel for a few days while Glenn looked for more hash, because what we had already wasn't enough to suit him. I sat in the air conditioning, nursing my rash. Besides, this was really his rodeo.

It was a Sikh taxi or rickshaw driver who came up with the next three or four kilos, and that was enough. We bought tickets to Amsterdam because I had read somewhere that prisoners in Amsterdam had their own private cells, each with a TV and three meals a day. That sounded pretty good, just in case.

We bought new clothes for the smuggle. I had had some dresses made in Kathmandu, some that weren't made of prayer shawls and were nice and modest and simple. I also bought some very fashionable vinyl heels that looked great in Delhi and like crap when I wore them in Amsterdam, but I felt very modern and invisible. Glenn had on some New York bell bottoms and a long white Indian shirt, clean, with short hair, like the young tourists we were.

Our friends, Australian Jim and his Spanish girlfriend we had shared meals and stories with in Penang, had shown up in Delhi, so they took us to the airport. We put our bags on the counter that said *Customs*, and they were taken to be loaded on the plane. Everything was in the bags this time, bricks of hash loosely layered in our clothes. It all looked cool, so we went up to the bar to have a drink and then our friends caught a taxi back to town.

When we turned to go into the Customs area we saw three rows of counters, each one manned by five or six very starched Indian civil servants in white uniforms. Ah, here was the organized work force Glenn had longed for, but at a very inopportune time for us! As each passenger came in, he identified his bag and put it on the counter. He then stepped back while the civil servants unzipped it, after which it was gone through by five pairs of rubber gloved hands, with a fine toothed comb. Glenn's knees buckled.

"Come on," I whispered, grabbing his elbow and dragging him behind the counter to our bags. We each took hold of our own bag, and just as we were about to turn toward the counter, there was a total commotion of excited yelling down at the last counter. They had found something!

Every single Customs Agent turned around and either walked or ran to see what it was. I grabbed Glenn again, "Come *ON*!" and dragged him through the double glass doors into the "Departure Lounge." He kept turning back in disbelief, almost willing them to come get him, but my will was stronger, and I dragged him through, bags in hand.

On the plane to Amsterdam, poor Glenn was a nervous wreck. Even though he had been the one to initiate the smuggle, even though the whole thing had been his idea, I don't think he had exactly thought it through. He curled up miserably in his seat while I ate apples and cheese (my first crunchy apple in over a year!) and chatted with the crew. I didn't even think about what we were doing. I just knew we were fine. I *KNEW*.

We got to Amsterdam, grabbed our bags from the carousel and waited for a taxi. I remember talking to some young guy at the airport who said, "Wow, you just came from India! Will you turn me on?" And Glenn actually wanted to get the hash out, right there at the airport!

Instead, we waited until we got to our room at the little B&B before we unzipped the bags. The first half inch opened on the zipper and the room filled with the smell of hash, heated to pungent fullness in the hold of the plane. The smell would have seriously permeated the airport lounge!

We smoked like chimneys. I had bought a whole bunch of chillums – small Indian pipes -- and I liked my hash that way, mixed with tobacco. We had sent about three hundred stone chillums back to the US from India, but had the ivory carved ones with us.

Amsterdam was a delight. Nobody noticed me. I could walk all over the city and not one man tried to grab my ass or any other part of me. I blended. I walked, alone, along the canals, in and out of coffee houses. After a year in Asia, being unnoticed and invisible was an absolute delight. I don't even remember doing much with Glenn, although we must have. I just remember being able to walk totally alone, totally unmolested.

After three days in Amsterdam we decided to go to Montreal. We had good friends living there: the guy was in med school and she was his cute sweet wife, both old friends of Glenn's from NYC. So we bought our tickets for the next day. We chose Montreal instead of New York because we figured customs would be less challenging there, not having read the latest Canadian papers about their fight against "La Drogue" (drugs) of which they considered hash to be one. They had just tightened up Customs at the airports and all points of entry, but, thankfully, I didn't know that.

We got to Montreal at exactly three in the afternoon, which was exactly when the shifts changed for Customs, so as the people in their booths greeted each other and changed their places, we grabbed our bags and walked right past them. If I were trying to combat La Drogue, I sure wouldn't schedule the customs agents to change over right when the plane came in from Amsterdam! But they didn't ask me. With Glenn turning around again and me dragging his arm, we cleared the airport and got a cab to our friends' apartment.

When we got there, it was obvious things were weird. She was having whispered conversations with her new lover on the phone, while we were all trying to pretend nothing was amiss. We smoked them out for breakfast, lunch and dinner, and I guess it was a bit much for them, what with the strain of their marriage falling apart and all. We were trying to figure out how to get to New York City when the husband volunteered, "I'll drive you." To this day, I look back at that and wonder why on earth he would put his entire future as a doctor at risk driving drug smugglers across the border, but he did. I think he may have wanted to:

1. impress his wife and get her to respect him more and stay;

2. get out of Dodge and away from those creepy whispered phone calls; or

3. just get us out of their house, with our incessant smoking.

In any case, we loaded up the Volvo and off we went, the men in the front and me in the back, groovin' along.

We got to Customs and our friend immediately blew it. "Good morning, Sir. How are you today, Sir?" The Customs guy told him to get out. They can spot a case of nerves faster than a dog. My husband turned to me, "<u>You</u> stay in the car!" They were both kind of nervous and edgy, and my nonchalance was wearing down every last nerve they had.

So I sat there listening to them grovel and blither with the Customs guy, who was pawing through all our stuff, until I just had enough.

"Excuse me," I said, climbing out of the back seat and joining the threesome on the sidewalk, going through our luggage, "but what *exactly* are you looking for?"

I got maximum glares from Glenn, and our friend looked like he had been Botoxed, with his face frozen into a terrified smile and his eyes glassy.

The Customs guy pulled out the box of chillums. "*What* are *these*?" he barked at me. "Those are native carvings," I told him, planting my high heel booted foot on top of my bag (where most of the shit was) and almost barking, myself.

"And what are *these*?" he barked again, pulling some Tampax out of a box, where I think we had just a touch of hash stashed for smoking on the trip down.

"Those," I told him, staring him in the eyes, "are Tampax."

I swear to God, he blushed! Then he put the Tampax back in the box, put the box back in the bag, said, "Ok, you can be on your way. Welcome to the U.S." or some such, and we were on our way.

The men got pretty puffed up by the time we got to New York about how they had shown that Customs man a thing or two, but I let them have at it, no argument. I really didn't care anymore; it just didn't matter because I knew I was close to done with this chapter.

We got to somebody's apartment and everyone came over. Everyone. There were about fifteen of our closest friends there. Well, his closest friends. And boy, were they impressed with how cool we were. His plan had worked.

I sat there, blending hash and tobacco, smoking chillums, all ninety six pounds of me. All of a sudden, this friend of his said to me, "You can't get away with this in New York, you know. This isn't India, this is New York, and you just can't act like this."

Bitch. And just like that, my bubble of light that had carried me from Kathmandu to Delhi to Amsterdam to Montreal to New York without the first problem or even moment of anxiety totally burst. I felt fear and paranoia flood in. From that day, I have rarely really enjoyed smoking hash or weed, and finally stopped. Even though, years later, I lived with smugglers of all kinds of stuff, I never tried it again. And, I got a divorce as soon as I could and I didn't look back.

I say that, but of course, I am looking back right now, thinking about smuggling. I smuggled two things in my life: hashish and statues of the Buddha. The story of my life, in a nutshell.

It's all over but the paperwork

After the smuggle adventure, it was obvious to me that I shouldn't stay with Glenn. The most important reason was that I didn't want to. I was too wild and free to live in New York as the prominent attorney's wife, which was the life he wanted.

It was on the beach in Penang that we *first* talked about what we wanted to do with our lives (life?). Seriously, our first conversation about it, which was a teeny bit ass backward since we'd been married a year or so by then. He told me he wanted to go back to New York City and become an attorney, live in a penthouse in the city and have a country home with a lake and a tennis court.

I was aghast. I could see it now: me with a stack of credit cards, shopping at Saks and Bloomies every day for some cute outfit to wear out that night, with my stiff sprayed hair from the hairdresser. I couldn't see me anywhere in that picture, and it wasn't a life I was remotely drawn to.

I had grown up in that life. My dad worked, my mom shopped and had her hair done. We had au pairs to raise us kids, and people to clean the house and do the yard work. I saw my mother's life looming into mine and I didn't want it. For many women I know it sounded like a dream come true, but for me, it was my nightmare.

"I just want to keep traveling!" I told him. "I love being out here."

Now it was his turn to be aghast.

There was little to be done, so we hung out in New York and at my parents' in Chappaqua, getting rid of chillums and hash, eating well and gaining weight and, we thought, getting healthier. And then, about two weeks in, the whites of his eyes turned yellow.

I had seen this before, when I was a student at BU. I was sitting in front of the student union and a friend, the same one I searched for years later in Sausalito, asked me out for a date. He later told me that he "finally got up (his) nerve to ask me out," and I looked him in the eyes and said, "You've got to be kidding. Go home and look at your eyes in the mirror."

I don't remember how I knew what gold colored eyes were about, but in both cases, it was hepatitis.

About sixty days prior, Glenn had gotten some vaccination in Malaysia, in Penang I think, at the public health department, as one of his vaccines was overdue. I don't know why mine weren't, or maybe they were but I didn't want the shot (smart me). It turned out the needle they used on him must have been improperly sterilized and he got hepatitis. Back in the day, for those of you who don't know, needles were used over and over after presumably spending the proper amount of time in an autoclave, being sterilized.

Glenn was hospitalized, and my mom and little brother Will were going to Liberia to visit my older brother

Rocky who was in the Peace Corps in Monrovia. Since Glenn was down for the count, and there was nothing I could do for him, said everybody, my mom asked me if I wanted to come, too.

All right! This was just what I had in mind: another trip! I was healthy again, after getting rid of some very pesky intestinal parasites and slowing down by about 99% on my smoking, so I was set to go. I may have even gotten shots for the trip, but with nice modern disposable needles. I know it sounds cold to leave my poor hepatic husband in the hospital, but he was getting the best of care and the very sexy Kip was coming to see him every day and I figured they'd be fine without me. Besides, we'd be back in two weeks and this was kind of my shot at a free trip to Africa.

So off we went for our two week jaunt to Monrovia (and then Paris to meet my dad), landing the very same day that President Tubman, who had led the country for forty seven years, died. The country was in an absolute uproar, but that didn't stop my mother, Gaham, from going out to mail her postcards after she spent the whole second day there writing them. As she turned the corner to the post office, an almost naked warrior painted orange came flying out at her, screaming bloody murder.

Who knows what he had on his heart? Maybe it was his way of mourning his now gone leader. Maybe he was wondering what in the world this country club lookin' lady was doing walking around his city while everyone was deep in mourning.

We'll never know, but I'll never forget the look on Gaham's face when she raced into Rocky's little house and told us what had happened. She did not go out again unless she went with Rocky. That was it for her Liberian adventures!

We took a taxi up country to see some other Peace Corps folks. We were obviously in high cotton, because we had our own car and did not share it with anyone else. The

121

seats were covered with thick vinyl which we stuck to as we sweated our way along, but we were all game. When we got to their house, they told us all about the "rain of baby cobras" that fell from their thatched roof the week before, probably *not* the wisest thing to discuss with nervous visitors to Liberia for the first time.

I love the Liberian people I know. My brother has stayed friends with many of them these last forty years. They threw him a crazy big 70th birthday party a few years ago and came from all over the eastern US to celebrate him. Liberians who never met my mother traveled hundreds of miles for her memorial service, out of respect and love for him and the woman who urged him to join the Peace Corps and improve people's lives. They have mostly been fun, lovely, wonderful friends to him and our family.

That said: Monrovia was awful. My brother's house was on a beach that was full of garbage, dead things, things that washed up and things that were dumped. To date the only comparable city I've seen.... No, forget I said that. Anyway, I had been all over Asia by then, and in India and Nepal, where I had watched the buzzards fighting over the dead donkeys and goats, and I *still* thought Monrovia was a shit hole. I think it's better now after a terrible civil war and then Ebola.

I had this wild desire to travel to Timbuktu and Ouagadougou. Nobody wanted to go with me, and I was scared to go alone. Taking my thirteen-year- old brother Will with me was probably also a bad idea, and so I abandoned the plan. Funny enough, both Rocky and my mom said, "OK, have fun, we'll meet up in Paris." So it's a kind of a regret, because that part of the world is too dangerous now for tourism, and I know I will never get to see it, but I just didn't have the nerve to go alone.

We took a little side trip to the Cote d'Ivoire (the Ivory Coast), which I remember as being colorful and extremely sweaty. I bought art there painted with camel dung and blood mixed together. It's been hanging in my house for forty years and has never faded a bit, which is probably proof of how hard it really is to get a blood stain out!

When it was time to go to Paris and meet my dad, who was there on business, it was hard to leave Rocky, but he honestly seemed really happy and in his element, which he proved by staying about ten more years.

Once we got to Paris, Bert told me that Glenn was well now, out of the hospital and was planning on meeting us there in Paris in a few days. My parents saw my face fall, and I came clean that I didn't want to be married to him anymore, that he wanted to live in NYC and I wanted to travel, that I didn't want him to come. Up to that moment, I'd been having so much fun with my family, orange warrior notwithstanding, and the news of my husband's impending arrival felt like a dead weight. I hadn't really thought about it until they said he was coming, but I felt my heart drop and knew I absolutely did not miss him one bit or want him there with me.

I don't think my parents were devastated, but they were very upset. They liked Glenn and they saw a good future with him, financially. They also knew me far too well to argue. Whatever Lola wants, Lola gets, kind of thing, but to their immense credit they did try to talk me out of being stupid.

In my mind, I wasn't being stupid. Stupid would have been staying with someone I didn't want to be with. Heedless and reckless would be leaving him, and my family, and having no skill or profession or money to speak of. So I was heedless and reckless, which was nothing new. My parents and Will were going back to New York before Glenn got to Paris. The scene was *not* going to be like Cher in Moonstruck when she says, "No, I need my family around me now." They were wisely staying the hell out of this one.

We had all been staying in the very nice apartment of my dad's business associate who was on the typical French one-month vacation, so after the rest of my family went back to the U.S., I had this great pad for the rest of the month! It was in a very ritzy part of Paris, and I was staying alone there when who should waltz back into my life but Patrick, my friend from Kathmandu. I had written him somewhere along the line that I was going to be in Paris, staying at this apartment, and suddenly there he was.

When Glenn and I were living in that hotel in Kathmandu, testing seemingly endless quantities of hash, Patrick used to come visit every day. He was this really kind and quiet Frenchman. He didn't talk much with me but was more chatty when Glenn was around, so I figured he was there more to see Glenn, that he was more his friend. He would just sit in the corner chair and talk softly with me, ask me how I was doing. At the time, I wasn't doing too great. I was shitting blood, had fever, and looked like a skeleton in a t-shirt; when I remember back, he talked to me like you would gentle down a skittish colt, softly, calming me down. I liked being around him, even if I couldn't figure out why he was there when Glenn wasn't.

Come to find out, he was just shy around me because he really liked me. He had good morals because he never made any kind of move or said anything suggestive. He had just gotten back to Paris, traveling by land while I had flown to Amsterdam and Montreal and Monrovia to get there, but we coincided. And I took a weekend trip out to the country with him.

That was all she wrote. We talked non-stop, he told me all his great theologies and philosophies about life and liberty and freedom. He played his sitar for me for hours, the sitar he pieced together with his friend Pierre after falling on it getting off the bus in Paris after 10,000 unscathed miles overland. He was different, romantic, and my ticket out of a life I did not want to go back to: the life of a New York City lawyer's wife. He was, for that moment, my Knight in

Shining Armor, offering travel and adventure instead of a wealthy settled life in New York.

Glenn came; Patrick disappeared, and Glenn and I had the conversation. Or several of them. I told Glenn it was over, and he didn't want it to be, so we dragged everything out and hashed it over. But you know, when one person doesn't want it, talking them into it only prolongs the inevitable. It was almost not personal. He represented a life I didn't want to be part of, and Patrick was part of a life I did want to experience. It wasn't fair or kind, and certainly not pretty.

And then we had a conversation that sealed the deal for me. We were talking about his practice of law, and who he wanted to represent and how. I asked, "What happens if you are hired to represent someone who you know is guilty, who you know did something wrong?"

And he told me, "It's not a matter of right and wrong, it's a matter of winning and losing. It's about winning your case."

That did it for me, although in truth it was already done.

Now I know his friends might say he wasn't like that, really, but that was what he told me. He's gone now so if I remember it wrong, I apologize.

Glenn went back to the States, became an attorney, divorced me for abandonment (fair enough) married the boss's daughter, had a daughter of his own, got very wealthy, got a divorce, remarried some time later to a much younger gold digger who took everything she could. When he died, she was barred from the funeral by his family, who despised her. They were divorced by then and I hope he is at peace.

I met back up with Patrick and we began the nomadic life together that I had romanticized.

The Book of Patrick

We Begin Our Life Together in Paris!
Autumn, 1972

How romantic! Here I was, back in Paris, a city I had longed to return to since my high school graduation trip. I was with a man I liked a great deal, even though I was never really in love with him. What I was in love with, or at least taken with, was that the way Patrick saw and lived life opened up a whole new world for me. At least I knew for sure I was going to experience a life with him that would not have been available had I gone back to New York with Glenn. My family had long since gone back to New York; their friend whose posh pad I had for a month had come home, and Patrick and I moved into his friend David's apartment for a month while David took a vacation in Morocco. This was going to be a breeze. Pat was working with his friend Thierry on a project, and I would cook and go for walks in this very nice Parisian neighborhood and take it easy. That was my plan, anyway, as much as I could be said to have any plan at all.

But we'd only been there a few days when Patrick got a phone call from a woman he had met traveling in India with her four children and her boyfriend. Her oldest son Timmy, who was only fourteen, had been busted in Turkey with her boyfriend, trying to smuggle a large amount of hashish through to Europe. Would Patrick be willing to take care of the three youngest children while she went back to Turkey to try to get Timmy out of prison? Her belief was that if she left the little ones in England with her family or friends, they would immediately be taken away and become wards of the state. She was desperate to find them a safe and stable place to stay out of the country, and she knew Patrick was both safe and stable.

What could he say? In one phone call we became temporary foster parents to Fudge, 10, Abigail, 4, and Judith, 6. What did we know about children?

Here's the story that made them famous, from the London news of the day:

Timothy Davey became the highest profile drug prisoner of his time when he was found guilty in an Istanbul court on March 1st 1972 of trafficking in hashish. He was arrested in 1971 trying to sell 25 kilos (56 lbs) to try and raise money for his family who had been on the hippie trail. He was sentenced to six years and three months imprisonment. Before the trial he had spent 7 months in Sagamilcar prison on remand. Billy Hayes told the London Evening News: "We were in the same cell block for a year and I got to know him very well." Timothy and his mother contrived an escape from prison after a few months by dressing him in girl's clothes. Rearrested at the border, he was sent back to a juvenile prison on the coast at Izmir. He was finally released in May 1974.

I don't remember the mother's name, but she was beautiful and gentle and absolutely distraught. Why else would she ask a childless Frenchman to watch her children for God knew how long while she did what she could to rescue her son? That was before she even knew he was with me. At least she knew for sure that Patrick was a kind and calm person. She was terrified and desperate. Having "lost" one of her brood, she was doing the best she could to keep the others safe and out of the clutches of the authorities. Whether or not we agreed with her belief that her children would be taken from her, we agreed to help her.

So there we were, Patrick and I, trying rather gamely to take care of these three little children who, God love them, were very very good and uncomplaining on the whole. I didn't know jack shit about being a parent, as I had mainly been raised by nannies and au pairs. I didn't know how to be tender and kind, because my mother didn't either. I didn't know about empathy. I knew about rules and unfortunately made too many for those poor little kids.

Patrick was working every day with Thierry. It was a project that lasted for months that today would take a couple of days. It would have all been plotted on a computer and cut out of adhesive backed vinyl by a machine, and then stuck on the boards. As it was, back in the day, everything was done by hand, letter by laborious letter. So they meticulously affixed these vinyl numbers and letters to boards for someone who would pay for it all in the end while I tried to think of what to do with the children.

Even though their project lasted for months, I never knew what it was or who it was for. Thierry had gotten the job and he and I were never friendly. First there was the language barrier, since my French was not good and his English nearly non-existent. Then there was a general feeling of just not liking each other very much. I was way too bourgeoise for him, and his Gauloises stank too much for me, for starters. So whatever they were doing over in their corner of the living room was their business, and I left well enough alone! But what that did was effectively put me in charge of everything about the children, since Pat could hardly do both, not being a woman.

When Timothy was imprisoned, Britain went nuts. A *fourteen*-year-old British boy in a foreign prison? It was unthinkable! It had to be remedied! The official outrage and wheels of diplomatic justice did not move anywhere near fast enough for his frantic mother, who took things into her own loving hands and smuggled him almost all the way out dressed as a girl, only to have him recaptured at the border.

He was eventually released, but by then she had long come back to Paris for the little ones, a joyful reunion for them and a big relief for me. By then, the British government was conducting the negotiations, and his release was an official government act, not an escape in disguise. The boyfriend was presumably left to fend for himself as best he could, which was a little cold, but understandable. We never heard another word about him, which is why we guessed he was just stuck there in that horrible prison.

So that was how we started out, me and Patrick. Not *quite* as romantique as I had envisioned! He was teaching me about macrobiotics, a diet for healing and for bringing the body into balance. I was making those kids eat rice all the time cause that's what we were eating, even when I used too much salt and we ate salty rice. I wish I had done better and been sweeter and more motherly, but they came along about forty years too early for that.

I did take them on little adventures, and told them stories at bedtime. We did all the stuff I knew to do for free, and I took them a few places in the city because I remember teaching them how to use the Metro, with the great boards that light up at each station, showing the route. Mainly we just maintained, which with five of us required quite a bit of shopping and cooking and laundry.

One afternoon some friends dropped by, and this young French woman knew *just* how to be with the kids. She hugged them and held them and cuddled them as I watched in amazement. Ahhh, so *that's* what you do with children!

I had not experienced that in my own childhood. I can actually remember two incidents in my whole life of my mother holding me close. This doesn't mean there weren't other times; these are the only two I remember.

One was on the way to have my foot stitched one night after I dropped a glass shard into it. We were in the kitchen, my parents, my older brother Rocky and me, and I got a bottle of milk out of the refrigerator. It was the old-school kind, glass with the crimped foil top. I was holding it by the top, and it slipped and shattered.

We never knew how my dad was going to react. He was hyper-reactive and flew into rages pretty easily. I have no way of knowing if he was like that before prison camp for two and a half years, but he was like that then. I froze in terror, then started to clean up the mess, when he barked, "Drop everything." Why would he say that? I dropped everything, which happened to be this long pointed piece of glass, which went right into my toe.

They all started racing around, got the car, bundled me up and put me in the back seat next to my mom, who held me close with her arm around me. And that's the sad part, that I was so happy that my mom had her arm around me, because it was so rare. I didn't even know where we were going or what was wrong, because I had no sensation of pain at all.

When we got to the doctor's office and he put me on the table, he said, "Well, look at that!" and like the good girl I was, I looked. *Immediately* I felt pain, where up to that second, there had been none at all. I am still in awe about that moment, that absolutely no pain could instantly become screaming, searing pain the moment I saw it.

Lately I was suffering yet another respiratory virus that I was convinced came on because I had been traveling and eating whatever seemed good, often dairy products. When I relived that moment with the milk bottle, how traumatized I was that my father might just explode, the realization came, "no wonder I can't 'handle' dairy!!!"

The only other time my mom hugged me was as we lay in the hammock on a summer night, waiting for the UFOs to come pick us up and take us away. That was her idea, not mine. I had zero desire to get picked up by aliens (again, and that's a whole other story) but it was *worth it* to have my mom hug me, to lie there in anticipation of being abducted by aliens! That gives a pretty clear picture of how little I was touched, and how hugging and loving on those little kids just wasn't in my personal experience. Touch was either about sex or punishment. I had no experience of simple holding and loving touch. As I'm sure I mentioned, I never saw my parents hug or touch. It just wasn't part of our family lexicon.

When David, the guy who lived in the apartment, came back from Morocco he was totally cool about these children living there. He didn't expect us to leave right away, and for a few days it was really crowded, but he, and Patrick, and seemingly everyone I met in that time, had a very live-and-let-live philosophy. What was happening was what was happening, and everyone just did their best to roll with it. Hashish undoubtedly helped.

David brought back a beautiful orange cape from Marrakech, and since I loved it so much he gave it to me. I wore it all the time, even after I made a dramatic entry somewhere by swirling my cape right through the heater flame and burning a big hole in it. Funny enough, I found it cleaning out my mom's shed after she died, still intact after more than forty years, with the hand crocheted patch I put on it after I burned the hole. I loved wearing it, a good thing since I didn't have a coat and by the time we moved again, fall was coming on.

We had to move, but where? David had been back a couple of weeks, and we were sleeping in his living room, even though he was super generous and nice about it. The kids had gone back to England with their ma, so it was just us. Once the British government took over Timothy's case and it became an official matter, there was nothing more the mom could do. By the same token, she felt sure that now they wouldn't take her children away because the whole family was something of a cause célèbre, suddenly well known. Even people who vehemently opposed drugs were rooting for this fourteen year old British boy in a Turkish prison, because he was fourteen *and* British.

And then one day, Thierry talked to a friend who was going out of town for five weeks and said, sure, we could stay at his place. Just like that, we packed our bags and headed across town to one of those farther out arrondissements, 17 or 18 or 19, where rents were cheap and streetlights few. Arrondissements are districts, and everyone in Paris knows what you mean when you say "I live in the 18th," or "I found the best shoe store in the 7th." Parisians know their arrondissements.

As we moved on into November, we started talking about spending the winter in Morocco because we were cold. It seemed like it was always raining in Paris, and even though the guys had been partially paid for their months' long job, and had a final payment coming when they finished in a few days, it wasn't going to be enough to last the winter in Paris. Maybe it would be enough if we kept camping out in people's apartments all over town, but that was getting old. And besides, as I mentioned, we were cold.

Thierry's friend's apartment was a cold water walk-up on the fifth floor of an old building. Every day, the guys would get the boards and panels out and work, while I ran downstairs to the street to shop at the daily market. I'd carry bags full of fresh vegetables and bread back up those five flights, and cook soup and great vegetarian meals for the three of us. Thierry made fun of my cooking because there was no meat in it. Ah, well, tant pis (TFB). He gladly ate it, didn't he?

The apartment had bare wood floors and a couple of beds, but what I remember most clearly is the cold water. There we were in November, and all we had was cold water. It's funny how a cold shower almost starts to feel warm once you get used to it. I would stand in that cold shower looking out the window at the rooftops of Paris.

It reminded me of a story I read once about a group of Jewish prisoners of the Nazis, stripped naked and made to stand in the cold November rain. The author said it was notable to him that in the midst of all that suffering and shock, no one got sick from it. Everyone was completely invested in surviving. It's one of the ways I have used for a long time to get through things that seem difficult. I think about something *really* hard that people endured, and whatever I am dealing with becomes a walk in the park.

Besides, it was *my* choice. Patrick and Thierry didn't take showers. In fact, they thought I was pretty funny, showering every day. Apparently it is something Americans are known and made fun of for. The French shop daily and bathe weekly, while we bathe daily and shop weekly. They retain more vitamin D and oils in their skin and eat fresher food. I don't really know what our advantage is since I don't remember ever noticing that people in France smelled bad, which is our big deal here. I'm sure a good compromise is possible, but that's a bigger social issue than I want to deal with. It was actually pretty cool that we even had a shower. Many apartments in Paris, especially in the economy sectors, didn't, as I had learned on my first trip to Paris six years before when I went to the apartment building with the room with the hole for a communal toilet.

Patrick confessed he had bathed daily in India, "washing" in the rivers because the weather was so hot. Considering what I saw floating in the Ganges, I would have taken a hot shower with disinfectant soap immediately, but he didn't have the same concerns. Maybe he saw some cleaner rivers than I did, but he was also plagued with all manner of tropical ailments before he got out of there, so I'm not putting money on it.

Anyway, I had no room to complain about anything. The apartment was free, like all the places we had stayed since I hooked up with Patrick, and even though it sometimes bothered me to put up with cold showers or other people, I didn't have much of a leg to stand on.

I had met Patrick while I was still on my honeymoon, so our coming together was a little less graceful than it could have been. We might not even have come together, honestly, if I hadn't been looking for a way out of my marriage with Glenn. The honeymoon was the coup de grace to a marriage that wouldn't have worked anyway and wouldn't have happened at all if we had talked about what we wanted in life before we got married, which we didn't. There was not going to be a settlement or alimony or any of that.

Long story short, I didn't have any money aside from a small amount my dad sent me every month, unbeknownst to my mom, who would have had a fit. He had traveled all over the world and seen most everything. He just didn't want me to become a prostitute or drug smuggler to stay alive. It wasn't much, but it worked; because of it I never had to do anything just to stay alive. It was enough to get me by. When I ran into Patrick in Paris, I just stayed. It was nothing I had planned; it was just the next thing that happened. That was how we did things back then, or at least I did.

The night the guys got paid, we decided to treat ourselves to a dinner out. Going out for couscous was our idea of a night on the town, and it was what we could afford. We lived in a North African neighborhood, and couscous restaurants were everywhere, and cheap. Besides, couscous was something Thierry and I could agree on. He could eat the little bit of meat that came on the top, and we could all share the rest, the grain and vegetables. The project had been completed that day; the guys had been paid; it was definitely worth a celebration!

A cold rain was falling, as usual, and the streets around our apartment were mostly dark, either unlit or poorly lit with a streetlight at each end. We walked on the uneven cobblestones, all slick and shiny in the rain, between narrow, shuttered buildings. I was wrapped tight in my burnoose, the big orange cape David brought back from Marrakech. It was a portent!

Down the block we saw light spilling out from a restaurant window, and we headed for it, walking fast and huddled together against the wet cold. As we walked in, I registered right away that I was the only woman, and we were the only non-Arabs in the place. Traveling for years had gotten me semi-used to this but it didn't always sit easily. Patrick and Thierry were completely at home though, just saying hi to the five or six men there and sitting down at a square wooden table away from the door.

Besides our table, there were four or five more in the front room, a storefront with big windows on the street. Against the back wall of the room was an old oak bar about twelve feet long, with a partially open heavy wooden door at the end nearest us. A couple of guys sat there at the bar, and the rest just seemed to stand around, or go in and out of the back room. We asked them if we could get couscous, and a bottle of red.

I thought things had gotten unnaturally quiet when we walked in, but Thierry and Patrick didn't seem to notice. They were already getting into their most regular rave, which was a leftover from their days in the student revolution of May 1968, full of barricades and bottle throwing, especially around the Sorbonne.

Bourgeois was one of their big words, and cops were always pigs. Thierry smoked those stinky fat Gauloises, very working class and authentic, which he was. My French was still in its developmental stage, despite four years in high school. Mostly I sat between them, either trying to figure out what they were saying, or trying to tune them out. Right now I could tell it was something about "Liberté" and how fucked up life was in Paris. Was it? It was cold, that was for sure, and there wasn't enough hot water in my life, but I was kind of enjoying the adventure.

Just like any French woman, I shopped for fresh food every day and cooked soup and ate fresh bread from the baker on the corner. Hauling that food up five flights of stairs was making me pretty healthy. With the macrobiotic diet Patrick had taught me, I felt healthy and balanced. All in all, Paris seemed ok to me.

But the guys were on a roll. Thierry always seemed angry, and used the word putain a lot, which basically translates as fucking, the adjective, not the verb. As a noun putain means whore, but that wasn't how he used it. The putain this, the putain that. I was glad I didn't get it all. Patrick would tell me later, "No, Thierry was not angry; it's just the way he talks," but I was never convinced. Probably some of it had to do with his black hair and dark eyes and bushy moustache. He looked angry when he got all expressive and jabbed at the air with his thick fingers. How was I to know?

Our food came, a big platter of couscous piled with vegetables and meat, and we dug in, eating with big spoons and bits of bread. All the men in the place had gotten really quiet, watching us. They hardly spoke at all, and it was starting to interfere with my appetite. I was feeling some weird vibes coming from those guys. Hey, je suis Americaine! We had Deliverance, and Charlie Manson, and all the other things Euros didn't used to know about. Just what were those guys planning?

Patrick and Thierry just kept eating and talking, drinking wine and when we got another bottle, Thierry uncharacteristically offered the guys sitting around a glass. "How 'all men are equal under God' of him," I thought, picturing him as more of an avowed racist. The men refused the wine, as surely he knew they would, but when we finished eating, and Thierry lit one of his cigs, one of them said something quietly to him. "Mais oui, bien sur!" he answered, a light in his eyes. We were shepherded into the back room, and I still didn't get it! Too much of the old New York paranoia in me, I guess. The thick oak door closed, but no one had said a word yet. And then those men all pulled out their little pouches of kif and their little pipes and got us high. No wonder they'd been casing us the whole time! They had to figure out if we were cool. So we passed, and all my worrying had been me, projecting a totally different scenario.

Later, we walked home happily full and high. The rain had stopped, and the night was cold. I was chattering on in my half French about how lovely it was that those guys didn't even know us and closed their little cafe just to sit with us and get high with us. Thierry looked at me all exasperated. "You know nussing! You Amerloques sont tous paranos!"

Well, he had me there. I was pretty paranoid compared to them, but couldn't that have been because I was the girl? Then Patrick chimed in about the beauties of the simple life with simple folk. At the time, I was unfamiliar with "idealization of Third World Cultures 101," but I caught on after a while. Along with free places to stay, it was a recurring theme.

There were practical reasons to go to Morocco. It would be warmer, for one big thing. Another was that the friend whose flat we were in would be returning in less than a week, so it was either find another place to crash in Paris or bail. Patrick and Thierry had been paid enough for us to live a couple of months in Paris, at best. In Morocco, the money would last all winter, even with paying our own rent. It was settled. We would go to Morocco, to a little village Thierry knew there on the coast called Diabet. We would all go in his girlfriend Claudine's twelve year old Deux Chevaux. The only person who wasn't in on the plan yet was Claudine, so Thierry asked us to go with him for support while he gave her the news. This was the first I ever heard of her!

To my eyes, Claudine was the perfect little bourgeoise Parisienne. She had a car, an apartment, and a real job that she went to every day from 9 to 5, wearing heels. What she was doing with Thierry was anybody's guess, but she seemed crazy about him. When he told her the plan that the four of us would go to Morocco for the winter in her car, her big blue doe-in-the-headlights eyes went even wider. Her apartment, she stammered, her job???!!! "Bon," he nodded, giving her a hug. It was a done deal. She just needed a little time to get things together, a couple of weeks.

"If you all need a place to stay until we leave," she offered matter of factly, "you can all stay here."

I looked around. It was kind of her to offer, but there was absolutely no room. Her apartment was the size of a large, walk-in closet with no shower or bathtub, either in the apartment or in the hall or anywhere in the building. My mind had a hard time wrapping around that, but she told me she didn't mind, she went to her parents on holidays and bathed. I figured to say nothing was the best option, because we couldn't all stay there anyway, with one little bed. Luck, or the spirit of Liberté was with us.

Within the week, we were Morocco bound, headed south with our bags of clothes in a twelve year old Deux Chevaux, the closest street-legal vehicle to a soap box racer.

The Trip South

Patrick didn't want to take his shoes. His time in India had done something to him, something good and also something weird. His clothes, mostly handmade things from India and Nepal, were packed in soft cloth shoulder bags that doubled as pillows. That was cool and useful as we chugged along in Claudine's ancient car. But the shoe thing -- was that about "Liberté" too?

"You really might need them," I told him. Last thing I wanted was to travel with a guy with no shoes, as much as I was enjoying my new macrobiotic health regime. So, as a concession to me, his little Americaine, he took them. The first time the car broke down, outside Madrid, it was snowing. No words, he dug around and found his shoes, because he ended up being the only one with a clue about how to get the car going again. That amazed me until I met

144

his parents the next year, and found out he came from this very practical, normal, middle class family. Go figure.

In fact, when I did meet his parents, they were very kind to me. We stayed at their apartment in Patrick's old room and did a week or two of the family thing. Like most mothers, his just flat out adored him, but his father said to me one day after lunch, "This. This is enough for you?" indicating his very own son and the itinerant lifestyle he had chosen. Of course I lied and said it was, but that was at least a year after this initial adventure to Morocco.

There was a definite agenda to this trip, and a developing hierarchy. Since Thierry had been to Morocco several times before, and since we were in *his* girlfriend's car, he became the boss. Patrick was definitely the lieutenant. Claudine and I were the girls. We got to stop to pee, or eat, things like that, but all the big decisions were made for us.

I'm pretty sure it was the jefe and his lieutenant who decided that we had to drive up into the Rif Mountains to score some kif before we went south because it would be so much cheaper to get up there. It was a very good plan. We all smoked so it made sense. So we headed for Chaouen, the mecca of Moroccan hash, kif and pot growing and selling.

As we climbed into the mountains, the terrain became rougher and wilder. Afternoon shadows lengthened and the air became noticeably cool. In the middle of a village about halfway to Chaouen, an elderly man held up his hand to stop us on the little main street. He stuck his face in the window, and in basic French remarkably like mine (yay! someone I can understand!) he asked us what we were looking for. He said, "Whatever you are looking for, you can find it here."

No games or bullshit here. We were in the just-about-middle-of-nowhere. "We're looking for kif," Thierry growled in his basso pirate voice. We are so authentic. All the other Euros come for hash, and the Americains, poor innocents that they are, actually buy grass, which cracks the Moroccans up since they won't even smoke it. But we come for the true smoke of the people. La Liberté gently raises an eyebrow.

"You need go no further," issues a low, coarse whisper from the old man, Monsieur Salah. "Here, I have everything you want. Come with me," he invites, opening the door to a house right on the street. Claudine wants to park the car in a more secure place (Paris?) but M. Salah reassures her. "Your car is safe here. This is my village. When you are with me, no one will harm you."

Well, that was kind of a yes and no. Did anyone ever really harm us? No. And certainly no one ever dared steal anything from a guest of M. Salah, because he was the undisputed Godfather. Patrick and I went back alone a few months later, in a VW van that we bought off some stranded Americans out of money. We slept in the back and when it was safe and the weather was good, we kept the back wide open so we could fall asleep looking at the stars.

Of course we didn't know any of this our first night there, that we would make friends, that we would come back, that we would even make it through the night. That last was my own nervous projection onto the list of possibilities. The Frenchies were more at ease. I had traveled a good bit, but stopping in this isolated mountain village to buy a kilo of kif put me on edge.

We had arrived during Ramadan, the holy month where *nothing* passes a practicing Muslim's lips from sunrise to sunset. I don't mean words, they get to talk, but they can't put anything in. No mint tea which they normally drink all day long, no food, and much more importantly, no smoke.

146

Meanwhile, we were getting the royal treatment, smoking up a storm of the finest (I guess) kif, passing the little sipsi around and around as M. Salah and his four or five young guys sat there drooling, watching us. "Mais non, vas y, vas y!" they insisted, urging us to feel free to keep smoking, even though they couldn't. "No problem, go ahead on."

It was getting dark in the little room, as the sun lowered. We were all sitting on banquettes built into the walls, like in a straw-bale/adobe house. At least an hour had passed while we smoked and talked and drank a little tea that arrived via small boy, the standard Moroccan delivery service.

All of a sudden, there was a banging on the door and it was officially sundown. Olly olly in free. M. Salah grabbed the sipsi out of Thierry's mouth, relit it and passed it. A couple of the guys brought out their sipsis, too, and everyone hungrily filled their pipes. Since kif is cut with tobacco, it was partly tobacco craving that was getting to everyone.

Once the immediate needs were satisfied, one of the young men got up and disappeared through a low door. A single lantern had been lit, and placed in the center of the room, which was the center of the circle of us. More tea was brought, and the sipsis kept being filled and smoked.

I quickly saw there was a whole art around the proper smoking of a sipsi. It is basically a one hitter, where you take your hit and then you blow the ash, a burning ball of it, out on the floor. It's ok. Everything's dirt or concrete anyway. If you don't blow at the right time, and with the appropriate velocity, the stuff gums up in there and has to be manually cleaned out. This slows down the action and annoys veteran sipsi smokers. I was not one but I was determined to learn.

147

The young man returned with a cardboard box top containing some chopped leafy green. He smiled at us, nodding, as he told us, "This is good kif." By now, it was pretty dark and pretty quiet and I got that old uh-oh feeling. I was once again in a New York state of mind. Thierry stuck his fingers into the pile, rubbing them speculatively together, feeling this stuff. "That's not kif," he tells them, "that's leaf."

Whoooooo. Stillness. A thick silence settled on the room, just about as thick as the shadows. I'm thinking it again: who would ever find us?

"Non, non, non, non, non," the young men insist. "That is good kif, our very best!" It's gotten remarkably serious in that little room, and I feel the creep of dread when Thierry laughs.

"No way, guys!" No way, dudes! The original Spiccoli. All of a sudden, they all laugh and smile, too. Somebody gets rid of that shitty leaf and they all laugh about how only the stupid Americains are dumb enough to smoke that shit, since all it does is make you crazy. Ha ha ha. All of a sudden we're all buds again, and the good kif comes out and we buy a kilo or two and everybody's happy as clams. And relieved, need I say.

And living with Thierry for the next few months, I never did figure out how he managed that. Did he know the Moroccans so well that he knew they'd try a scam, or did he know his kif so well that, in the dark, he could tell the difference. Maybe he was smarter than I gave him credit for.

There were no unguarded roads south. Every road leaving the mountains had a checkpoint. Guards would catch people with dope and arrest them, getting a big bribe and smoking the dope themselves, or selling it back to the dealers.

Sometimes growers didn't like their customers, so they'd sell them out to the cops, get their dope back and probably make their quota. The worst spectre, of course, was the possibility of going to jail there. I could only imagine how enlightened the woman's prison system must be.

But M. Salah and his guys had a plan, and I felt like we were all on the same team, that they would do all they could to keep us safe. Part of it was, well I wanted to think it was the novelty of getting high with two young Euro women, but they didn't really give a shit about that. They liked us and all, but these guys were *stoners*. What they really dug about us was that Thierry kept his head, and knew his kif, and turned everything into a joke. He earned their respect for all of us, and their guarantee of safe passage, if a guarantee could be had.

About an hour before dawn, having half slept huddled together on the banquettes under some blankets they lent us, we got in the car and headed south. Two of the young guys went with us, in another car or a truck. I was really hoping we wouldn't have to outrun anything in this old hulk of a car. A bicycle maybe, but nothing more. There was some elaborate plan concocted for subterfuge, but when we got to the customs shack, it was empty. Hallelujah!!! With six huge grins and lots of waving goodbye, we left our friends and headed south.

Welcome to Diabet, or as it's called on maps Diabat.

Diabet, the village we were aiming for, is about ten kilometers outside the town of Essaouira, a town concocted of the incredible architecture that makes Morocco look like a fantasy world. Essaouira has arches and color patterns and everything is mosaic tiled and absolutely beautiful. We stopped for lunch at the Hippy Cafe, a marvel of blue and white tiles and arches built around a central open courtyard that served as the main body of the cafe.

Apparently Jimi Hendrix had hung out there a few years before, and he was still blasting away on the sound system. Lots of Europeans and Americans, smoking and stoned, were hanging out. It was way more of a scene than we were looking for, I was quickly to discover, because as soon as we'd eaten and checked it out, we were off for Diabet.

It was too soon for me. I liked the Hippy Cafe. I liked seeing people from America. No, I liked being with people I could talk to who had similar backgrounds to mine. Basically, I was pretty tired of always having to speak French, unless I was alone with Patrick, who spoke totally excellent English.

I felt really disappointed to leave so quickly. My French wasn't that good, Claudine and I didn't have much in common, and Thierry the same. I felt lonely since the only person I talked to much was Patrick, who also had to interpret what was going on sometimes when the French flew thick and fast. At the same time, I didn't try to stay in town longer because what would I have said, "I want to be around people who speak English, even if I don't know them?!" I just got back in the car.

I haven't said much about Patrick lately, I know. Besides being a revolutionary kind of guy who had spent a couple of years in India, he was a pretty good musician and artist. He had brought a sitar home from India, carrying it overland all those miles of busses and trains, only to trip getting off the bus in Paris, shattering one of the two gourds. Typical of him, he and his friend Pierre, who was coming to Diabet soon, pieced the whole thing back together. It took endless patience, which Patrick had. What he didn't have was ambition, or drive, or motivation, which was surely what his father referred to when he asked me if this was enough for me. Patrick could sit in total stillness longer than anyone I had ever met. While I admired the talent, it sometimes got on my nerves like crazy. Someone I knew once told me this about loving another human: the things that we are initially attracted to, that we think are so cute, are often the same things that eventually drive us crazy. And so it was.

You would have thought that with all that sitting still, (whittling little Buddhas was about as physically active as he got, given his druthers) Patrick would have been a fat kind of guy, but au contraire, mon ami. He was skinny as a stick. I could barely squeeze into his cool bell bottoms he'd had made in India. I was thin as a rail and he was thinner. He wore little John Lennon glasses and his hair was almost to his waist. And he had bad French teeth they get from drinking wine when they are babies, instead of drinking cow's milk, like good American kids.

What I liked about him was his sense of freedom and possibility, his love of art and music, his intimate connection with Liberté herself. He had introduced me to a whole new world: macrobiotics, which was changing my life, and Morocco, which was to be discovered.

When he was first teaching me macrobiotics, he pushed the old-school agenda. For the first ten days I ate *only* diet #7. This was the direct teaching from George

Oshawa, the Japanese man who brought macrobiotics to the west. It was very popular in France, where people love this kind of thing.

Diet #7 involved eating *only* brown rice. No veggies, no beans, no sauce, no nothin' else for ten days. You got to drink three cups of liquid a day, either water or green or bancha tea. Period. And you chewed. Lord knows you chewed. Every mouthful was chewed something like a hundred times until it was liquefied.

That diet was something else. It was sanctified! One day, about day three of Diet#7, when we were still in Paris, I was standing out on the balcony of David's apartment, looking out at the city. I saw energy in waves coming toward me from left and right, and when the waves met in me they merged and streamed out from me, out before me, in one smooth, harmonious band. Now you don't get *that* from eating hot dogs, believe you me! And I wasn't high on anything but brown rice.

Speaking of brown rice: a woman caught my eye in the Hippy Café, a thin blond woman veiled like a Moroccan. Later, we made an important connection over a bag of brown rice, but that day, I watched her, transfixed like most everyone else except the hippies too stoned to care. You could just see wisps of her blond hair. Of her face, only her beautiful blue eyes showed. I can feel her moving when I think of her today, floating like a breeze, gracefully and modestly. She spoke briefly to the leering proprietor,

and left. Quick, quiet, like a soft wind passing through. Light. I was intrigued by her, and she changed our time in Diabet in a sweet way I couldn't have foreseen.

Diabet was the filthiest little village I had ever seen, or at least planned to live in! The one lane that ran through the village, down to the village well and back up the other side, was lined with barbed wire and uneven wooden slat fence, with prickly pear cactus growing over the sides. From every barb in the wire, from every thorn in the cactus, from every snag in the fence hung nasty old dirty plastic bags, and scraps of tissue paper. Could this really all be toilet paper? Please tell me no!

Everywhere you looked there was garbage. You know how people say, "This place looks like a dump?" They were talking about Diabet. The whole place was the town dump. Right in the middle of town, just on the way to the river and conveniently located across the street from our soon to be new home, was the little field everyone on that end of town used for a bathroom. Although that might conjure up visions of rows and rows of porta-potties, it was just a field, with some well-worn paths, and trees. The trees afforded the only privacy there was, and yet, I never saw another person down there. Moroccans were natural people, and some things were just private.

I was having some very strong issues about moving to a garbage dump, but Thierry had heard there was a big house for rent right in the middle of town, a house big enough for the four of us and Pierre and Catherine when they came from Paris. Pierre was a professor at the Sorbonne, which always amazed me because Patrick and Thierry were so *not* mainstream. With all their radical politics, I never thought they'd be such close friends with professors and office workers until I spoke enough French to realize they all held the same basic views and had all been on the same side in '68.

Our new house was easy enough to spot. In a bend in the road leading down to the single village well was a long whitewashed wall with a partially open blue door in it. Blue is the spirit color, painted on doors and windows to keep the evil out. In this case, we knocked and entered into the lower courtyard where our soon-to-be landlord, Mohammed Boumie, was standing on a wooden crate, repairing a bit of loose plaster. He was thrilled to see us, and to find out we wanted to rent his house for a few months.

By Diabet standards, this was a really big house. There were six rooms on three separate courtyards. The first courtyard, where we met, was the public entranceway, with three rooms opening onto it. Through a crooked archway, up a few stairs and we were in the second courtyard, with one large room and one very small one. A gate led through a short arched passageway to a large, single room guarded by the small third courtyard. Thierry and Claudine immediately claimed that by Divine Right. Patrick and I really didn't care. Thierry's head had swollen to an uncomfortable size after our successful kif hunt, so I figured it was best if he kept it back there in its own courtyard.

One thing that was getting a bit strange was that Thierry still had all the kif. What was up with that when we had put in half the money? I could only ask Pat, and I was hesitant because I kept feeling that there was some cultural thing going on that sooner or later I would understand. After not too long, it was clear that it wasn't a cultural thing, just a bullshit thing, and it got resolved and we split it up.

But in the meantime, we were meeting down in the lower courtyard to get high, since Thierry and Claudine had all but barricaded the top gate. It was either the second or third day in the house, and the four of us were relaxing in the courtyard, having an afternoon smoke when there was a rapid-fire knocking on the front door. When I opened it, a young village woman stood there, wild-eyed and talking so fast I had to bring her in for the others to translate.

Her toddler, a little boy about two years old, had turned the cooking coals over on his leg and was badly burned. She was frantic, looking for a ride to the hospital in town, about fifteen kilometers away.

Thierry turned away. Putaines Moroccaines! No way was this little dark-skinned drama going to cut into his pleasant afternoon of getting high. I couldn't believe my eyes and ears. He and Claudine went back to where they had been lounging and proceeded to ignore this woman, as if she had come to sell Amway. I looked at Patrick, and God bless him, he really was "for the people."

He got the keys from a grudging Claudine, and off we went to the hospital in town, the woman sitting in the back with a whimpering, shocked baby. It was four kilometers down a bumpy dirt road, then ten more to the hospital, but that baby was pretty quiet as the mother constantly shushed him. The whole thing was so amazing, that someone could refuse her need, especially someone I was sort of friends with! Ok, I lived with them, but I didn't have to like them!

After about an hour of waiting, she came out with the little boy in her arms. His leg was smeared with grease, then covered with fine charcoal. It looked very funky to me, but she was completely self-possessed by then. Her baby was going to be fine, and she was not in the mood for any commentary from a skinny hippy girl who didn't even have a baby!

Even though you could tell she had little use for foreign women, she was still plenty grateful, because she could tell I had had a whole lot to do with getting her baby taken care of. And so, in a sense, she adopted me.

Getting adopted, becoming her friend, was an entrée into the world of Moroccan village women. Few Western women went there, mostly because they were not invited. It was a closed world, but even if they had been welcome, I'm not sure how many would have been interested.

It amazed me how many women went to Morocco to live like they were still in London, sunbathing naked and then wondering why the village men wouldn't leave them alone. Hello! But the village women's society was tight and private, for their eyes only. All day long, they hung out together, with and without children. At night, the men were home and had to be taken care of, but the days were their own.

It never seemed to me that the village women were very serious. Tough, yes. Hardworking and strong, yes. But serious? Hardly. They loved to play. If you saw a woman carrying her empty pail to the well, most likely she would be playing it like a drum. And she'd be good at it, too.

In the village, the women never wore veils. They dressed in baggy knickers made of floral printed flannel or cotton, with a big brocade tunic over. It was only when they  went into town, into Essaouira, that they put on their ugly gray or gray/blue chadors or niqabs, covering everything but their eyes, hands and feet.

The village women loved to run up to me in Essaouira, at the market or in the street, while they were veiled. It was a big joke to see if I had any idea who they were. When I finally gave up, because I could never tell who it was, they would quickly lift up the veil and have the most mischievous, mad grin on at what a great joke they had pulled!

My first play day in Diabet came just a few days after our ride to the hospital. My new young friend, the boy's mother, showed up at our door to ask if I wanted to come out and play, basically. Sure, I did. We went to have grain ground. You may not think that sounds like much fun, but I was curious and so happy to be invited, especially knowing how rare it was.

An older woman, probably close to fifty and thereby entitled to veneration as an elder in the village, did the grinding. Her equipment consisted of two very large stones, the top one with a stout, well-smoothed stick stuck in it to use as the turning handle. She sat on the floor, turning the top stone around and around with one hand, while with the other she scooped up handfuls of grain and poured them into a hole in the top. The weight of the large top stone crushed the grain into fine flour that streamed steadily down a chute cut in the lower stone, filling a large bowl resting on the floor. Her mill could have been hundreds of years old, or brand new. It was as if nothing had changed for centuries.

The other women sat around, turning the bowl automatically as one side became full, bringing an empty bowl when needed, taking an occasional turn of the stones so she could rest. But mostly they laughed and talked, and even though they were kind to me, there was an air of slight ridicule, that even though I was obviously ok because of the hospital trip, they really didn't know if I was good for anything.

The "old" woman (even though I'm now older than she was, she was definitely the oldest woman in the room that day) seemed to never have known a moment of self-doubt. Her confidence and strength were palpable, as were her shrewdness and sense of humor. As she laughed and talked, turning the big stone with remarkable ease, her eyes took in everyone and everything in the room, sizing up the energy, watching with great humor and mischief. Suddenly she stopped turning and motioned to me. "Here," she gestured, "your turn!"

Not wanting to offend, wanting to be a good sport, even though I really didn't want to spend my afternoon grinding their grain, I grabbed that handle and gave it a good hard pull. Whomp! I fell back on my ass, and that stone hadn't budged one inch. Did they laugh?! What do you think?! Their suspicions were confirmed. I was not only pale and puny, but useless as well. Well, at least if I couldn't *do* anything, they could improve my looks.

Out came the bottle of kohl, and the little stick to apply it. They showed me, you dip the stick into the black powder and then, closing your eye on it, you pull it along the length of your eyelid, lining both the top and bottom. OUCH! When they did it, it burned and it hurt. I think that's because they did everything a little rough, and because they were into some one- up-woman-ship.

I once saw a woman with a baby in Morocco teaching it to toughen up, quick. She nuzzled and snuggled it, getting it to laugh, and when it did, she slapped it in the face. The shocked baby cried and cried, and she nuzzled and snuggled it until it laughed again, at which point she slapped it again.

Messages from this: Don't trust anyone, especially someone seeming to love you? Never let your guard down?

The people closest to you will hurt you the most? I might not have known much about being a parent, but at least I knew better than that!

I was getting to see things other Westerner travelers didn't. The village women did not interact much with the foreigners. They made hash candy, called majun, since they didn't smoke. They ate majun for a good time. It could be pretty strong. One night I ate some for an overnight bus ride and slept all night cuddled up against some Moroccan guy in the seat next to me. Testament to the stoniness of the whole country, he just seemed to take it all in stride and made nothing of it. It was a great trip, mainly because I slept all night and woke up relaxed and refreshed, rare for a long bus ride.

It reminds me of the only other overnight bus I took, years later, from Eureka, California back to the Bay Area. My friends told me, "Take the overnight bus. You can sleep all night and wake up in Oakland." Excuse me, but, my ass! All night long these two junkies behind me were fussing and messing around.

"You gave me too much! You gave me too much!" one of them loudly whispered to the other. I never slept a wink. It was not at all like eating majun and sleeping through the overnighter in Morocco.

For those village women, my hair, long and loose, would not do. Moroccan women wore theirs tied back, and hennaed. I started using henna in my hair after that day. I liked the smell, and the reddish color it added. The village girls would draw designs with the paste on my hands and arms that made faint tattoo-like orange marks if I sat still in the sun with it long enough. At first, I thought kohl and henna were just cosmetics, but after a while, I understood

159

that they had medicinal properties, too. Many of the men were afflicted with eye problems from the wind and dust, but the women, who used kohl every day, were essentially cleaning out their eyes with the powder. And henna kept away lice, a constant problem for the long haired and unhennaed. Moroccan men solved that problem by shaving their heads.

Speaking of shaving their heads, the little boy with the burned leg got his head shaved on his next birthday. I don't remember if he was just turning two or three, but it was the birthday when traditionally boys get their hair cut off. Like most Moroccan children, his hair had been thick and black and glossy, a mass of curls that framed his sweet face and showed off his huge dark eyes.

He was a sweet seeming little boy, and I went to see him now and then as his leg healed. It healed without a scar of any kind, no limp or any handicap from a bad burn that had covered nearly the entire back of one leg. So much for grease and charcoal!

But the day after he got his head shaved, I didn't even recognize him. In the place of the soft, gentle little boy who would smile shyly when I came in was an aggressive militant boy with no hint of softness to him. The desired transformation had been made.

Sometime along in all this, Pierre and Catherine arrived from Paris and moved into the best of the rooms on the lower courtyard. They only had about three weeks there, or maybe even less, which was ok with me. Pierre was an angel, a Gemini with the same birthday as Patrick, and so patient and kind. He had to be. He lived with the Witch of the West. Catherine was as sharp as a razor. She didn't like me, even though she'd just met me, so everything she said about me was demeaning. I tried to stay away from her, but I liked to hang around with Pierre. He didn't speak a word of English, so we just didn't talk much. His presence was a comfort, unless he was with her.

Pierre's job was about to change, and they were going to live in the south of France, leaving Paris to live in a medieval village and study the ancient architecture of the area. Later, we lived there with them for a couple of months, in spite of what a bitch she was to me. Their farm was so dark and closed in feeling, both the land and the architecture, and her control and anger spilled out over everything. But even there, I managed to be gone most of the time, walking in the mountains all day with the goats, coming home just as the sun went down. That's where I learned to breathe my way up a mountain. I remember taking really deep breaths that seemed to carry me up the mountain, so I arrived at the top breathing comfortably and easily. I breathed in through my nose and let my belly expand on the inhale. I had learned that at yoga class back in New York years before. I exhaled however felt best, nose or mouth. I'm guessing part of it was being forty years younger and in great shape from pure food and no alcohol.

The Macrobiotic Restaurant of Diabet

Patrick and I decided to stay on in Diabet, even though the others were leaving. Pierre and Catherine had planned to go back to Paris, so we knew about that, but Thierry and Claudine surprised us. We had thought they would stay all winter with us, but the lure of smooth walls and right angles and Claudine's steady paycheck proved too strong.

That left Patrick and me with a six bedroom house, more than we wanted to deal with, and no car, a luxury we had become accustomed to. We did get Thierry and Claudine's straw mattress, which we considered quite a step up in the world since we had been sleeping like the Biblical prophets on sheepskins on a woven straw mat!

Even though the rent was something like 100 dirhams, about $20 a month, it was more than we wanted to handle alone. But Providence had something up her sleeve for us.

The veiled European woman I had seen in the Hippy Cafe on that first day was a beautiful and gentle woman from Denmark. She wore the veil for two reasons. First, she told me, was out of respect and solidarity for the Moroccan women. Secondly was to keep men at some distance. She was

162

a bit slim for the Moroccan ideal, as they liked their women chunky, but she was extraordinarily beautiful. For her, the veil was a refuge, and she never went out in Essaouira without it.

Right about the time of the mass exodus from our house, her neurons began a mass movement of their own. As her nervous system imploded, she made the wise decision to return to Denmark and her family, who sounded loving and supportive. Her parting gift to us was a fifty pound bag of brown rice she had brought to sustain her through the winter. We gave her some money for it and decided: we have rice, let's open a macrobiotic restaurant. It only seemed logical, or as my good friend Jeanne Brown likes to say, "It seemed reasonable at the time..."

But first, before we opened a restaurant, we had to be able to get food from the market in Essaouira to our house. We were nothing if not planners! A car was out of the question. Buying one was beyond us, where to buy one another issue, and borrowing was way too haphazard and unreliable. So we decided to do what everyone else did. We bought donkeys.

A camel and donkey market in the desert is a rare treat. I'm sure we were the only Westerners there, for want of a better term, but we were dressed in our woolen djallabas, just like everyone else. I was the only female I saw, besides the animals, but that was understandable given the kind of market it was. Women went to buy food, not big purchases like donkeys and camels. We didn't hang out much in touristy areas, so being the only non-Moroccan people at the market wasn't strange or uncomfortable. After a long bus ride to get there, we went first to have tea.

The ceiling of this tea house was very low. Some of the men had to stoop to enter. It was built on two levels, the lower one at the entrance and an upper one with a step up of about two feet. People were less concerned there with possible lawsuits if someone fell off that step, and besides, someone there would catch you if you did. It was more common sense, definitely less litigious.

On the upper level, there were no chairs, just straw mats on the floor around low wooden tables. Tea houses are also smoke houses, so while Patrick smoked sipsis with some men, I looked around and sipped my tea. Moroccan tea is always a green gunpowder tea, boiled strong and then poured into a silver teapot crammed with fresh mint leaves and a *big* fat chunk of sugar. Since we were still trying to be macrobiotic, and didn't like the jumpy, itchy feeling all that sugar gave us, we always asked for our tea with no sugar. That created a bit of a stir, since it was an unusual request. In fact, it was something of a sacrilege.

I sat quietly, sipping my high voltage but sugarless tea and watching. Nobody paid much attention to me. These men were camel traders and donkey sellers. They were some of the thinnest men I saw in Morocco, hungrily eating pieces of flat brown bread dipped in oil from a small bowl on their table. Just bread, oil and tea, and I knew that was pretty much it for them for the day. You could tell, because they were so gaunt. But they had their kif, and everybody toked up before and after the market.

In a field just off the road, like a Southern yard sale, was the camel and donkey market. About a hundred camels were tethered by one foot or tied by the nose to a line along with lots of donkeys, young, old, fat and thin. Everyone stopped and stared admiringly when a white baby camel was trotted out.

Dust swirled around every time a truck or bus passed up on the highway, the main road between Essaouira and Marrakech. Up and down the donkey pen we walked, looking into their eyes while everyone else checked things like backs and legs. Finally, we chose two donkeys, a sturdy little grey one, and a knock kneed dark brown one, because she had such beautiful eyes. Nobody else would have bought her, since they were not a sentimental people and would have noticed that her hocks knocked together when she trotted. But I fell in love with her, and that was that.

We hired a truck to drive the donkeys to our house in Diabet, since it would have taken us all day, and half the night, to ride them home, and we went home to get a place together for them. It was decided that in the day, we would take them to town or they could run around, and at night they would sleep in the lower courtyard on a bunch of straw we got for them. We hadn't counted on the ire of Monsieur Boumie, our landlord. When he heard we had donkeys living in the courtyard, he pitched a fit.

Arriving at our house a few days later from Essaouira, M. Boumie began right away ranting about how we could not keep donkeys in the courtyard. Patrick, about half his size, told him to fuck off, we paid the rent, it was our house now. "Oh boy," I thought, "That's a good one." "Besides," Patrick went on, "what about that ram living in your kitchen in Essaouira?"

Pat had a little teeny problem with property rights. Whatever he thought was his business that the Boumies had a ram in their kitchen, I couldn't figure, but somehow, it seemed to make some sense to M. Boumie. He started to back down; then Patrick called him a "putain mendiant," a fucking beggar. Does that make sense, that the renter calls the landlord a fucking beggar because he objects to the donkeys in the courtyard?

I was nonplussed, and sat there in the courtyard, watching the show, probably with my mouth hanging open. Boumie seized a big board and raised it over his head to bash in Patrick's skull, and again Patrick, his skinny arm raised to protect his head, barked out, "Putain mendiant!"

M. Boumie put the board down with a smile and shook Pat's hand. We never heard another word about the donkeys. I could barely make heads or tails of what had just happened. The ram, by the way, didn't live in the kitchen in Essaouira forever. He was just being fattened up for the feast that ends Ramadan, which ended his last, plush days.

Almost immediately it became clear that riding a donkey was worse than walking. The first day we had them, we took a practice ride down in the forest that separated Diabet from the Atlantic Ocean. At least, there used to be a forest that separated Diabet from the Atlantic Ocean. In pictures now, that forest has been replaced by not one but *two* golf courses, God help us. But back in the day, it was a wild and wooly forest.

It was a pretty ride down the forest paths and out onto the windy beach. Even though it was really uncomfortable and jiggly, I was glad to be on a donkey since I knew there were lots of wild boar in the forest that occasionally charged people. But the riding thing wore off that day, and except for riding to cross the river, we mostly walked the donkeys to town and let them carry all the stuff back in big straw panniers that went across their backs.

We already had some of what we needed to cook on and in; we just needed more. Charcoal braziers, like little barbeque grills, were our stoves, with big hand-thrown clay pots to cook in. Every day or two, we went to town to buy vegetables and fruits, honey and oil, grains and fish. And charcoal, a big dirty bag from a man all covered in black dust.

It would have taken us all day to gather enough wood to cook every night, but I always tried to get Patrick to go alone to the charcoal man. He was dirty and creepy and he liked to leer at me from his black crusted face. I'd flash back to the eye of Quasimoto in the Million Dollar Movie version of the "Hunchback of Notre Dame", which kept me up, terrified and sleepless, for about a week when I was twelve and insisted on watching it every single night!

The market was full of beautiful produce, artistically piled in glowing mountains of color. In the back of the market, one guy caught our fancy. His stuff was excellent and fresh, and his prices fair. He didn't try to rip us off because we were foreigners. He probably figured any foreigner who arrived on a knock-kneed donkey needed all the help she could get.

Anyway, after a while we just went straight to him, and once the restaurant started, our purchases became fairly sizable. We had to allow at least an hour, sometimes more, because when we arrived, no matter the time, so would food. If it was midday, his wife would show up with a delicious couscous, and if it was earlier or later, a tray with tea and delicate almond cookies.

After we got the bulk of our stuff from him, we would check out fish. If someone had very fresh, just caught sardines, we might grill them that night. At the bakery we bought fresh flat brown bread, and sometimes at a nearby stall we got some dried opium poppy pods to make tea later in the night. Our donkeys' panniers would be loaded with carrots and onions, shiny tomatoes and peppers, squashes and big sprays of fresh fragrant spearmint. Paper cones of green tea and couscous were stuffed in, along with those huge cones of sugar everyone else loved. When we started the long trek home, we'd have to hustle to arrive in time to start the dinner.

The division of labor worked fine. I went to the well and got buckets of water while Patrick got the fires going. Every night was brown rice, and a big plat tagine of vegetables roasted in olive oil, and sometimes fish, or a sweet. Sometimes with hash in the dessert, sometimes not. Sometimes we'd make a big thick soup, full of handmade noodles we'd dried all day in the sun. It was never fancy, but it was good, and people came from all over the village to eat our 1 dirham dinners, about 20 cents. Word began to spread, and people tired of town actually made the trip to Diabet to eat at the famous Macrobiotic Restaurant of Diabet. It was lots of work, but it was fun, too. It gave us a purpose to stay there and it paid the rent. Sitting around smoking and drawing little pictures was fun for awhile, but I needed a project, and the restaurant fit the bill.

It was truly a beautiful restaurant, especially if you consider that we had no tables, and no chairs, and no running water or electricity. After all that brouhaha, the donkeys had moved to a neighbor's courtyard, made for animals, and their corner was cleaned out and made into the cooking corner. The menu, such as it was, was written in chalk on the wall behind me as I sat in my corner, stirring pots and chopping vegetables.

Patrick talked to people, greeting them and taking their dirhams. Benches lined the courtyard, where everyone sat and talked or smoked while they waited. People brought instruments, and played exquisite music while the food cooked, and after eating. On full moon nights, you could literally read by the moon, it was so light. Everyone would stand, silently watching the moon rise over the hills to the  east, and not a word would be spoken to break her spell until she had passed the horizon and entered the black and open sky.

For a month or so we made dinner every night for about ten to fifteen people. With our facilities, that was really enough. We only had eighteen bowls, so if anyone more came, they'd have to wait for someone to finish eating so we could wash a bowl and spoon. But usually, ten people would be about it. And then one night, we became famous.

Welcome to the Festival of Light!

Californians of a certain type, on the road, were always easy to spot. They had the most amazing neon blue eyes, blond hair, were always tallish and usually great looking. Sometimes they were also pretty intense, like the young woman who wanted to tell me about Jesus at the beginning of my journey, when all I had wanted to do was buy some acid for the freighter trip. To be fair, I also met Australians who looked like this, kind of electric.

169

I don't remember this particular freak's name, but he was a Californian of that ilk, wrapped in an old blanket, wandering around with a mission: to create a "gathering of light" that would draw all high beings together for a night of peace and love. Or whatever. A night of acid and drumming was more like it. We're two donkey-riding hippies, really not part of any big social scene, and one day we run into a guy who thinks he is a prophet. We had seen him before since he basically lived on the beach near the village in a blanket that was both his clothing and his bed.

On this day, his hair was stiff and standing straight up from salt water, his skin leathery and tanned, and he had those bright electric blue eyes. And what excitement! He had come to tell us about this wonderful event that would be happening that very night!

"Have you heard about the Festival of Light?" he asked us, eyes glowing, with a great deal of enthusiasm and expectation in his voice.

"No, no, we haven't, what's that?" answered Patrick, very politely.

And he told us, in the most extravagant terms, about bringing together the lovers of peace and harmony in one beautiful, Earth-changing, planet-reviving night of love and celebration. He would've waved his arms, but they were holding up his blanket, his only clothing.

"Great, great, that sounds wonderful!" We both nodded and assented the way you do when someone is all excited inviting you to something and you know perfectly well you're not going to go. "Where's it going to be?"

He smiled at us benignly. He had saved the best news for last: "It's tonight, at your restaurant, when the sun goes down."

That night, as the full moon rose over the little village of Diabet, four hundred hippies from Essaouira and beyond gathered in the village. They crammed into our courtyard, all tripping and stoned, but peaceful. Those that couldn't fit into the courtyard settled out on the hillsides surrounding the village, building fires, drumming and dancing wild dances and screaming their delight into the night. Since I was powerless to do anything, and it was so out of any control that there was nothing that could be done anyway, I sat in my corner, cooking, and watching. It was pretty peaceful, for being so crowded, until the cops came.

Someone in Diabet had contacted the police in Essaouira, and suddenly, there they were at our door. Patrick, who had been cruising the crowd as Director of Good Vibrations, like the cruise director on a ship, met them at the door. He was calm. He explained that we were a bit surprised by all the people, but everyone was having a good time and there was no evil intent.

The Diabetans were terrified by all the fires and chanting, but Pat convinced the cops that it was just a way of partying, that there was nothing dark going on. He kept the vibe nice and high and easy, so that the hundred or so people tripping in our courtyard stayed nice and easy, too, and none of those bad currents were allowed to start. It worked. The cops left, unbelievably leaving all those nuts in our hands! What did they think they were going to do, anyway? Four cops to four hundred tripping howling hippies!

But someone picked up a bad vibe. A young Moroccan, high on acid and probably a little unsteady anyway, had gotten spooked. It wasn't enough to get four hundred people all to Diabet; part of all this "Festival of Light" theology was acid for everyone who wanted it, whether they were already a bit fried or not. So this guy, tripping and freaking, grabbed my big chopping knife that was lying near me. I had been so focused on the police at the door I hadn't noticed, and all of a sudden, he was armed. Glazed and threatening, he swung around, brandishing the knife at everyone near him. People pressed against the walls, and panic started. Just the scenario you want to *never* be in.

And then, there was Patrick, slowly and quietly walking toward this guy with his hand outstretched, telling him he'd be fine, just give him the knife. Over and over, his voice low and soothing, Patrick said, "You're safe here; nothing bad can happen to you here; just take it easy and give me the knife." He walked straight up to the guy, as everyone else backed away, and gently put his hand on the guy's shoulder, taking the knife from him. Handing me the knife, he led the guy up the stairs to a more private courtyard so he could help him calm down. When they finally came back down, most of the people were gone. That was fine with me. Ever after, that guy called Pat "Jesus Christ."

What I Loved about Patrick

That. Even though he had no ambition to do anything other than just "be", he managed to be pretty cool and kind when the chips were down. He didn't require much in the way of maintenance, just some dope and food. He was self-entertaining, and could always be counted on to stay calm and calm other people down. I had arrived in Paris a fairly typical New York divorcee (for someone whose honeymoon had been an around the world freighter trip that outlasted the marriage), and he was showing me a whole other world, full of exotic places and new ideas. That whole other world was what I loved about him, along with his calm, quiet nature and his radically liberal ideas about Liberte.

People and their Food Trips

I should talk. I've got as many food trips as anyone, but having a restaurant, people talked to me about food, or else that's what I listened for. Even when I was a kid, my dad would come home from a trip to some exotic country and mainly I wanted to hear about the food. I'd sit on his bed while he unpacked and he'd tell me about fabulous and disgusting food he had eaten, like monkey brain and sugar mice. The most disgusting stuff was always in China.

When I read travel guides, the first thing I look up is food. Morocco was a great country for eating. As a pretty much vegetarian, I never lacked for something healthy and tasty to eat. There was couscous, a grain cooked with a pile of vegetables and a teeny bit of meat. There was the plat tagine which was cooked with oil and steam in a special cooker. There were many varieties of breads and there were desserts, which I don't remember because thankfully they never have interested me. And then there were people's personal dietary trips.

Like Mohammed, a skinny Jewish kid from New Jersey who came around late every afternoon as the sun began to set. He was a diminutive, argumentative guy that reminded me of guys I had met in Brooklyn, so I figured he was a refugee from some really heavy Jewish home and rebelling for him came in the form of calling himself Mohammed.

Mohammed's deal was food preparation and mono-food diets. He was living on fresh figs. Period. At least that's what he told me. Macrobiotics taught me that food, and everything else in the universe, is either yin or yang or some percentage of either or both. One yin attribute is talking, and figs are very yin. Mohammed would talk without coming up for air, on and on about the importance of only eating one food at a time, and about not eating or preparing food at sunrise or sunset.

He would generally show up around sunset, as I prepared food for the meal that night, but that didn't seem to bother him a bit. Oblivious, he would talk on and on and on, telling me that sunset and sunrise were times for prayer and worship, not for eating. We never addressed the obvious; I just kept cooking and chopping as he talked. Besides the fact that he talked all the time, Mohammed didn't look too good. He had open sores on his arms and legs that never seemed to heal.

I had seen those sores before on people doing lots of drugs, especially in India and Nepal, where things could be very dirty. Mohammed swore he didn't take drugs. I was amazed. If he was telling the truth, he was getting really screwed up eating just figs!

Learning macrobiotics meant learning balance. I saw it as a great and peaceful way of being, not just a way of eating. It kept us healthy. When a plague of hepatitis struck Diabet, nearly half the village was stricken. There were lots of scared kids far from home lying in these mud-walled houses with no running water, no guaranteed clean water, and nobody around to take care of them and get them the clean food and drink they needed. I started taking cooked brown rice around to them, and washing their dishes and sitting and keeping them company. I never once thought I would get sick; I had so much faith in my way of living that I was sure it would keep me healthy. And it did.

The Moroccans didn't seem to get sick much, but then, that would have been hard to know. After the first few flings with the women, we didn't hang out, so I rarely went to their homes or they to mine. But my impression of them was that they were a strong and sturdy bunch. Even though they ate huge quantities of food, about 98% of it was grains, fruits and vegetables. If they made a couscous, the amount of meat in it, which always went either to the guests or the father (and mother?) was less than 1/2 what a normal American would have on a sandwich. They did eat sugar, drink it actually in their never-ending green tea, but they didn't drink alcohol, so the sugar thing probably about evened out.

One night, the Boumie family invited us to their home in Essaouira for couscous. Patrick and I went, along with their other tenants, a pair of sanctimonious vegetarians from San Francisco. We were seated on the floor, the four of us with M. Boumie, when Fatima, his wife, brought in the huge steaming tray of couscous. It was a mountain of the grain, topped with all manner of vegetables, and on top, a piece of lamb about the size of a silver dollar. It was the size my brother would have eaten at least ten of when he was growing up. The meat was offered to us all, but we all declined except Patrick, who would eat anything to be polite, as long as it was prepared with love. He split it with Boumie, who seemed pleased with the arrangement. When it came time to dig into the rest, the two vegetarians refused to eat. "We don't eat vegetables cooked in the steam of meat," was their puckered faced explanation. The Boumies faces fell in disappointment, after all the trouble and expense they had gone to making a wonderful big dinner.

Those goody-goodies left. I was so glad. Too much purity tends to stink. After dinner the Boumies asked us if we wanted to spend the night. Sure! I wanted to see how this was going to work, where everyone slept and all.

The banquettes that extended around the whole room were about straw bale width. They may have been made of straw bales, stuccoed over. In one corner, they made a bed with something, maybe the table, so the whole corner was one solid bed. As the younger kids got sleepy, they were put in bed, littlest first, until the outer space was for the oldest son, a stupid looking teenage boy who stared wistfully at me whenever he saw me. Everyone just lay down in their clothes.

Patrick and I made a bed of something in another corner and lay down, stuffed with couscous, to sleep. In the middle of the night, we were awakened by the strangest sight. Madame Boumie, the little fat Fatima, was holding her crying little daughter as M. Boumie force fed the crying, protesting little baby cookies and tea. I sat up, "What are you doing to that baby?" They explained that they wanted her to be healthy. Whatever. I was in their house, their guest, and knew whatever I said would be pissing in the wind. As far as women were concerned, fat was healthy, desirable and good. I turned my bony ass over and went back to sleep.

Nightlife

In Diabet, all the nightlife I knew about was going on right at our little restaurant. Some of the most wonderful musicians came by with instruments, and those nights would go on and on, often with the addition of poppy tea. Poppy tea was, no kidding, how Moroccans put cranky babies to sleep. I'm sure they made it weaker than we did, or at least I hope so. For about a dime, you could buy a bag of dried opium poppies at any market stand. That made enough tea for a bunch of folks to get seriously fucked up. Then the music would become truly transcendent, as melodies and harmonies blended softly in the night.

Sometimes, of course, things got more than transcendent. A Canadian couple who rented a room from us developed quite a taste for the tea. Late at night in their room, which was the little one next to ours, you would hear a big crash as one or the other stumbled against something or fell. For all you youngsters out there: I'm sure it's illegal by now. It would have to be. It was *way* too easy and accessible.

Once in a while, we found ourselves in town at night, either in Essaouira or Marrakech. It wasn't often, since we had so much going on at home, but when we went, it was great. My favorite place late at night in Essaouira was not finally the Hippy Cafe, but a coffee stand under the arches right near the bus station. There, a coffee artist worked caffeinated visual wonder. He would start with a tiny little spouted pan of thick black coffee, and pour it quickly into a thick tall glass. Next he poured hot milk into the glass, then poured it overhead in a streaming arc of hot liquid, from glass to glass, back and forth until it was all foamy. Watching the hot, steaming cafe au lait stream back and forth over his head was an amazing show of dexterity and unswerving skill. I didn't even like coffee, but I always ordered it. Just the thing for the long trip home.

The trip home at night was always by car, or else we didn't go. No way I was going to walk through that river at night, and totally never would I cross the bridge at night. By day, the bridge was a nightmare.

After the donkeys were stolen, which happened only a couple of months after we got them, we were back on foot for our trips to town. It wasn't that there was some dramatic theft; the donkeys simply disappeared. I know it's because we let them run free during the day when we didn't need them to go to town. Some kids must have grabbed them and hidden them; we decided we were *never* going to find them. I was comforted by the knowledge that in their little bit of time with us, they had the best treatment, most freedom and food they were likely to have again, but I wish we had tried to get them back. We didn't believe we would, so we didn't try.

The restaurant actually didn't last too much longer than the donkey ownership, but while it did, we still had to bring home the bacon. With no car, it was a foot trip, or partly, with a chance of catching a ride on the other side of the bridge. The worst thing about the bridge was that it was only about one third there, or less. It had once been a stone bridge that spanned the river, about thirty feet high over the rocky river bed where it widened to join the sea. Little by little, I suppose, the bridge had eroded, until all that remained for about fifty feet was a raised lip, about eighteen inches wide, with a little stub of the original roadway, about the same width. We were invariably stoned coming from town. I am not overly coordinated at the best of times, and have a horror of heights. Add to that a big woolen djallabah flapping against me in the stiff sea breeze, and a basket of vegetables bouncing on my hip. It was perilously close to more than I could manage.

"Well," Patrick told me, "we could always go through the river." It was winter, chilly and windy, and the thought of hiking through the cold river at sunset was too awful. The bridge was so much shorter. Ok, I agreed, we'd do the bridge.

It was my last time. Patrick strode comfortably ahead in his usual fearless manner. I got to the broken part and sat down. The riverbed was so far below, the wind was blowing so hard, and I was nearly petrified with terror. Slowly, I began to inch my butt across, dragging my basket beside me. God, this was going to take for fucking ever! Suddenly there was an insistent ringing behind me, and I turned my head to see one of the village men coming home from work on his bicycle, riding calmly across the broken bridge, probably for the five thousandth time, at least. I had to inch my butt off the ledge, onto the little bit of broken roadway that remained, to let him pass. It was humiliating, scary, and when I finally inched my ass over to the other side, I announced that I would *never* do that again. And I didn't.

Since I refused to cross that bridge again, Patrick started doing the market run for the restaurant. By then, a German guy was living in the house, one in a long string of colorful characters that rented rooms from us. He was helping with the restaurant, so he would go do the market thing, too. But it was getting old, hauling all the water from the well, and the worst of it was having to do it every single night. The macrobiotic restaurant of Diabet was well known; people depended on having dinner there. We either had to be there every night, or quit. That was an easy choice.

Well actually, first Pat quit. He told me one morning he wasn't doing it anymore, and returned to his previous vocation of rolling little cigarettes with local tabac and smoking them. He was just warming up for whittling. The German and I kept it going for a few more days, but the thrill was gone and we closed. Hallelujah!!! What a blessing! We hopped a bus for a trip to Marrakech.

Marrakech

There we were, riding on the Marrakech Express, the direct bus from Essaouira to Marrakech. We got there in the middle of the day, with plenty of time to go find a cheap hotel room and stash our bags. Then we went to see the sights on the square.

Marrakech is a day at the circus, or it was then. The main square was full of the most amazing assortment of buskers. There was a guy playing with cobras who would occasionally pick one up and bite it on its hood. Another guy took boiling kettles off the fire and poured the liquid straight down his throat. All this was for money, so you'd put a coin in the basket. When a beggar approached us, a Moroccan would step between us, putting a coin in the beggar's hand and steering him away.

Around the square were stalls where we saw men making pipes with little lathes they ran with their feet, and we bought some beautiful old caftans that still hang in my closet. There were rugs and brassware and beautiful carvings and tiles, but the thing that was most powerful for me was watching a woman at the stand where we were eating dinner.

At sunset, all over the square, people set up food stalls with big pots of meat and vegetables on open charcoal fires, like our place in Diabet, only much bigger and more organized and with tables and chairs. And meat. A group of raggedy young boys, maybe seven to ten years old, had been hanging around, begging for food, begging for money. They were all barefoot and their clothes were full of holes, but they had happy mischievous grins. Every time they got close to the stand where we were sitting, the owner got rid of them, threatening them, yelling at them or having one of his helpers chase them off with a stick.

A woman approached the stand, and everyone got quiet. I had seen her earlier, an ethereally beautiful blonde woman getting out of a van with an English-speaking guy who sounded exasperated. He sounded like he wanted her to do what he wanted her to do, and she simply walked away, unmoved by his anger or desperation. Now, with the same air of serenity and self-possession, she approached the stall, and some men rushed to brush off a chair for her. The cadre of little boys stared at her. Everyone stared at her. I stared at her; I couldn't help it. She was so beautiful and calm. Finally, the cook's wits snapped back in and he asked her what she wanted, so she ordered a dish of something. There were about ten choices, each one costing one dirham, which was the equivalent of about twenty US cents.

She took a bite, then handed the plate to the little boys, who devoured it. The owner started to say something, then stopped when he saw the look in her eyes. She ordered another dish. Another dirham, and she took another bite, then again passed the dish to the boys. Nobody talked or moved as she repeated the same order for four or five more dishes. The owner was in thrall. With each order, he piled more food on the dish. The attention was making her blush with each order, but she didn't stop until all those little boys

181

had eaten their fill. Then, quietly, she got up, paid for her food, and went back to the van she had emerged from.

I felt like I had seen an angel. She was more beautiful than a regular human, and her goodness radiated out in the Marrakesh square, stopping all that poverty and meanness, if only for that night, or that moment, and giving all of us an example of how to give and how to love.

Marrakech was done for me, after that. Morocco was done for me. We had already extended our visas once, or maybe I had to but Patrick didn't, being French. I didn't relish the thought of another interview with a fat uniformed Moroccan guy in the old castle that looked like a dungeon, leering at me suggestively about how I could extend my visa. I'd had enough. We had nothing to do: the donkeys had been stolen into thin air; spring was coming; most of the possible tenants were headed north and there was nothing to hold us.

We headed north, spending time in Tangiers, one of my favorite places for mystery and intrigue. Some stranded hippies needed to sell their VW van, so we bought it for something like $500. It was just what we needed to make the trip north. Besides, Patrick had just gotten an invitation to a wedding in London that we didn't want to miss.

London, spring of 1972

Patrick was full of surprises. One was that he had gone to a very upscale boarding school and made friends with a boy named Tim Healey, whose dad was about to be Britain's next Chancellor of the Exchequer, Denis Healey, aka "the Greatest Prime Minister Britain Never Had." We were invited to Tim's wedding in London and of course we wanted to go. Patrick wanted to see his old friend, and I had never been to England. I had one dress, a long slinky thing that I wore most of the time. I was young. It would do.

The Channel crossing by Hovercraft was horrendous, rough and bumpy. We had chosen the Hovercraft because it seemed it would be much smoother, from the pictures. Maybe the first Hovercrafts, those little bitty ones that took thirty eight passengers, were smoother. After all, we were riding on a cushion of air pressure, so it was supposed to be an easy trip. But by the time we rode, in 1972, those little Hovers had been replaced by much bigger ones that carried cars, trucks, VW vans and up to four hundred people. In theory, it should have been smooth, but the water was very rough that day and the craft followed every wave, rising up and crashing back down, over and over and over.

Everyone except Patrick was throwing up, including the attendants. Pat was at the time smoking Balkan Sobrani, a brand of tobacco with little black bits of something nasty in it that he rolled himself. To this day if I smell it I want to throw up.

We had our VW van to stay in, so we parked close to the neighborhood of the wedding, right down the main street from Buckingham Palace. We could see the front gates from where we parked, just a couple blocks away. We had to park on a slope because of course the damn thing never started without a jump or a push, so there we were, in this lovely area, sleeping and eating and brushing our teeth in the street.

The morning of the wedding we cleaned up as best we could, made our little breakfast, because being as skinny as he was, if Patrick didn't eat he might die, and went to start the van. All morning long, as we cooked breakfast in the van on our little Coleman camp stove, and bushed our teeth and washed our dishes out on the curb, using water from the big camp jug we always carried, people walked by just as nice as could be. A few said cheery "good mornings" to us, but mostly they just minded their own business and walked on by. It was very refreshing. No one accosted us for being hippies sleeping in our van on the street. Naturally the van wouldn't start, but with the cheery help of several men passing by, we got her rolling and headed off to the wedding.

What I remember most of the whole affair, besides the glorious hats and Denis Healey's booming voice and fabulous famous eyebrows, was the woman who leaned in to me and asked, "Where are you staying?"

"In our van, down the street from the palace," I told her.

"Oh, how kicky!" was her reply.

I so wanted to ask her to trade. She could stay in our van, with or without Patrick, and I could go to her house and take a lovely hot bath and sleep in a proper bed! But I didn't.

From the high-society frothiness of the wedding we went to spend the night with Pat's other friends in London, Daniel and Hope, who were living in Hope's widowed dad's house. Daniel was a government-maintained heroin junkie. Every morning he went to the center where he was given his allotment of heroin for the day, then went to his friend's house where they both shot up and hung out. I only saw him briefly as he was not particularly sociable or present, being a heroin addict. Being a junkie was his occupation, something he did all day long.

Hope, on the other hand, was extremely sociable and present. It was a cruel name for her, as she didn't have much left. She was a beautiful, short cherub of a woman, blond with huge clear blue eyes. She and Daniel had a two year old son, a gorgeous little boy with his mother's blue eyes and a head full of blond curls. Hope told us that they could never leave, and life would never get better because Daniel could get heroin every day, free, from the government. They would never get their own house, and he would never have the ambition to better himself, finish his education, get a real occupation. He would never have the incentive to kick his habit, a painful and arduous process, because it was just too easy not to.

186

Meanwhile they lived in the house that belonged to her father, a haunted-looking wraith of a man who darted by, briefly, but did not speak. He looked ancient and wizened and much too old to be her father. He had been a progressive educator who tried to bring more enlightened teaching methods to the school system and, as a result, had been ridiculed and hounded out of the profession. Now he darted furtively around the house. He didn't come to meet us or have any curiosity about who we were. He didn't look at anyone.

It was a house of ghosts: a broken old man, a junkie, a sweet baby and the woman trying with all her teeny might to keep it together. It didn't seem so bad to me, but hey, I was living in a van that had to be parked on a hill every night. Their phone was a pay phone on the wall in the hallway so that no one made calls unless they paid for them. The house was comfortable enough, but shabby. And it was never going to change.

As much as I had ever thought about heroin and junkies, I had always believed it was for the best they be given an allotment and kept off the streets, to control crime and disease. What I saw in London was the other side of the coin, how maintenance was a form of enabling that removed the incentive to get clean by making addiction so easy.

So if anyone asks me if I've been to London, I can honestly say that in three days I felt like I saw the extremes: a "kicky" high society wedding, the kind politeness of strangers, and in one household, the hopeless result of a government program created surely with the best intentions. We got in our van and headed back south.

Back to Morocco, the States, and France

In the USA it's a big deal to go from country to country because the USA and Canada and Mexico are so big, but the trip from London to Morocco was just few days drive, so we took a lovely detour to visit Patrick's parents. They lived in the port city of St. Nazaire, in an apartment that overlooked the locks. We could sit on the balcony and watch ships come in. His parents were easy going and nice to be around. His mom was jolly, fat, and busy, busy, busy, always shopping and cooking and talking and laughing. She was enthusiastic about everything, especially her son and Tupperware, which she sold like crazy and had stacked up in her cabinets. His dad was quieter, more considered. This was the trip where he asked me if this life with Patrick was enough for me. I said yes, but I had my fingers crossed behind my back. I was trying to be polite, but I'm pretty sure he saw through it.

We wanted to see M. Salah again, the grand patron of the kif world in the mountains, and just have a little walkabout in Northern Morocco, so we drove back down, heading south through France and Spain. It was a pretty uneventful trip. Since it was on highways, we split the drive and it went fast. In those days, we'd just pull off the road when we got tired and sleep in our van and nobody bothered us. We caught the ferry from Algeciras, the southern tip of Spain, to Tangiers. Actually, the port is about forty kilometers (about twenty five miles) east of the city of Tangiers, which suited us just fine because it put us on the road up into the Rif Mountains, back toward the village where M. Salah lived, halfway to Chefchaouen.

They were happy to see us back in the village. Most "tourists" probably didn't stop there but just went on to Chefchaouen, which is well known for beautiful handicrafts and in those days, kif and hash and all forms of marijuana. Since visitors were relatively few, we were welcomed warmly and treated to a lovely dinner at a nearby café.

We sat for hours that night at the little cafe in town. Someone had a flute and someone else had a drum and someone else had a ball of the blackest hash I had ever seen. All day long he had worked it in his palm to give to me that night, a perfect ball of the most potent, perfect hash.

I got it right away: this was not about love or romance. This was entertainment. That guy was young. He would make a thousand more balls of hash like that in his lifetime, maybe ten thousand. But who knew when he would get a chance to get loaded with an American girl again?

Whoo Wee. We had fun. The black sky was spinning stars, and they spilled out down the street and all over the ground and through the air. The drummer and the flute player and my new friend the hash maker and probably more walked me and Patrick out to the field outside town where our van was parked. Nothing had been touched, of course. It was well understood: we were guests of M. Salah and *not* to be troubled or violated. We fell asleep with the back hatch wide open, looking up at the stars.

Sometime in the middle of the night, sound asleep, I felt someone kissing me *hard* on the side of my face. "Pat, what the fuck!" I turned over to say to him, and there he was, sound asleep on the other side of the van bed. Whoa. Slowly, slowly I raised my eyes, and there, leering over me, was a man in a hood, his face all but invisible in the dark shadow of his djallaba. "Patrick!!!" I screamed, shaking him awake, "This man's been kissing me on my face!!!"

"You're dreaming," he murmured, rolling back over to sleep. The mystery midnight kisser had vanished into the night with the first scream. I had felt sorry for the women anyway, with the veils and all. After that creepy kiss, I felt even sorrier for them, if that was any indication of Moroccan romance.

Anyway, I told M. Salah the next day. I was pissed, and I knew he wouldn't want anyone or anything messing up the good thing he had going there. Sure enough, Romeo had already bragged, for which he probably got his ass kicked. I know he got his ass kicked. The other guys told me. Getting me stoned was one thing. It was good for business. The other was way over the line.

So there we were, driving around, camping and sightseeing and having a grand time until the van broke down outside Tetouan. Our luck went south; we asked a Moroccan mechanic to fix the van and he pretended he knew how.

By the time we met a couple of young mechanics who knew how to fix it for real, the first guy had experimented too much. It would work for a little while, then break down. Still, it got us around most of the time, and we decided we could make it to Paris. We had only wanted to spend a few weeks in Morocco anyway.

We had just started talking about leaving when I got this telegram from my dad: "Your mother and I divorcing. She needs you. Wiring $200 to Banc de Maroc in Tangiers. Please come home." $200 was the price of a ticket back to New York in those days, maybe even a round trip ticket.

Well crap! That settled that. We'd drive to Paris, sell the van, get to the USA and rescue my mother. It's weird and typical that instead of calling her "Gaham" or even just saying, "divorcing," since I would be able to guess who pretty easily, he said it like that. They weren't very connected as a couple, as I've mentioned.

I was upset for her, and honestly, by then I didn't mind getting a little direction! It's funny looking back that I so jumped to save her, considering we never had a very loving relationship. I wanted one, a loving relationship. I wanted to feel loved by her, and to the day she died, we kept trying, she and I. We just didn't connect very well.

It's also funny that *she* didn't ask me to come back. She *never* would have, not necessarily because she didn't want me there, but because it just wasn't in her nature to ask. She wouldn't dream of interrupting my life to take care of hers. It was my dad, asking me to take over his responsibility, which I was willing to do because we were so emotionally entangled. My mom would've *shit* if she'd known he asked me to come back. That would have pissed her off royally, probably more than whatever she was divorcing him for. Even when my mom was dying in the downstairs of my house, forty three years later, she became completely indignant when a friend of mine said she was glad to see my mom getting such good help.

"Help? Who do you think is helping me???!!" she replied, deeply offended at the suggestion that *she* needed help as she lay in her hospital bed for the tenth day in a row, unable to get up. That was my mom. She didn't ask for help.

When Patrick and I got to the bank in Tangiers, they told me they didn't have the money yet, but would in a day or so, so we went out to Kasim's place, a little café on a bluff overlooking the ocean just a few miles outside of Tangiers. When I say a little café, I mean one or maybe two tables in a little shack. Kasim lived in a room behind the café. Patrick knew him, somehow, and knew about a room Kasim had built into the cliffside, overlooking the beach and the sea. We stayed there for a couple of weeks, waiting for that damn money, which mysteriously would not arrive. Kasim would make us tea or food, or we'd go into town to pick up supplies every couple of days when we went to check on the money. We always had our little Coleman camping stove so Patrick could eat his requisite four or five little meals a day.

We did ok in that little room. It was actually more of a cave with a door. The only light came in from the open door, and the sound of the waves crashing on the beach, which was originally soothing, became teeth-gnashingly grating after a while. We met some German hippies who came to stay for a few days. The only "English" they knew was "up-ke-fuckt," naturally meaning fucked up. They said that pretty often, "allis up ke fuckt!" meaning it's all fucked up. Patrick spoke enough German so they could have a conversation, and they were sweet, if not terribly good conversationalists for me.

One day I was out walking on the beach and started talking with a Moroccan guy also walking the beach. He told me his name was Mohammed M'rabet and that he had just published his book <u>M' Hashish</u>. Then he told me how he wrote it: every night he would meet his friends and smoke hashish and get good and stoned, then he would go home and tell stories into his tape recorder. In the morning he took the tapes to his typist/transcriber and voila, he had this amazing book. Just hearing that opened up a world of possibility. Writing a book didn't sound so hard if all I had to do was get stoned and talk! I already did plenty of that.

He became a very famous author, friends with Paul Bowles, even mentioned in Patti Smith's brilliant book, <u>M Train.</u> I had a copy of <u>M'Hashish</u> once upon a time, but it went the way of so many things. When I went to order a replacement from Amazon for nostalgia's sake, it was something like $70. So I didn't.

We got tired of living in the cliff and went back to check at the bank, but we were *one day* too late. There had been a clerical error that reported the transfer as $2,000, but it was noticed and fixed *the day before!* Damn. We could have traveled a long time on that, in those days. Or as my dad later said, "I told them at the bank if they gave you $2000 I'd never see my daughter again!"

We made it to a small town by the side of the road in Spain before the engine gave up the ghost. There was nothing left to grind. Morocco had taken it all. We needed a new engine. Hmmm. This was a problem.

Meanwhile we were lucky enough to be at a mechanic's (who let us keep sleeping in our van at his shop) thankfully right across the street from a place where you could go fill your wine bottles every day with cold fresh-pressed white wine from a huge oaken vat, so that softened the blow. Still, we needed to fix this. Leaving the van with the very accommodating mechanic, our plan was to hitchhike to Germany, get an engine *and* a cheap car to drive back, get back to Spain, fix the van, and sell both vehicles somewhere and get to New York to, as I've mentioned, rescue my mother.

We did make it to Germany, stopping in Geneva along the way to ask my dad's wealthy friend Geoff to loan us some money, to make it easier. Oddly, we couldn't get my dad on the phone, and Geoff took one look at Patrick with his bell bottoms and his waist length hair and refused to lend me anything without Bert's word. Geeze Louise, I was asking for a couple of hundred dollars, and they probably ate that in osso buco every month. We got nada, zip, zilch.

Happily, Patrick spoke passable German, and we got a little VW station wagon and an engine for the camper, which we had to smuggle into Spain under some old quilts and blankets that we got along the way. Spain was still under Franco and very strict, even though he was nearing a million years old and things had to change soon. Spanish friends I knew couldn't even get passports, so they couldn't leave the country, and we couldn't bring in an engine without hiding and smuggling it. What a stupid exhausting adventure, but we did it. We had built it up so huge in our minds about smuggling this engine into Spain, but when we got to the border they just waved us through and never ever checked inside the car. We had even picked up other hippie hitchhikers on the way back, a really sweet American couple from Massachusetts, so the four of us were just four young hippies on holiday!

Our plan worked. We got the new smuggled engine into the van, which we sold on a promise from the American hippies that the guy's grandmother would send us a check to my parents' address in Chappaqua, NY and that the money would be waiting.

We took their word. They told the truth. We sold the little station wagon the first day in Paris and flew to New York. We just went into a travel agent and said, "We want to go to New York on the next flight" and they made it happen. No penalties, no 14 day plans. We were on the next plane.

I had sent a telegram, but there was no one to meet us, which was odd. It was late summertime, 1972. Finally I called our neighbor and Bert's best buddy Whitey, who came to pick us up. He was a great guy, very laid back, and he didn't know either why I hadn't been able to get my parents on the phone. Patrick had to go through the official "welcome process" of entering the US, which took a couple of hours, so we didn't have long to wait after that for Whitey to show up, driving the two hours or so from Chappaqua. Our entrance/immigration policies are among the least friendly and least helpful I have encountered in the world. It was embarrassing, but it did fill in the time we would have been waiting.

I found the hidden key, let us in, and then we kind of camped out there for a week. No parents, no little brother, no note, no phone call. This was very unusual. Maybe those UFO's had shown up, after all!

And then, after a week or ten days, they appeared. Instead of getting a divorce, they had gone on a family vacation. Thanks guys.

Patrick and I took our money from the last car sale and bought another VW camper. That was all we needed for our life, since we didn't have any household stuff. Being with my parents and Patrick under one roof wasn't all that comfortable, so we went up to Woodstock (NY) to visit with Martine and baby Jesse, living on Ohayo Mountain Road in a big old house rented by some guys who were out on tour with Martine's husband, DJ.

Patrick wanted to see the USA so a road trip seemed in order. Friends he had met in India lived in California, and I wanted to see my old Brooklyn pal Lenny, his lady Val and baby Josh in Tahoe. We already had the VW van, so we could travel in the style to which we were accustomed.

We were headed first to Boulder because Paul Butterfield was playing there; DJ was his road manager and told us to come along. From my parents' in New York, we were driving across country to go to a free show! It was good, the Volkswagen van we bought ran well and after the disaster of the Moroccan mechanic, Patrick had bought the Volkswagen for the Complete Idiot book and learned to fix any little things that went wrong. We stopped to sleep in Nebraska or Kansas, identical flat states (sorry!) on the second night, and woke up to an ice storm. All the windows of the van were iced over, on the inside! I began to cry. It must have been November by then.

In his calm and reassuring way, Patrick said, "Look, we'll turn on the cook stove and boil water and the steam will warm up the windows and melt the ice." He did, it did, I stopped crying and we were on our way.

Years later I had a spontaneous past life memory during an intense bodywork session. It was related to my leg, where the therapist was working, how I became disabled and died in the snow. Patrick wasn't afraid of freezing to death in Kansas, but I was. I'm going to blame it on that other lifetime and our immediate self-rescue on *always* having a way of cooking Patrick's four or five little meals.

Boulder was wonderful. What a hip little town back then! DJ put us up in the hotel with the band and we went to see the show for a couple of nights. Then they all left town for the next gig in some other cool town. You know I wanted to get on that big bus with them, but instead I went into a little hippie bakery to get muffins and coffee and ran into my friend Nancy Hazen, who was working there. I knew Nancy from Boston or Cambridge back in the day, and maybe I knew she was there and looked her up. We went to stay with her in a cabin in the hills outside Boulder. It was my first experience of Western winter mountains, where you can lie in the sun in a t shirt when it is thirty degrees out and be perfectly comfortable.

That cabin was a trip. It belonged to some friend of hers who led us up there, us in our VW van, chugging along, and him in his Jeep, driving like he was on a clear paved road instead of packed snow! After a few days, we all decided it would be a nice gesture to really clean his cabin for him. When we lifted the tablecloth, the ubiquitous soft Indian bedspread of the times, there was so much weed that had filtered through over time the table was completely covered with a thick dusting of fine powder! Needless to say, that made the rest of our stay even more fun!

From Boulder we headed north to pick up I-80 West to Lake Tahoe to visit Lenny, Valerie and baby Josh who was about a year old. It was beautiful there, cold, sunny and snowy, and wonderful to be with Lenny, who had rescued me when Buzzy wanted to kill me, among other adventures. He was the only one of all our friends who stayed equally friends with me and Glenn. Since Glenn wouldn't talk to me anymore, Lenny was my link for the next forty years or so to find out how he was and what he was doing. He was the one who called to tell me when Glenn died, alone in a hotel room in Connecticut.

Leaving Tahoe on our way down to the Bay Area, Patrick wanted to cross the Donner Pass. It's a famous, high elevation pass where a wagon train got stuck in November of 1846 because of bad weather. Out of eighty one people who started the journey to the coast of California, only forty five made it, and they did because the living ate the dead. Or some of the living ate the dead. Obviously that was a very big deal, and very well known. People will talk. There have been books and a movie about it, thankfully none of which I'd read or seen at the time. Anyway, that's the Donner Pass, and since this was probably going to be Patrick's only chance to see it, that's the road we took.

Don't take the Donner Pass in winter. Interstate 80 was bad enough. We were lucky we made it through, me with white knuckles and wearing every last thing I owned to stay warm enough in that van, Patrick just his usual calm self, driving through blizzard conditions on a slippery road, happy as a lark. Once we got over the pass, the western side was much easier and more gradual. VW vans were always cold and poorly insulated, back in the day.

Since Patrick had friends in Berkeley that he had met in India, that's where we headed next. We camped outside their house for a week or so, and during the day what I remember doing is lazing around their living room. They had couches all around the room covered with Indian print bedspreads and saris. It was quintessential hippie decor.

There were dogs coming and going, too. A beautiful black lab jumped in our van and pretty much stayed there, sleeping with us at night, hanging out on the Indian bedspreads during the day. She didn't seem to belong to anyone, so when we left, she left with us. Sorry if I took your dog, but you didn't seem to be paying much attention to her. We called her Bougie, French for candle.

We headed south, picking up an insane hitchhiker in Big Sur, outside the Esalen Institute. Bougie growled. The Esalen Institute is a very well-known training center for cutting edge therapies, the Human Potential Movement and personal growth modalities. It attracted great healers and their students from all over the world, and of course it attracted some kooks, too. We got one. Should'a listened to the dog!

Bougie's growl should have been our clue to not let him in, but we did anyway. He was doing some seriously crazy shit that made Patrick struggle to keep the van on the road, and since we were on the 101, a curvy, twisty road along the sea cliffs, going off would have been grim. Energy would ripple through the van from the back and I'd feel all the muscles of my back and neck tighten. And then it would release, only to start again a few minutes later. I think we were both too scared to say, "Look Asshole, either cut it out or you're getting out here."

As soon as we got to somewhere, some little town, we dropped him off. A whole dark cloud of energy, that black magic kind of energy, got out with him. It prejudiced me against the Esalen Institute even more than I was now prejudiced against Kansas and Nebraska! I never wanted to go to Esalen, even when I became a massage therapist and got into energy healing and so many people told me what a wonderful place it is. That weird guy might have just been trying to get in there and they might have told him what we couldn't, "No way, asshole. Keep moving." And then we came along!

As Christmas neared I wanted to head back and be with my family. We had gone down to Los Angeles, where at least it was warm. We spent a couple of days with my Aunt Lizzie, former fashion model and diva at her house in Pasadena. Lizzie was always a big inspiration for me, with her Norma Desmond sweeping staircase and her walk through closet full of gorgeous designer clothes. She was the great model in New York who got my mom and several of her sisters up there working. Lizzie was the only one of them with enough serious attitude to become a big name in her day.

My cousin Mike was there and he took us up into the mountains into the snow, up toward Big Bear. I learned that day that in California it was a *law* that if you had three or more cars following you, you had to pull over and let them pass. It seems so obvious, but Cousin Mike very kindly told us that it was time to pull over as our van struggled up the mountains, a line of cars building behind us. After cavorting around in the snow, which was really fun in the warm sunshine, we turned around and went to the Pacific Ocean for a swim. That was all in two hours, which is part of the magic of California.

Pat ran into an old friend from Kathmandu in Topanga Canyon. He didn't have a place we could stay, we didn't have much money, and I felt strongly that we didn't belong there, that I didn't have any connection there. Aunt Lizzie didn't want us camping in her posh driveway for too long, and I didn't want Patrick to start any shit about her being a capitalist. Besides, I wanted to go back to Chappaqua to satisfy this nostalgic holiday feeling.

We drove across country for four or five days to surprise my family by arriving for Christmas. The weather was warmer on the southern route, from LA to NY, and we didn't hit any ice storms, gratefully. It turned out to be an illusory bit of sentiment that wore off quickly once back in Chappaqua. Bougie fit right in, Patrick less so. He argued with my father in his own house, telling him he was a "dirty capitalist" while simultaneously eating his food.

We moved into a spare bedroom downstairs where nobody ever went, anyway. There were seven bedrooms in the house, most of them huge, and just my parents and Will living there, so we could stay out of the way. I got a part time job in a nearby health food store and Patrick sat by the fire, since our room had a fireplace, and whittled adorable little Buddhas. Really, they were great. One of the things that amazed me about working in that store was the faith people put in *me,* in my answers about their sometimes really serious health problems. One guy asked me what vitamins he should take because he had been diagnosed with cancer. Cancer! How the fuck was I supposed to know? All I did was sell the stuff, even though I had studied my mom's Adele Davis books since I was a kid. But cancer? People were desperate and knew the answer didn't lie solely in conventional medicine, even then.

I would get home in the evening and Patrick would have made us some macrobiotic food, some rice and veggies that the rest of my family didn't want to eat. I think we ate downstairs most of the time and didn't interact too much. I'm sure it drove my parents absolutely nuts to see me go off to work while this long haired Frenchman sat downstairs and whittled, or cooked his little pots of gruel and rolled his little cigarettes, smoking them by the fire.

Around late February or early March, I got a call from Martine, who was living in Woodstock, NY again. DJ was out on the road with Paul Butterfield again, and she was alone with little Jesse in the same huge old house on Ohayo Mountain Road. Did we want to come stay with her? Well yeah, bien sur. For one thing, she was my favorite friend. For another, I love Woodstock. And finally, we'd get out of my parents' hair for awhile, which would be healthy for all of us. The health food store people were great and told me to come back whenever I could.

The guys from The Band, good friends with DJ and Martine, came by every couple of days to make sure we were ok and had enough weed, what with DJ out of town and all. Martine and I cooked and laughed and had a great time. Sometimes other guys came "home" as this was somebody else's house. I remember a guy named Gary who wanted me to sleep with him, even though Patrick was there in the next room. It was a rock 'n roll kind of theology. On the road, off the road, beer and tequila and weed and coke, easy sex with pretty girls, back on the road for more. Martine never got hit on, of course. She was DJ's old lady and he was one of them, but I don't think any of them thought much of a long-haired Buddha-whittling Frenchman. He didn't really fit in that lifestyle or mindset, as serious and quiet as he was. PS. I didn't. Sleep with Gary. For the record.

Our friend Carl came to visit. Carl's in and out of this story: he asked me out at Boston U. when his eyes were shining yellow with hepatitis, and we looked for him in Sausalito when we were hunting acid. He was always one of my favorite people, very kind, very funny and off the charts smart.

One morning when he was staying at the house, this girl he knew from Sausalito came drifting down the stairs. Martha was her name, a very pretty long haired brunette who had a maniacal fan obsession with Dylan but was in "our" house by virtue of currently sleeping with Gary. Gary was *gonna* be sleeping with somebody! Word was she had walked into Dylan's house while he and Sarah and the kids were having breakfast. Woodstock was one of those places where you just didn't bother famous people. There were tons of them, and everyone's privacy got respected by people who weren't nuts.

As she drifted down the stairs, she took us all in, smelled the breakfast cooking and imperiously declared, "No bacon for me, thanks." We still laugh about it.

When the guys came off the road, there was really no room for me and Patrick to stay. All the rooms were taken by people who actually paid the rent there, so we headed back to Chappaqua, to my parents' house.

I appreciated my parents' letting us stay as long as they did, but after a few months of détente, with me going upstairs to hang with my family some, and Patrick staying down in our room, my parents told me they loved me and I could be there whenever I wanted but Patrick had to go. I felt kind of badly because his family had been so nice and welcoming to me, but I could see that this was just not working at all. Besides, in all honesty, I was nicer to be around. I never criticized his parents, for starters.

We loaded up again and went to see Lonny and Maj, friends of mine who lived out in the Poconos. They had rented a really cool old farmhouse on 200 acres in western

New Jersey and invited us to stay. They lived downstairs with their baby Ilse. Patrick and I lived upstairs and got jobs at a little health food store in the Poconos town of Delaware Water Gap.

It was an amazing health food store right at the foot of the Appalachian Trail, a meeting place for hippies and hikers and tourists and bikers and everyone in between. The Italian guy who owned the store made wine in his cellar and stuffed the casks with coca leaves he brought back from his voyages to Colombia. The reason that's important or figures in this story was that when we needed to work late, he'd give us a glass of his wine. It was amazing. We'd get a nice buzz from the wine, but an effervescent high from the coca that gave us energy for hours! It was a smart way to get maximum mileage out of us.

This guy, let's call him Enrico, had a big kitchen in his store with an ancient Hobart mixer and a huge pizza oven, and he was looking for someone to come in and cook for the season, which was just starting. Happily enough, I was a great cook looking for a job, along with my French boyfriend, who was also a good cook although difficult to get motivated.

I may have mentioned before that he didn't like to move much, this French boyfriend. Patrick was quiet, still, inward, skinny, and lazy. He could sit still all day long, rolling his little cigarettes and carving little Buddhas, which were awesome but did not exactly bring in the bacon. When we first met I was mesmerized by his seeming familiarity with all the great spiritual truths, but that fascination dimmed over time in the light of his inactivity, especially in the area of fiscal responsibility. He was also one of those people who could justify just about anything he did in light of some great cosmic or societal truth. In other words, bullshit.

Lonny and Maj's farm was about a thirty minute drive to the store. We brought food from the store for our rent. It was summer; there was food all around, gardens, and Rolling Rock beer, which was new and popular because we all believed it was made with pure water, so we drank it like a health beverage!

After a while, Lonny and Maj wanted their house back. We weren't really in their way, but I think a month or two had gone by and I might have driven them nuts, and I know Patrick did. Besides being lazy, he was also very judgmental. Even though he didn't bring in much money, he always had judgments about capitalists, preferring to live off the fruits of other people's labor under the guise of some pretense to purity. He had already had a fight with our landlord in Morocco over property rights, then had fights with my dad, calling him a dirty capitalist in his own house. He was of the "what's yours is mine and what's mine is mine" school, a convenient position since he didn't have much.

All my friends waited 'til we had separated for good to tell me what a jerk they thought he was. I lacked the self-confidence to counter his accusations of being bourgeoise and middle-class. No one had ever told me I was ok just being me. In fact, my upbringing was a mess of criticism and not-good-enoughness, so Patrick's criticism of my upper-middle-class background sounded familiar to me. I didn't realize he was just being a jerk; whether I was too bourgeoise and middle-class or not had nothing to do with it!

Where were we going to live as we worked in the health food store? Since we were working all the time anyway, and since we were no longer getting paid, which I'll explain in a minute, we moved onto the back porch of the store, the perfect solution in the warm summer season. At least we had a place to sleep and all the food we wanted. I guess there was a shower there, or we went down to the river to wash, which surely suited Patrick just fine.

The river was a site of great social and political import at that time, since The Valley it ran through was full of very old farms and farmhouses that had been bought up cheaply by the government to build a recreational reservoir. Here were these places, hundreds of years old, all going to be flooded so people could jet ski.

The land was beautiful, rich and fertile. Wild berries grew in rich abundance. After The Valley had been acquired for pennies on the dollar by the government, squeezing out all the old farmers to make way for vacationers, the hippies moved in. These hardy, healthy, happy souls moved into the old farmhouses and set up housekeeping. The ideology was political, ecological and conservation based. There were babies and goats and ponies and dogs, long skirts, long hair and canning jars full of homegrown and homemade preserves. There was music and laughter and lots and lots of love. People had lived there for nearly three years by the time we came along. And then there were the bulldozers.

Every once in a while the government guys would come in their big bulldozers and the squatters would throw their "'dozer boards" against the sides of their houses and scramble up to the roof, men, women and children. With a bunch of people on the roof, the bulldozers would back down. Until the next time.

Meanwhile, in the courtroom, the fight to save The Valley went on. As it was waged, back and forth, life continued there, with no electricity (that should get rid of those stinkin' hippies!) or running water for most folks, who learned to live just like a hundred years before, pumping water or carrying it from the river, burning candles or kerosene lanterns.

Those were good times, going down to the river behind our friend Dorothy's house, watching tube riders fly by in the fast current, swimming near the edge to keep from getting swept off to New Jersey on the not too distant shore. All that ended after a valiant four year court battle. As for us, we had settled in to the back porch of the store very comfortably. We were kind of the straight hippies, me and Patrick, since we had a job that we got paid for. Well, at least in the beginning we got paid.

We were definitely the straight hippies. The river folks were pretty much cash free except for Dorothy, who worked in the store a couple days a week. That's how we knew her and got an in to The Valley. There was also the Turkey Ridge crew, Peter Coyote and Nicole Wills. I was, like any sensible female, in awe of Peter, even though I hardly knew him. Just watching him and hearing his voice was enough. He could charm a Goddess out of her underpants! But I never got to know them all very well. They'd come in the store and float around. Rumor had it heroin was the preferred substance up there, so while I was making pizzas and sweating in the ovens, they were ethereally floating along, seemingly untouchable.

The other friends were organic gardeners and music people. Rita and Bill Goodwin lived on an old farm. Rita gardened, Bill played jazz. They were kind of the normal end of things, with their own homes, like Lonnie and Maj, and a decent livelihood and new babies coming along. Patrick and I were in the middle. We had jobs, but as I mentioned, we weren't getting paid.

Thing is, Patrick and Enrico did *not* get along. It may have had something to do with Enrico getting totally pissed off at paying an employee who did nothing. He said as much to me, that I was A-OK in his book, but what the fuck was with the French guy? I said I didn't know, and went back to making granola.

A couple of times on a Friday night, Enrico would give us a glass of his "special" infused wine, especially if we were facing a really busy weekend and needed to stay up late and cook. It was wonderful. We cooked until two or three a.m., then got up all cheerful at seven a.m. to do more! We didn't get that wine very often, but it was memorable for how great we felt. Will work for wine.

Granola was definitely a specialité de la maison. I mixed fifty pounds of oats with honey and oil and whatever else was going in, spread it on huge cookie sheets and baked it at some ridiculously hot degrees in the six foot pizza oven. Buddy, it was hot back there, and my arms were just fried from being in and out of the oven, especially since it was summer and already hot enough in the kitchen.

Someone, not me, had set up the granola barrel, a fifty gallon tan drum, next to the garbage barrel, an identical fifty gallon tan drum, you know the kind: heavy cardboard with metal bands. I never thought that would be a problem until someone brought in their bag of granola with a huge shard of glass in it. Oh whoops! I moved them apart and hoped I didn't make that mistake again.

Thankfully, people were less litigious in those days.

From time to time we heard about altercations in the valley, and brushes with the police in general, especially since the counterculture was so easy to spot. Moving through a sea of beige and crew-cuts and sprayed hair and polyester was this current of beaded, fringed, long-haired, dancing, singing, smoking, laughing craziness. We stood out. We drove painted vans and cars, wore handmade clothes and shoes, ate granola!

Police were on the alert. For what, they weren't really sure. Were we un-American? Enemies of the State? Going to steal their children? *Hell, we were their children!!!* Whatever we were up to, straight America was by turns amused and afraid. One of our long haired friends, driving on the New Jersey Turnpike in a VW van (just like ours) got pulled over, hauled out and beaten to serious hospitalization. It put everyone on edge.

Then Patrick got pulled over, with hash and a hash pipe, and a French driver's license, in New Jersey, the epicenter of hostile police and policies. They did not know what to make of him, since he acted like he didn't speak English very well. When they showed him the hash and hash pipe he said, "Is zis a problem? In my country, zis is legal, no problem." Finally, they let him go. I think they even gave the pipe back, and kept the hash. *Lucky* him, with his hair half down his back!

Since we were living on the back porch already, and we weren't getting paid anyway, we started having dinner parties out there every night, using the food that was already cooked and had to get eaten at first, and eventually just using whatever we wanted from the store. Hikers would come in off the Appalachian Trail to an amazing meal. People from the area came over. Of course Enrico never came. He would have been furious to see ten or fifteen people a night eating his food. But his wife did! She came for dinner every night, and brought the kids!

And then it ended. Summer was over, it got too cold for the porch, and it was time to move on. We didn't have anything else to do in the States and Patrick's visa, which had been renewed once, was almost up. With huge heartbreak I found Bougie a new home with a little girl who adored her, and got on the plane to France. In retrospect, I should have stayed with the dog and let him go, but I wasn't quite through with whatever we had to do together.

Medieval times in the Cevennes

When Patrick and I went back to France from the U.S. in the fall of 1973, we didn't want to live in Paris again. For one thing, we couldn't afford it. Paris is so expensive, and, as usual, we were hand-to-mouth. I remember landing in Paris and falling asleep on a public bench outside a restaurant. While Pat ran around using the phone and getting us a place to stay, I got comfy right there on that bench in the middle of that little square in front of the restaurant that let him use the phone and fell asleep leaning on our suitcases. Thank you, Angels. Those were definitely kinder, gentler, safer times.

He got in touch with Pierre, who was glad to invite us back, since he loved us both. First we would go visit Patrick's family in St. Nazaire, out on the Brittany coast, and then we would join Pierre and his witchy wife and help them continue their experiment in medieval living.

Patrick's family lived like most French families. They had one bathroom with a bidet and a tub and a sink, and then the toilet in a separate enclosure. They took baths on Saturday night. That was it. Lots of people used to live like that, I know, but I love taking a bath every night and then supplementing with Vitamin D. Now that Vitamin D is big news, we all know we need more of it, and that it washes away with hot water. Long ago, people didn't bathe much, and hot water was hard to come by, but now it's easy so we wash away our Vitamin D with every hot bath or shower. Of course, things change when you live with little water but that wasn't an issue. They just only bathed once a week, but they did wash their butts every day with the bidet, which is a lot more hygienic than toilet paper, when you think about it. Anyway, they didn't weird out too much that I bathed so often. It confirmed what everyone knew, that Americans were sort of crazy.

The family ate really well. Pat's mom went to the market every day for fresh bread, veggies and meat. They all ate meat but me. Before dinner those who wished had a small bit of Dubonnet in a glass with one ice cube. I still like it. They drank a glass or two of wine with lunch and dinner and took naps after lunch; it was highly civilized. They talked at every meal, really talked to each other, really listened. I'd never known a family like it. If my family talked at dinner, it was usually my father giving me shit about something, everyone looking down at their plates, and me leaving the table to go throw up. This was such an amazing experience, so normal and kind, even if I struggled sometimes to engage in the conversation. I was fine with most conversational French, but slang was a challenge, and I was still slow.

After a week or two, it was time to move on. Patrick's grandma gave him a car. It was a cute little thing. I think I drove once the whole length of France, for about an hour, and that was enough for him! It was tricky navigating those narrow old roads *and* watching for stop signs, so when I didn't see one of the signs (just one) he said, "Pull over here, I'll drive," and he drove the rest of the time, which was fine by me.

We drove through the Loire Valley, past vineyard after vineyard. I didn't drink wine in those days, except for an occasional sip of Dubonnet, so we just drove by and admired the beauty, since he didn't want to stop just for himself, and besides we were, as usual, watching our centimes.

When we got to the Cevennes, where Pierre and Catherine lived, they put us up in a little room off the kitchen of the old house they were restoring. It was a bit of a hovel, but certainly no worse than the house in Diabet had been, or a VW van, or a back porch of a store. Patrick was comfortable with Pierre and they were working on a project so I ended up being around Catherine a lot while they did whatever they were up to. She and I cooked and ate, because that's what we could do most civilly while the guys did a building project for the goats or the bunnies.

I've been eating imbalanced since I was a little girl. When I was about six or seven, I stopped eating. I was a pissed off little girl, and so for the third time in my young life, doctors told my mother I was probably going to die unless they could do something to make me eat. The first time was when I was born, then when I was two and got sick, and then when I wouldn't eat. I have this feeling, knowing myself as I do now, that eventually I would have eaten, especially if they had quit trying to *make* me, but who knows?

Having lost a baby just before I was born, little Katie, my mother was pretty much a nervous wreck when it came to the possibility of losing another one. I believe that's why she never bonded with me, or really loved me fully; she didn't want to lose again and risk that pain. She told the doctor to have at it, come up with something, anything that would make me eat

He did. He came up with a tonic and an appetite stimulant. I think it was probably a sedative and some cannabis product, because after about a month, I could not *stop* eating. I ate anything and everything in sight. One time I thought the top of the furniture polish jar was mayonnaise and I licked that. I mean, that is how wacked out my eating sensor got.

I didn't get my eating under control for years, and I still get off balance when I am stressed out or anxious. From fat I became bulimic (all the girls in high school told me how *good* I looked!) where I threw up any time I felt I'd eaten too much, or something not good for me like ice cream. Family dinners had been my training ground for that, and throwing up when I felt full became the new normal for several years. My weight went up and down, up and down. It was rare for me to feel "right" in my body, and I used drugs and starving myself to keep at the weight I wanted. Since Pierre's wife Catherine was in a constant struggle with her weight, I should have just told her about Dexamyl, or to just go throw up.

She and Pierre had moved to a tiny village outside a medieval town to study the effects of architecture on the local culture. At least, that was the story Pierre gave the Sorbonne to get the grant to do it.

The streets of the town were narrow and dark, kind of like the townspeople. It was culturally interesting to be in a place where the buildings and the people and their language and ideas and clothing hadn't changed for hundreds of years, but after a while, their hundred-year-old morality and closed-mindedness started to annoy me. The thing I remember and liked best was the cloth: they had the most beautiful cotton cloth, always prints on a black background, to make the women's dresses and skirts. The food was great, the cloth was great, but the people were generally dour and unsmiling.

By now, I spoke French fluently enough to be taken for a German or a Swede. Never a Francaise, but at least, not an Amerloque either! That was good in some ways, but now that I could understand everything, some people were more irritating than before. Catherine was definitely one of them.

All that muttering under her breath, which I used to be able to ignore, was now understandable. She still didn't like me, and only because I was younger and thinner. Her reptilian brain didn't get much beyond that, and I couldn't figure out why Pierre stayed with her, except that she was really pretty and was willing to live in weird places and experiment.

Things I learned while living there included:

1. You can kill an animal in front of all the other farm animals and have it be so peaceful the others never even notice. Pierre did it all the time with the rabbits they raised for fur and meat. He learned how from an old farmer. If the farmer had to kill something big, like a pig, he got it good and drunk first, so it would be relaxed.

2. There is a thing to put on the bottom of the pan of milk so it won't boil over.

3. Goat milk tastes like shit after the first day, or more exactly, like you'd imagine a goat's foot to taste.

4. How to make goat cheese, which unfortunately I don't remember but could easily learn from YouTube.

5. And how to follow a herd of goats up a mountain at the end of a long day and keep up with them without getting tired or running out of breath. I called it breathing my way up the mountain, and I would literally ride my breath uphill, taking such deep breaths that the oxygen fed me. I could walk fast from the bottom of the mountain to the farm, near the top, and feel energized. Of course, forty years might make some of the difference!

Pierre and Catherine were generally so busy with their little farm that we had minimal interaction. I couldn't see anything he was doing to report on the influence of architecture on the local mentality. They had become farmers of the Cevennes, selling their delicious herb-wrapped goat cheese at the local market along with their rabbit pate, which I never tasted, much to Catherine's disdain. Then we had a visitor who changed everything.

Anna arrived from Paris. She was a young beautiful friend of Pierre's who was delighted to find Patrick there, too, as they had started on a journey from Paris to India together four years before. She had stopped in Afghanistan, falling in love with a guy she met there and traveling across that country for almost a year by horseback. After that experience, nothing much fazed her, and it was impossible to get bullshit by her.

Her stories about Afghanistan were spellbinding. She said they learned right away that if they rode at a normal pace all day, even across barren lands, around sunset they would arrive at a town. Everything was spaced one day's ride away.

In one little village her boyfriend got arrested for having hash. That was obviously a scam because everyone had hash and at the time, it was probably responsible for half the GNP of the country! The cops were about to take him away when Anna said, "If you take him, you have to take me, too."

They tried to talk their way around this new dilemma, but Anna insisted. "I'm not going to stay here alone without him, so if you take him to jail, I am going, too."

Apparently she had a big effect on them, because they let the boyfriend go and gave them their hash back if they would just promise to leave town in the morning.

Obviously, Anna was the bomb. She was clear-thinking, beautiful and smart as hell and Catherine decided that Anna was going to be her new best friend. All it took was one of Catherine's nasty comments to or about me and Anna turned to me, "You let her talk to you like that? Are you crazy?" I remember the power of that simple comment. I couldn't just pretend anymore that I didn't care or couldn't understand. It was out in the open now, Catherine's shitty comments to me, and I was ready to leave the next day.

It took about a week for us to leave, for the guys to finish whatever they were into and for Anna to be ready to go back to Paris with Pierre, who had to report in at the Sorbonne. Patrick and I both loved spending time with her.

Catherine was suddenly trying to be my friend but I wasn't having it. Leaving her to kill the bunnies and stew in her own juice, we headed next to *my* choice of venue, a commune in Draguignan, in beautiful Provence. Au revoir, bitch!

Miles on the Phone

We had met some people from a commune at some gathering
or other in Essaouira the year before, and as was common in
those days, they invited us to come stay. I actually still do
that when I meet people I like who are thinking of coming to
the US. The commune was big and had lots of room so
inviting people was not unusual for them.

An American girl, raised in France, had been given a
beautiful old farmhouse and farm by her family, who had
moved back to America in the hopes that she and her band of
hippies wouldn't follow. She and her six-year-old daughter
lived there with her lover Gerard, the undisputed alpha male
of the commune, his former wife Christine and their son, and
four or five other people. All the women who lived there
eventually became Gerard's lover if they appealed to him. It
was understood.

After eating non-stop at Patrick's family home, and
then at Pierre and Catherine's farm, when we got to the
commune, I just flat out stopped. I remember the first night

we got there. Everyone was eating dinner around a big table. They invited us, of course, but I wasn't hungry. The next day I wasn't hungry either, or the next or the next few weeks after that. I just stopped eating, something I'd wanted to do since I was six and they gave me that damn tonic! After a few weeks, the king of the commune said, "What happened to you? You came here with a big ass and now look at you..."

I must have looked how he thought I should, because I became another of his lovers. His girlfriend, the American who owned the place, was none too pleased with this arrangement, but he got his way, all the time.

Patrick wanted no part of any of this craziness and retired to a little room or hut or something up the hill while I slept down in "the big house." This was really typical of him, that he would just remove himself from the situation rather than have any confrontation. Objectively I respected how he did that, because no matter what he said I probably would have done what I wanted anyway, so any argument would have been wasted air. But as his girlfriend, I wanted more. I wanted him to step in, not exactly fight for me, but....yeah, sort of.

Now that I think of it, he did tell me he thought that was pretty stupid, for me to sleep down there with Gerard when he wanted me to sleep with him *and* it was private in his little hut. But the appeal was, for whatever reason, too great. It was a wild time for me. I guess they were all used to sleeping with each other in varying combinations, but that was a first for me.

The first and last time it happened, my new lover, Gerard, wanted me and his girlfriend in the bed with him. Ok, I could roll with that, it was something new. But when he wanted us to kiss??? Hello, we didn't even *like* each other!

I'm sure he was envisioning something a lot more blissy than he got, and that pissed him off. He wasn't getting what he wanted (she would do *anything* he said, but I sure wouldn't.) She wasn't happy, Patrick wasn't happy, and it was a mess.

So when talk started about a trip to Morocco, I was all in. We couldn't keep going the way we were. Something had to give.

We were on our way to Morocco in a big blue Mercedes van: my boyfriend, my lover, his girlfriend, his ex-girlfriend, their son, his girlfriend's daughter, and maybe some others. There were bunks built into the walls of the van and mattresses on the floor.

A few kilometers out of Barcelona, I said, I'll be getting off here. I had friends from the US staying in Formentera and they had told me it would be simple to find them once I got there. I had to get out of that van.

Everybody except the girlfriend tried to talk me out of it, telling me how we'd have such a great time in Morocco together, but I already wasn't having a great time together. My boyfriend was sad all the time because I had this other thing going on. My new lover was on a power trip and wanted everyone to jump when he said. His girlfriend was sad and didn't like me but he wouldn't allow her to say it, and his ex-wife was the only one who seemed pretty happy, since she had nothing to lose. I actually liked her a lot, Christine. She had long glossy black hair to her waist and she made all their clothes, drapey velvet dresses and tunics that she whipped up on her sewing machine with no patterns or anything.

I had a little bag of clothes, my passport and $7, the exact fare to get to Ibiza. I figured once I got on the overnight ferry I'd be ok, so when they dropped me off at the pier and drove away, I felt nothing but relief. I had no idea there were multiple possibilities of *not* finding my friends, or that I might end up having to walk all over an island to find them. I was running on faith, which turned out fine, thank God.

I turned to go in to buy my ticket and saw the sign. The next ferry for Ibiza was *the next day*. They ran every *other* day. I had twenty-four hours to figure out and no overnight cash to figure it out with. Hmmmmmm....

Near the entrance to the pier was a little plaza with room to sit in the sun. Some American girls were sitting there, three or four of them together, looking very healthy and well fed. I went over and sat down with them. If it came down to it, I knew they'd feed me and give me a place to sleep.

We had just started talking and introducing ourselves when I looked up to see a good looking guy in jeans, a white shirt and a ponytail walking up to us, out of the blue. "Any of you girls want to see a Miles Davis concert tonight?" Uh, excuse me, where does a bear shit? I started walking with him, the other girls walking behind. His name was James and he was Miles' road manager.

That night I went to a Miles Davis/BB King double bill show at the Palau de la Musica Catalana, an amazing old rococo theatre that looked like a wedding cake. It was November 13, 1973. I know because I've watched the footage on YouTube. I don't remember where I watched from, where I sat, but I remember Miles and BB on stage together, playing together.

Miles played for *forty four* seconds, while BB held the whole show together. I know this was in Miles' heroin days, or daze, and that's pretty obvious watching the footage. BB probably wanted to smack him silly, pun intended. No wonder I didn't remember much of it! There wasn't much of it.

Afterward James and I went back to his room at the Ritz Carlton. I was taking a bath in the biggest bathtub maybe in the world when the phone rang. "It's Miles," James winked at me, and held the phone close so I could hear what he was saying.

In a voice like velvet and gravel, Miles whispered, "I heard you have a girl with you...." And then some other stuff about James having this girl with him and me thinking I was pretty hot stuff that Miles Davis is talking about me, even if he doesn't know me.

The next day, when we got up and it was time to go, James said, "I would love to take you with me, but I don't want to interfere with (or was it interrupt?) your journey." Inside of course I was weighing the options: room service in five star hotels listening to totally great music with a really sweet guy, or traveling alone and penniless to God knows where again.

If I were that kind of girl, I would've begged, "No, fuck my journey! Please, take me with you."

But of course, I didn't, 'cause I'm sort of not. It was hardly an invitation, anyway, just a polite good-bye. I think I found him years later in Texas. You can Google anything.

Ibiza

The boat to Ibiza did come in that day, and I got on it with a couple of hundred other people. I probably traveled deck class, which meant spreading out a sleeping bag somewhere and trying to sleep. It was a fun party and I met people I would later go live with for a few months, a French guy named Jean Luc and his Australian wife, Jan and their chubby little baby girl. When we docked at the port in Ibiza the next day, I was invited by my new friends to stay the night with them since the next boat to Formentera wasn't 'til the following afternoon.

Their house was an old, unrestored farmhouse pretty far out of town, but we got out there and had a great night together, talking half the night and becoming friends. The next day they got me back to the pier for the boat to Formentera, and there were my friends Marsha and David and their baby Amos from New York, just about to board! David was an old friend of Glenn's from Brooklyn College. We had a polite détente, since I had left Glenn and since I didn't like the way he treated Marsha. So we were simply polite, all the time, and Marsha was my real friend. The odds of finding them like that were super slim, especially considering they almost *never* went over to Ibiza, but this one time they had come over in the morning and were just then headed back.

When we got to Formentera and I saw how *far* the port was from the towns, and then how *far* their house was from the nearest town (once I knew which town to go to and got there) I realized there was just *no way* I would have been able to find them in any linear fashion. It was again, pure Grace. I don't believe I would have made it through if not for Grace.

From the time I met Marsha and David in Park Slope in Brooklyn, where I lived with Glenn, I had heard stories of Formentera. David and I didn't talk much, but Marsha was full of enthusiasm and love for Formentera, the magical little island, little sister to the much larger island of Ibiza. And it *was* magical. Just finding them in that way was magical.

Marsha and David were staying with their old friends from previous visits to the islands, a Welsh guy Deri and his German wife, Emilia, in their little cottage in Formentera about an hour's walk from town. (I *never* would have found them.) Deri and Emilia also had a much bigger house in Ibiza where they usually stayed, and where we visited once or twice. The Formentera house was too little for all of us.

One night we all went over to Ibiza and Deri got out a guitar. I know we all got high, that was a given, probably smoking hash and/or opium, which was very common there, or drinking wine, or all of the above. Emilia and their little five year old daughter Ana, and baby Amos had all gone to bed, and the four of us, Deri, Marsha, David and I, went out

225

to a studio room or small room Deri had built apart from the main house. I began to play and sing. He might have had a microphone, maybe not. I remember playing for hours. I sang every song that driver knew, and then some. It's funny to look back at, because there are times when I didn't play guitar and sing for ten, twenty years, and I regret it now. Yeah, I was doing something else, but I could have been a bona fide guitar player if I had stuck with it!

Marsha and David and baby Amos stayed for about two more weeks. Mostly we hung out in Formentera, took walks, cooked, and were together. David is gone now, and so, tragically, is Amos, who was in his early thirties when he died very suddenly. It was heartbreaking for the whole community of friends, and shattered Marsha and David for years to come.

When they went back to the States, Deri and Emilia said I could just stay on in the Formentera house since they hardly ever used it. It was awesome to have my own little house. I usually slept in the "reading nook," which had a big picture window so I could see the stars. The old houses in Formentera and Ibiza had thick walls and teeny windows. While this made for great insulation, it also made for living in partial darkness, like a cave. People who owned their houses and could afford it generally remodeled them to let in more light, putting in big windows where before there were just really tiny ones.

Late every afternoon I walked into town because that was where all the expats on that end of the island met up. An hour or so before sunset, everyone congregated at the little tienda and either had a chamomile tea or a glass of hierbas, the local liquor. Hierbas was named that because it was full of herbs. It was sweetened with honey and was very alcoholic and delicious.

In Formentera, hardly anyone I knew had a car, so when we were going somewhere night or daytime, we walked. I wore Earth Shoes (I was the first person I knew who had them) and Indian ankle bracelets that jingled as I took my heel-lower-than-toes Earth Shoe walks. I could walk for hours back then.

If it was night time, it was a good idea to have a flashlight because in those days there were no lights except in town, and maybe an occasional street light if you lived near a "main" road, of which there were two. Mostly we traveled narrow lanes bordered on both sides by stone walls surrounding fields where sheep grazed. The farmhouses, in the middle of the fields, were pretty far from each other, and of course without ambient light, the nights were pitch black dark.

One day Deri and Emilia and Ana arrived from Ibiza to spend a couple of days. Of course they arrived unannounced because there were no phones back then. That was cool; I was ready for some company by then, Marsha and David and Amos having long since gone back to the States. Besides, it *was* their house. I didn't know these folks very well. He was tall and good looking and she was a gorgeous blond. Ana was five years old.

That night, as I was curled up in my window alcove falling asleep, I heard whispering.

"You're not a man; you're not a real man," then a dull thud as she hit the wall.

"You think that hurt? A real man would never have to hit a woman..." Thud.

"You'll never be a real man...." Thud...

Their daughter woke up, crying. I was 100% freaked out. I had never been around *this* kind of circus before. Not only was he hitting her, something I had zero experience with, but she was egging and goading him on, getting him to do it again, and all in the presence of their child.

As fast as I could I pulled on more clothes. This might be where I formulated my theology to only wear clothes comfortable enough to sleep in! I cracked open the door and ran.

By this time I had met some of the people on the island from the hippy expat community. There was a couple living in a similar little stone house, just a few fields away, a Hungarian woman and her American boyfriend, and I headed there. They had dropped in on me a couple of times in the middle of the night when they were stoned and cruising around. I knew they'd be good with my showing up out of the blue in the pitch black, black and blue being kind of the theme of the night.

In my mad rush to get the hell out of the house, I hadn't taken a flashlight, but I could see in front of me. I turned to see where the light was coming from, but there was no moon or light source. Still, as I looked ahead, the light shone in front of me enough for me to see ahead a few feet as I crossed fields and climbed over several stone walls to their house.

I noticed it after that whenever I had occasion to be out in the night. I didn't often go out alone walking after dark, but when I did the way was lit before me. It was a golden light that never failed to appear when I needed it, and I have absolutely no explanation for it except that Formentera really was a magical island.

Having those folks fighting in the house moved me right along. I definitely didn't want to spend another night there, so I went back, got my little bag of clothes, and moved into the home of English Tony. There I began my life of leisure, since he had a car. The whole time I had been living in the little house, when I walked an hour into town every night, I never got sick. Then I moved into English Tony's house and he drove into town every evening, so I started riding with him. And got my first cold. Of course, it wasn't bad enough to make me start walking again!

Eventually I moved over to Ibiza. I had gotten a note from Jan, Jean Luc's wife, who I liked very much, saying life was kind of lonely for her and they had an extra bedroom if I wanted to come stay. By then I had gotten myself into multiple romantic entanglements and it seemed like a good time to change scenery.

They lived way out of the main town, almost at the end of the road. Their old farmhouse was so dark we had to burn lamps inside in the daytime; of course we had no electricity. I had a bedroom off the main entrance room, and they had a big bedroom with their little baby daughter, who was about one. This was one of those unrestored farmhouses with the teeniest little windows so that all the rooms were basically dark, all day long.

We had an agreement: they paid the rent and stayed home and worked. They had lived in Mexico before Ibiza and learned to make traditional huaraches. Along with leather bags this is what they made and sold to earn their living. My "rent" was to go into town and get groceries. Going to town meant hitching a ride, which usually went easily enough. Coming back was the trick. We were all the way at the end of the island. Going in, most everyone was going to town, but coming home, not that many people came out as far.

Coming back from town one day I caught a ride with a very rich German man in his gorgeous sleek car, something like a Jaguar. The man might have been about fifty, which seemed old at the time, dressed impeccably, quite polite and friendly. He said he would be glad to drive me home, all the way home. I told him the road was rough to the house, but he said that was ok. Ha! Little did he imagine how rough it was, but once we got on the narrow part of the drive with all the roots and ruts, it was too late to turn back, since there was no place to turn around. He was very politely hitting on me, and I was so grateful to have a ride that I invited him in for tea.

I knew it was a huge stretch for him, coming in to this dark kitchen, sitting on a cushion on the floor with us, but he was rolling with it remarkably well until the baby woke from her nap, crawled over to us and got mashed banana all over his lovely expensive sunglasses. He was quite gracious about it and insisted it was ok, even though I could tell he was trying to be polite *and* get the fuck out of there.

It was a shame to let him go. Although I couldn't really imagine a relationship, it would have been nice to date someone who had money. It was obvious he was rich by the way he dressed and the car he drove. Then he told me when he came from Germany and got his first piece of land, he had a tower built, went to the top of it and bought all the land he could see. I wonder whatever happened to him, since that land must be worth a pretty pfennig by now!

Most of the really old houses in Ibiza were haunted. My own theory was that it was all that darkness; without windows there just wasn't enough light and people went nuts. Of course there was also a very limited gene pool back in the day, and that probably contributed. In any case, one night at Jean Luc and Jan's house, I was just falling asleep in my bed, alone, when a shimmering blue form, the shape of a man, began to emerge through the wall. I pulled the covers over my head and fell instantly asleep, so God only knows... Having had sex with a ghost growing up, I have zero fascination with them and just want them to go away and leave me alone. Sticking my head under the covers and passing out usually works. Well, it did that time.

Home Again

Eventually, within a couple of months, Patrick showed up from the Moroccan adventure and moved to Ibiza. He got a caretaker position at a huge old house with a big irrigation pool that made lovely swimming. I ran into him a few places because he planned it that way, and he offered me a place to live so he could try to win my heart again. Of course I moved in there. Lots of people came through  and lived there. There were a couple of very handsome Argentinians, and Manou the Russian tap dancer. And there was Bernard, beautiful Bernard who became a lifelong friend for the rest of his too short life. I cooked and sold food at the Hippy Market and walked a lot, since I didn't have a car.

When I met Bernard, he was living in the old town of Ibiza and supporting himself as an artist for tourists, doing oil paintings of the harbor with palette knives instead of brushes. I stopped to admire his work and we started talking. He constantly belittled his paintings, saying he was not an artist, that this was just mechanical shit. But watching him, it was obvious how talented and artful he was.

He also had a huge thing about dying. He would take acid in his apartment and lie in the pitch black dark and "practice dying." This was not something I ever wanted to do with him, even though I adored and revered him. He was gorgeous and funny and so deeply self-deprecating and lovely, there was just no way not to love him. Even though Patrick knew the crush I had on him, he also loved it when Bernard came around because he was just one of those guys that everyone liked.

One day Bernard took me to meet some friends of his, an aristocratic couple from Paris, lovely, ethereal creatures. The man was very tall with curly brown hair and soft eyes, and she was one of those gorgeous feline women that slid and floated rather than walk. I felt I had fallen into a Fellini movie. As the wife moved around the room, she blew gently on the shelves. "Look at her." her husband murmured adoringly, "She's doing the housework, dusting."

Bernard also had a thing for really crazy women. I was definitely crazy enough, but apparently not violent enough to fit the bill.

After I'd known him a while, he disappeared up to Paris, where he kidnapped his cute little two-year-old daughter Sita. The mother knew where he lived in the old town, so he came to live with me and Pat in this big house out in the country.

One night I went into town -- a rarity for me -- to the big new disco that had just opened. I had eaten a little ball of opium, the drug of choice around those parts, and was

233

wearing my long flowy white gown that, from pictorial evidence, I appear to have lived in. I was out on the dance floor floating around, having the time of my life, when all of a sudden, out of the fucking absolute *blue*, I was being dragged by my hair by a screaming hellion from the fires themselves.

Bernard immediately appeared and collared her; that was Sita's mommy, just in from Paris. She was convinced that I was with Bernard and that was why he took the baby, and of course as pissed off as she was, there was no talking her out of it! There was no talking, just dragging bodies here and there. I remember the next day my scalp hurt like hell, the pain killing effects of the opium having worn off.

The next day she appeared at our house. Information of who lived where was easy to get. She had a knife with a 12" blade in her hand and she went for Bernard. Ah, those passionate Parisians! He disarmed her, but the upshot was that she took Sita back to Paris with her, and after she did, Bernard moved back to his apartment in the old town to take acid and practice dying.

Years later, it came in handy, I hope. He was living in South America, in Colombia, with his second Colombian wife and their baby. I hadn't seen him for a couple of years by then, but they took a vacation to Argentina and were in a horrific accident. She and the baby were eventually fine, but he was badly hurt and no help came for a couple of days, and he died out there at the scene of the wreck. The only solace I found for him, knowing he had been out there for a couple of really bad days, was that he had all that practice at letting go, as if he had a premonition that he would someday need to know how to "die well."

The owners of the little farm where I lived with Patrick showed up one day. We knew they were coming, but they needed almost all the rooms, which is why I went back to sleeping with Patrick instead of having my own room and how we more or less got together again for a while. They were German coke dealers, big and loud and rough, but nice, not bad people. Just big and loud and rough.

I wanted to leave, but I was afraid they would eat my goat. That's how rough. Their vacation was mercifully brief, and before they went back to Germany, one of them told me his sure fire way to get rid of a cold:

"Get in a very hot bath, drink a *bottle* of vodka while in the bath, then get out and wrap in blankets. You will sweat and break the fever and be well."

That's the kind of constitution they had. The cure would kill lesser mortals.

I got a letter from Heinrich saying he was coming. We had written regularly while he was in jail in Australia. He and I had been so attracted to each other, even to the point of declaring our affections on a rooftop in Kathmandu (how's *that* for romantic?!) but I was married at the time, and he was with the lovely Patty who subsequently sent him off to prison, so nothing had ever come of it. I looked forward so much to seeing him again, Heinrich of the huge blonde Afro and the piercing blue eyes, one of the freest spirits I had encountered in those years of free-spirited globe-trotting. Or as my father told people, "My daughter will be back some day. She's busy walking around the world."

When Heinrich came, we gave him a small room off the kitchen because it was kind of private and quiet. He was shattered. He'd ask me if he could go for a walk, or if he could get something to eat. I told him, "This is your house, you can do whatever you want here. Walk when you want to, eat when you want to. You're not in prison anymore, you have freedom to choose now.." but whatever they had done to him had really gotten deep. I understood, from my own brief experience in New York, how you could go from totally free and carefree to completely contracted and paranoid, so the fact that his transformation took three years of prison made me hurt for whatever they had done to him. I wanted to do more, but all I could do was love him and be his friend.

After a couple of months, he got an idea in his head about something he wanted to do, which was an *excellent* sign. It had to do with running a transport for hippies to India from somewhere in Europe, and once he left we pretty much lost contact after a few years. He was one of my favorite people I met on these journeys, and I searched for him once the Internet got invented. Even though he had a really long and unusual last name and there were other people with that name in his home country, I never found him again.

I got tired of trying to get along with Patrick. We were just so constitutionally unsuited to each other, although when we weren't trying to be a couple, we loved and admired each other for our stellar good points, which were creativity and fun and depth of understanding on a spiritual soul level. I spent time in town, first at Bernard's and then sometimes staying with this German Baroness and her Aryan lover, Peter. They were a trip. She had been having sex with either her father or her brother or both since she was really young and wanted to know right off the bat if I had sex with my brother. I recoiled and was immediately called uptight and bourgeoise. When she was twelve, her father had taken her on a tour of the erotic temples of India. You can't make this shit up.

I had my second and last attempt at group sex with her and Peter. I had sex with him, with her total blessing, once in a while. One time, she came in the room and slid in the bed with us. Euuew! I did not want that, one bit, and that was pretty much the end of that.

The other thing I remember from their house was the night I slept there and the German junkie girl was there, too. When we got up in the morning, she went staggering by me, gray and sick and miserable, into the bathroom. Through a crack in the door, I saw her shooting up. Right after, she came out totally chipper and cheerful, smiling and shining. I've seen people go from 0 to 60 over their morning caffeine, and it makes me think of her.

Suddenly, I was pregnant with Patrick's child, just when I knew I had to get away from him and get a life that didn't involve whittling little Buddhas as a major pastime. I wanted more, and here I was, pregnant. He wanted me to have the baby and be together forever and ever. I was absolutely certain this could not happen.

We went to Paris, because in Spain, a Catholic country, there was no abortion. In Paris there was a new movement to teach women to give themselves an abortion so that working class women, who couldn't necessarily afford a doctor, could abort a child they could not care for. I knew I couldn't have this baby. I had no home, no income, and didn't want to be with the father. I had the maternal instincts of a bivalve. Seriously, the last thing I wanted was a baby. And so I had that abortion. As it turns out, it's a lot harder and more painful than they were leading me to believe, those learn-to-do-it-yourselfers. I ended up telling the doctor, "I won't scream if you'll just do it, but I'll never be able to do this." In French. And so he did.

I didn't regret it. I personally think abortion is the best solution to a problem that has no good solution, better than bringing an unwanted child into the world. Other people feel differently, I know. God bless and love us all.

It was always easy to find a place to stay in Paris since Patrick had so many friends there. This time we stayed with a young couple I had never met before with a toddler and an infant. The mother was a frazzled mess. One day the toddler hit the baby. The young mother hit the toddler, screaming, "Don't hit!" It wasn't a big thing, but we'd already spent a long week there and I was ready to go. The fact that I had chosen to abort Patrick's and my fetus was a clear indication that I was about done with him, and it certainly did not make me more patient or willing to put up with anything. I was nauseous and anxious and sad and angry, and after I had the abortion, I was just sad and tired.

I wasn't ready to begin another round of living in other people's apartments, and I missed my family. Besides, I was really sick of watching Patrick sit there, calmly rolling little cigarettes, hour after hour, day after day. I remember when I was pregnant the smell almost made me throw up. All I wanted was to go home to New York to my daddy, who was really probably at the heart of most of my craziness. And so I did.

My dad worked for a company with an office in Paris, so I went over there. The man I saw, a good friend of my father's apparently, insisted on giving me a huge check for a wedding present, because he had missed my wedding. "But," I told him, "I'm not even married to that guy anymore! We've been separated for over three years!" No matter, he said, the money was for me. It was great. I had the money to get home.

As Patrick sat in that apartment smoking, I bought a ticket back to the States. The flight left in two days. I had to give him that much consideration and myself enough time to gather my wits. Paris was in the middle of a garbage strike, city wide, and there were piles of garbage everywhere as I walked from the metro back to the apartment that afternoon. It was chilly, which kept down the rats and the smell. Yuck.

I walked into the apartment and saw Patrick, sitting there calmly, smoking one of his skinny little cigarettes. "I bought a ticket to New York," I said. "I leave the day after tomorrow." He couldn't believe I could leave him and our life together, but I did.

The day I left for the airport, I left alone. He wasn't into helping me with my stuff, getting me to the airport, any of that. His heart was broken, he told me.

I walked out of the apartment building and turned for what I thought would be one last look. Someone had died in the building the day before, and the entire facade of the building was draped in black. That's the French way, or it was then. There were huge black cloths draped on either side of the entrance doors, and black swathed across the whole front, wrapping the whole building in mourning. I picked my way past the growing mounds of garbage, turning around again and again, not believing my eyes.

I saw my years in Europe, my years with Pat, dying in front of my eyes. My whole identity for the last three years trailed and diminished with each step I took toward the airport. I was surrounded by garbage and rot, and I was in mourning. But I didn't stop. Numb and frozen, I somehow got myself onto the plane, where I curled up on my seat.

What was I doing? I was leaving behind so much of myself, going back to what? The steward came by to urge me to eat my meal. "You have to eat it; it's Thanksgiving Dinner!"

Thanksgiving? Thanksgiving. I hadn't had a clue when I bought the ticket, didn't even think about my father driving in the holiday traffic the two hours to pick me up.

And then, after the eight hour flight, I was off the plane and there stood my dad with my little brother, so much more grown up and shy than when I left over a year earlier. In front of him, my dad held open my old fur coat. "Put this on," he said, wrapping me in the soft warm fur. "I thought you might be cold."

THE BOOK OF DOUG

Honeymoons

I might be the Queen of the short marriage, long honeymoon. Or else, I think the honeymoon is going to go on and on, and it doesn't. Case in point is when I came back from Europe: my dad was all there for me, my parents were happy to have me "home", everything was fabulous. Then the honeymoon came to an abrupt end. I got back on Thanksgiving Day, so it wasn't long before Christmas was coming along. I had just spent a few years in Europe where I wasn't near family at Christmas, and I knew how lonely that felt.

My friend Bernard, the one who had been in Ibiza practicing dying, was living in New York City with some other French guys I had met and liked. I asked my parents if I could invite two or three of them out for Christmas. After all, we had three extra bedrooms at that time and I was in a sharing mentality.

That house in Chappaqua had been an inn in the 1800's and early 1900's. The old dining hall was now our huge living room, with massive old rafters where my parents' friend Fels climbed up and danced at their many parties. The pass through from the kitchen to the dining hall became a well-stocked bar between the kitchen and the living room. I think of it now as the heart of the house, a place where I did some informal experimenting as a kid, a place where more than one cleaning lady did the same, the place where one of them experimented until she had to take a nap, right there on the floor in the bar. My mom found her sleeping there so she didn't come to clean any more after that.

I loved that house. I had been there since 4th grade and had my first and second sexual experiences there, the first being with a ghost. I felt it was my home. At least it was the only home I had ever had.

My mother informed me that not only could I not invite my friends out to the house for Christmas, but that I needed to remember it was my parents' house, not mine. As she imperiously put it, and she was big on imperiousness, "You need to remember, this is our house, not yours."

And so, fuck me, I didn't have a home. I thought it was my home, too. I thought that was how family worked. That's how it's worked with my sons and me, but not with my parents.

I called my friends near Northhampton, Massachusetts who were living in a commune with a weird artist guy and his daughter and the next day I caught a bus and moved out again.

The Massachusetts interlude was all well and good. I immediately slept with the owner and then immediately regretted that lapse in judgment as he was needier and weirder than even I was. He was an artist who painted by sliding through the paint on huge, room length canvasses. He also took baths with his little daughter, which I don't have a problem with, and let her play with his penis, which I definitely do (have a problem with). The reason I know is we only had one bathroom, and so we were totally casual, the four "adults" there (and I use that term loosely) walking in and out pretty much as we needed.

One night I walked in while they were in the bath. She was saying, "Make it bigger, Daddy!" which he was obliging with a large erection, all the while giving me a sheepish look like, "What could I do? She wanted to play with it!" His place, his rodeo: we all knew about it, but didn't do anything except move out, one by one. I was first.

My friend Carl came to visit from Connecticut from time to time, bringing both opium and a breath of the outside world. We took rides in his big Mercedes, the one that looked like something officials of the Third Reich would have driven, one time riding up to Vermont to visit Rutland. Carl wanted to show me the town because all the electrical wires were underground, and had been since 1910 or so. It so impressed me, how wonderful not to see wires strung overhead, that the one time I built my own house, I made sure all the electrical wires were underground, too. We smoked Thai sticks and picked up hitchhikers and laughed all day. Against all odds, Carl became sane as the years went by, with a hugely successful career as a psychoanalyst. Nobody in those days would have bet on it.

We had some fun there, we communards, but winter seemed to last for fucking ever. One March morning, as I looked out on a *foot* of ice on the long driveway and took my frozen glass of bedside water down to the kitchen to thaw, my friend Martine called from Atlanta.

"The daffodils are blooming here. You should come."

Within two days, I was there. Life was easier and more spontaneous before you had to buy air tickets in advance. I've never adjusted well to that, as I've mentioned. When pre-planned travel became the rule, it really cramped my style.

Georgia

Martine and David's house was great, a typical Atlanta brick ranch house in the upscale neighborhood called Buckhead that used to be safe and affordable. Their baby son Jesse was a toddler, so Martine and I would take him for late night walks in his stroller, the only people in the neighborhood out walkin' after midnight. One night we put sunglasses on him and laughed about being out walking our little freak. Lenox Square was a close walk, a manageable little mall about a tenth the size it is now, if that.

Since I didn't have a car, and they just had one that David needed to get to work, I hitchhiked all over Atlanta. People picked me up outside grocery stores, men mainly, and drove me to my door *and* carried in the groceries for me. People were so polite and kind and I started to make some friends and meet like-minded folks at places like the food co-op in Little Five Points, the hippie mecca.

It was early springtime in Atlanta, a beautiful time of blooming dogwoods and warm days and cool nights before the hot wet blanket of summer descended. David and Martine's house was right around the corner from Broadview Plaza, home of the Great Southeast Music Hall. In the 70's it was the most amazing venue, with acts like Jimmy Buffett, Tom Waits, Emmylou Harris, Muddy Waters, Nitty Gritty Dirt Band, Doobie Brothers and New Riders of the Purple Sage. On April 17, 1975, the Legion of Mary came to town, the side band Jerry Garcia and Merl Saunders had started.

David and Martine had moved to Atlanta specifically for David to work on the music end of things for a guy named Mike Thevis, whose main business was porn. He had started with "Playboy" in the 50's, but when he realized the profit potential, moved into really heavy duty hardcore porn, from bondage to bestiality to child porn. I never met him, for which I am thankful because he sounds like a horrible guy. Years later we unknowingly bought and moved into a little house in the North Georgia mountains where Thevis hid out from the FBI when he was wanted for a couple of murders. What are the chances of that? David worked at General

Recording Company, one of several businesses Thevis opened to launder money and create a legal front.

On that day in April, David asked me if I'd be willing to take Merl Saunders around town for a few hours and show him Atlanta. I was totally in, even though I wasn't sure at the time just who Merl Saunders was, or what he had done. I had no idea what David was really doing, either, or who Mike Thevis really was, besides the guy who got busted for selling Playboy. That didn't sound too hard core to me. Little did I know! What I knew was that whenever Martine did laundry or looked through David's pockets, she usually found little packets of coke. We would snort it up for proper motivation to do stuff like shop and sweep. Or just to sit around and talk.

David brought Merl over to the house. We took David back to his office, then Merl and I drove around. We talked and stopped at Lennox for him to buy some stuff, because being on the road it's hard to get what you want outside of hotel gift shops. We went back in time to have one of Martine's amazing French gourmet dinners then down to the music hall. I walked in with him so nobody asked anything. I felt like an escort girl, only not to have sex. I remember his quizzical looks at me, and my equally quizzical feelings, like, is there a script I didn't get here? Still and all, we had an ok afternoon.

Backstage was a lounge area with a closed door, and a room in the back. It was nothing fancy, plywood walls painted black and some sofas. We sat in there having a drink. I was pretty mute, just watching. A few people came and went, but everybody knocked first. I didn't see Jerry, who was the big name even I knew. He was hanging out in that back room and the band guys occasionally went in there for a while.

There was a knock at the door. Just as it was opening, Jerry called out from the back, "Hey, is that the guy with the cocaine?" Funny enough, it was the Mayor's brother.

Maynard Jackson was the thirty-something year old first black mayor of Atlanta, and here was his brother at the door, come to say hi. He just laughed. I'm *sure* he'd heard worse.

The show was great, and what I remember most is that Jerry Garcia did not move. I mean it. He rocked back and forth a teeny bit once in a while, but he'd play these insane guitar riffs and stay totally still except for his hands.

After the show, David, Merl and I headed down to the Bistro, a club on W. Peachtree St. owned by David's friend Jimmy McGinn. Or Ginn. Flood, a local band David was managing, was playing that night and David had convinced Merl to come hear them. When he agreed to sit in with them and play, in that tiny little club, they were over the moon. They *definitely* knew who *he* was. Jay was on the keyboards, and he was just thrilled to turn them over to Merl. What did I know?

Soon after that, I got a job at The Bistro as the cook! Jimmy probably hired me just as a favor, to give me something to do and let me make a little money. It couldn't have been much since I made organic, handmade, vegetarian sandwiches on bread I baked myself, healthy food in a beer-drinking, meat-eating culture. In the land of barbeque and Little Debby's and RC colas, I was peddling hummus and juices, light years ahead of the curve. The guys in the bands bought my sandwiches, especially the Flood boys, who were basically healthy hippy musicians. And that's how I met Doug.

I had my little food booth open for an event at Chastain Park, Atlanta's outdoor music venue where Flood was playing, when their sound engineer caught my eye. I saw him going back and forth backstage with his tools and wires and stainless steel aura and felt a coldness surrounding him. Turns out, it was just the cocaine. Go figure why that would intrigue me, but I do like a challenge.

There was a woman named Lesley who worked at the Bistro as the only waitress. Every night she came in with her son, who was about six or seven, and put him up in Jimmy's office to sleep while she worked. We didn't talk much but we were friendly enough.

When I started hanging out with Doug in Atlanta, I told him I worked three or four nights a week at Jimmy's Bistro.

"You know a woman who works there, Lesley?"

"Yeah, sure. I see her every time I'm there. She puts her son up in Jimmy's office to sleep while she works."

"You know who she is?"

I thought about it. Come to think of it, Lesley and Doug did look a lot alike. They were both short and blond and had squinty kind of eyes, so I took a guess. "Your sister?"

"Naw. She's my ex-wife, and that's my kid."

What are the fucking chances of that?

"You've got to be kidding me," said Martine when she first met Doug. Martine was like my sister, a year older than me, also very much a Virgo, and a mom a few years before I became one. She's French and like me, way beyond liberal, so she was very happy when I came down to stay. Southern culture had her confused and unhappy.

One of her first experiences in Atlanta, David's new work partner invited them out to his in-laws' pecan plantation south of Atlanta. Martine asked about the picking process and was told it was done by little pick ninnies who were weighed before and after picking so they didn't steal pecans by eating them.

Horrified, she never fit in or wanted to fit in with Southerners. So when she first met Doug, cute, short, and totally Southern, totally not my usual style, she was not a fan. It was hot summer and he wore blue jeans with a big ass belt buckle and cowboy boots.

"Just wait," I told her. "Get to know him. You're going to love him."

And of course, I was right. He was the most loveable and annoying person, agreeable and funny and charming. In those days, he always had coke and he always shared, which made him really popular. He was always late, for everyone and everything; he made *everyone* wait. But when he finally arrived, he was so fun and nice you couldn't stay mad.

Well, at first.

Eventually I could, but that took some time.

Climbing the tower at the Fox Theatre

"The Night I Fell in Love with your Father" is the title I first gave this story, when I was writing it just for Rasta and Pablo, because it was.

When I first met Doug, I certainly didn't fall in love with him right away. That first night at Chastain Park, when he was running the sound for Flood's show, I don't think we were introduced or that we even said hello. I noticed him, and of course was intrigued by his energy, which was intense and inward and extremely focused. Let it be noted for the record that I am habitually drawn to the unusual.

I was still living with David and Martine and baby Jesse in their house in Buckhead. Since David was in the music business, I got to meet musicians and go to shows pretty much all the time. All the guys in Flood, a band he was promoting, were from St. Simons Island, a place I really wanted to see since they made it sound so beautiful. The guys were around the house a lot, especially when invited to one of Martine's amazing French dinners. When a couple of them said they were going down to St. Simons for a few days to see their families, I asked if I could go along for the ride.

It was summertime and *hot*. The drummer for the band showed up around midnight with Doug, and off we went, me with the one guy in the band I barely knew, the drummer, and this silent one, Doug. I got in the back seat, planning to sleep my way through.

We were driving for hours on two lane highways through mangrove swamps, where houses could be miles apart, down to the coast. They were "doing" Ketamine, which I think was an elephant tranquilizer, up in the front seat. I don't remember how that was ingested -- smoked or snorted -- but it was being ingested in the front seat big time. We were in an old Suburban, and I was sort of asleep when all of a sudden we had a flat tire or a blowout. We didn't go sliding off the road or anything, but we definitely needed to pull over and change the tire.

Paranoia strikes deep, and of course what we needed wasn't there: the handle for the jack. No problem though; they used a hash pipe, which luckily they did have! They were a little nervous about someone coming along, but no one did. We probably passed three cars on the six-hour drive, once we left what little highway there was in those days.

By the time we got to St. Simons, Doug and I had somehow connected. I don't remember how it happened, more Karma than Kismet, truth be told, but we were definitely into each other. He was staying with the drummer and his wife and daughter and I was staying next door, at the house of their friend Victor, where there was more room.

Victor was educated, liberal, feminist, handsome, smart, funny, accessible and kind, with curly red hair and a

 great sense of humor. He made his living making bags and cool shoes out of leather, and his vibe was peaceful and gentle. He really wanted me to stay with him and I liked him, too; it would have been so easy. Since Victor was actually

able to feel his feelings and express them, being with him threatened true intimacy. The more I look back on my relationships, the more I wonder at my compulsion to create relationships with wounded or otherwise unavailable men.

When the time came to choose, after a summer spent going back and forth between St. Simons and Atlanta, I chose to be with Doug. I really loved them both but was drawn to Doug in a way I couldn't resist. Karma. Loving men who aren't emotionally available. Loving men who don't dare feel their feelings, just like my dad. Whoopee. Enigma solved!

One of my back and forth trips makes me drop to my knees and thank the Powers That Be that I am still alive. I was headed to St. Simons to hang out with Victor, with an extra dress, a kitten on a long scarf, and a vial of coke, Doug's gift for a happy trip. No one can accuse him of not taking care of me! (And I mean that in the least sincere way!)

Someone, maybe Doug, dropped me off on I-20 East and I stuck out my thumb. A man almost immediately pulled over and picked me up. I got in. He had swollen track marks up and down both arms, blistery looking injection sites, but he was nice to me. He asked, "Where are you going?"

And I told him, "St. Simons."

"You're on the wrong road. You need to be on 75 South," he told me, and then he took me there. We didn't talk, but he didn't scare me at all. He probably didn't believe I didn't bail when I looked at his arms, but sometimes crazy is the ticket. We had a comfortable silence, believe it or not.

Once I got on I-75 S, along came a Volkswagen bus driven by a little Israeli hippy who tried to put his hand on my thigh for a while. I told him if he'd stop, he could have a place to stay in St. Simons, so he did. Once we got there, he hit on Agnes, the other woman in the house, so he got off my case. Victor's house was like that, pretty much open to anyone who behaved, and this guy was basically nice and harmless.

We used to have huge communal fish dinners. Agnes worked as a cook on a shrimp boat, an industry that was going great guns in those days. When they pull in the nets, they discard anything that's not shrimp, so Agnes came home every two or three days with a big bag full of fish, and we'd start cooking and invite everyone over. The saying was, "I wonder what the poor people are eating tonight?" We were all cash poor, but fish rich!

At Victor's, everything was communal and cooperative. My friend Bernard, the French guy who practiced dying in Ibiza, came down when he heard I was living on an island; he and Victor became fast and lifelong friends. He almost got arrested for indecent exposure on the beach when his thin cotton drawstring pants got wet, but luckily he managed to talk his way out of it with his charming manner and his French accent.

We went out in the fields and picked psychedelic mushrooms, which used to grow prolifically in cow poop, before they started feeding the cows mushroom-killing feed. I remember eating them on a rainy day, sitting alone in Victor's room and crying in a really grateful, cleansing way over how beautiful everything was.

But Doug had an attraction I couldn't resist, as much as I loved Victor and the ease and grace of life at his house. These things must just be karma, karmic relationships that need completing, since they make no sense at all. That's my story, anyway...

And then, sometime in late September, still hot in St. Simons so I remember it as summer, I got pregnant, an event that no one had planned or seen coming. I had to choose.

When I told Doug, his response was stellar: "Look," he told me, "I don't care whose baby this is. I will help you raise it. I already have two kids, and I want to be with you."

Sometimes he sure did know the right thing to say. I was *pretty sure* the baby was his, but one thing I was 100% sure of: I wanted this baby. It was time. I was twenty seven. I wasn't going to ever have a child if I didn't do it now. I didn't know much about babies, but Doug did, so we were good.

Doug was funny as hell and really smart, but people and feelings were not his major interest, except when it came to me. I tried, overtly and covertly, to help him feel his feelings, something I was trained in from toddler age since my dad didn't dare feel his. And, conveniently, while I was concentrating on his, I could ignore mine! It's taken me decades to even recognize the pattern, since all these wounded men *seem* so different, one from the next.

Doug was an engineer with a focused scientist personality. He would get so engrossed in figuring something out that the people in his world didn't even exist. At first this was charming and kind of endearing because it was new for me. At first.

One time a few years later we were living in Woodstock, NY, and visitors arrived from Guatemala, where we had all met. They had come all that way to see us, so I called Doug down at Bearsville Studios where he worked as a recording engineer and told him James and Samantha had just arrived. They were sitting in the living room with me when he got home. Without a word of greeting, he walked right through the room, right past us to his workbench where he bent over whatever project he had going. Samantha looked at him, then me, in absolute bewilderment. "How can you stand that?" she wanted to know.

"It doesn't bother me," I told her, and it was true. He didn't nag at me about anything and I was, in those days, the same. Oh, if only *that* had lasted!

Eventually he finished his thought process, turned around and was his sweet, friendly self. What's wrong with that?

After a later trip to St. Simons, I rode back to Atlanta with Doug to see Bruce Springsteen at Alex Cooley's Electric Ballroom, a big venue downtown across from the Fox Theatre. I *thought* we were going to see Bruce Springsteen, but as soon as we got there, Doug left me at a table out front to listen to the way-too-loud music and get hit on while he disappeared into the backstage area.

I was a little slow on the uptake, maybe; it took me a few shows to realize Doug was selling coke.

This was 1975, and cocaine was extremely popular and accessible. Sometimes we had to do it just to go to the grocery store, except whoops, we rarely made it since in those days, stores closed about when we were getting ourselves up and out. Coke was supposed to speed things up, and it did make you go kind of fast, only mostly in circles. I remember countless hours spent getting ready to go do something, which is when we started saying, "I'm fixing to...." That was part of Doug's endless procrastination, which continued long after his cocaine use ended.

When he *finally* came back to where I was sitting, it was late, like 2 a.m. We went out into the parking lot and there, staring us in the face, was the Fox Theatre with its majestic tower rising about five stories on the back corner of the building. "C'mon," he said, taking my hand, "there's something I want to show you."

We climbed up the fire escape ladders, up the side of the Fox Theatre and ran across the roof to the next ladder. Eventually, a few ladders and rooftops later, we stood at the foot of the tower. Every time I wavered, Doug held a spoon of powder under my nose (a teeny spoon!) and we kept going. I thought this was really fun, not too scary, but the best was yet to come.

Inside the tower was a narrow ladder to the top. I'm going to say it was 12" wide, which seems really teeny, but it was. We climbed and climbed and when we got to the top, there was a little door. We ducked through and we were standing on the parapet, the domed top of the tower. We leaned our backs against the top and there was a little ledge about 6" high to put our feet against, running around the bottom.

To say I was terrified would be a total understatement. I am scared of many physical challenges, and heights might be right up at the top. I was barely breathing and stiff as a board.

And here was Doug's challenge to me as he rolled onto his right side to face me: "What's the point of doing all that yoga and everything else you do if you can't do this?"

What indeed?

When I told one of my friends this, her response was, "So you let him bully you into it!"

I didn't see it that way. I was raised in a high conflict alcoholic home, so peace and serenity were a lot more threatening and unfamiliar than chaos. I required a strong challenge to get and keep my attention. As soon as things got easy and comfortable, I bailed.

And at that moment I remember thinking, if I am afraid of death, which a tumble from the tower would undoubtedly bring, then what *was* the point of all the yoga and everything else I did? Forty-some years later, I think maybe that was pretty ridiculous, but at the time, it made sense. Now I'd just do yoga to be flexible, you know, not to risk my life to see if I've transcended my fear of death. Or I might even recognize that I'm not all that afraid of death without putting it to the test. Or that I am, and let that be ok. But of course, I don't do coke now, or climb towers, so it's a moot point.

We leaned our backs against the top of the tower and inched our way around. The city was spread out below us, twinkling lights and neon. He was pointing out sights in the city, his city where he was born and raised, and alternately sticking that little spoon of courage under my nose. I was obligingly snorting the coke as I convinced myself to keep both breathing and moving. Obviously we made it around, because I'm writing it here, forty-three years later. It was paralyzingly frightening, and yet I did it. Without Doug's little bottle of artificial courage, I doubt I would have, but I wouldn't have been up there in the first place. I would have frozen in fear, period, although he said he and his friends had been going up there since high school.

When we started back down, I was flying. I had just done the scariest thing I'd ever done, and headed back to base camp like I had been shot out of a cannon. A helicopter came by and shined lights on us, but we were already down. I lost a shoe. We were running and laughing like lunatics, crossing from roof to roof to roof until we were on the ground again.

That did it for me. Victor offered stability of sorts, and was much more like me in background and education, but Doug had won my heart. And of course, when this little baby came along and looked exactly like Doug's dad, that sealed the deal. No more shadows of doubts, although by then, I didn't have any.

We had both been through the Vietnam War and seen what the draft did to people. We wanted our boy to be safe, in case this baby was a boy, so we decided to have him or her outside the USA, in case there was still a draft when he turned eighteen. Honestly, it seemed like a totally reasonable idea at the time.

Macon

I would be remiss if I didn't tell about the Macon connection, or what I know of it from Doug's telling and my own few experiences of it. Doug had been the Allman Brothers sound and light guy for a while, back in the day. He never met an electrical connection he couldn't figure out and get to work right, and he pretty much idolized those guys. He worked for them after Duane died in the motorcycle accident in 1971, during that year before Berry Oakley died, the same way, almost to the day in 1972.

Anyone who wants to know about the Allman Brothers can look up just about anything on Wikipedia. I like their music better now than I did back then, when it all sounded like too much noise. When I came home from France on Thanksgiving, 1972, the first thing my fourteen year old brother Will did was drag me into the living room saying with great urgency, "You've gotta listen to *this!*" It was "Eat a Peach." It was ok, kind of noisy for me, but he was over the moon with it. He's always had a great ear for music like that. I had lived most recently in Morocco with no electricity and only acoustic music when we had it at all. All that amplification was too much for me. It still is.

261

Doug still had connections in Macon from those times, even though he had only stayed a year or so and then moved back to Atlanta. So a few times in the summer of 1975 we went down there, before I was pregnant or sure I was going to stay with him. Doug drove a black Cadillac limousine, an older one, not a stretch or anything like that. Sometimes at night I was the driver, since I was the only one who didn't drink alcohol. I'd wear a black fedora to look official, like a real limo driver. I liked to snort a little coke and I smoked hash when we could get it, because weed made me nervous and paranoid, just as the Moroccans had said it would.

Mostly I liked to draw and paint. When we got together with people to do coke, everyone else would snort it all night long, tell each other five thousand times how much they loved them, drink along with it, have to take something else to come down and go to sleep, and generally feel like shit the next day. I liked to snort one line and leave the room, go find a quiet corner and paint or draw, and go to sleep at dawn like everyone else, only without needing to take another drug to do it. I'm pretty homeopathic when it comes to drugs and alcohol, meaning I can do about a tenth or even less of what most people can and it's plenty for me.

The first time we went to Macon, we went to see Doug's friend Jack at the Iron Gardens, this big junkyard Jack owned with his parents. He lived in a little house in the center of it all, surrounded by washing machines and car parts and piles of metal scrap. There were pit bulls wandering around, but they were very well behaved. They were probably scared of Jack, who was a rough and grizzled fellow. I took off my shoes before I went in his house and left them on the rough wood porch. In those days, I always did that. Jack and his mother were in the house, drinking whiskey and talking junk yard business. Neither of them had ever seen anyone take off their shoes at the door, especially the front door of a wooden shack in the middle of a junkyard, so they thought I was a total trip. I'm sure I was.

After we left Jack's, we drove around looking at the places Doug was connected to in Macon, and then we picked up his friend Kim Payne. Kim had been a roadie with the Allmans but appeared to have fallen on harder times, or at least on harder drugs that night. He was high on something that made him sweat like a pig and paw at me. Doug said he was doing heroin, but I didn't see him do any drugs, so I don't know. I was in the middle on the front seat of the Caddie, Doug was driving, and Kim was on my right. He'd lean into me, his face all sweaty, drops of sweat hanging on the ends of his greasy dark hair. All the while he was ranting about how he wrote "Midnight Rider," which at the time was attributed to Gregg, or that he co-wrote it and never got any credit or money. It's funny because when you read about the Allmans, and all of them living together in "the Big House," their insistence on a fair and communal distribution of earnings was a big deal. "All for one and one for all," was a band motto. It's possible that when the earnings got bigger, that philosophy suffered, since it did with most every other band.

I didn't like the Allmans, categorically, just because this sweating guy had his hands all over me and was simultaneously telling me why I shouldn't like them, because they stole his song. Come to find out, thanks to Wikipedia, that Kim was telling the truth. The whole story's there of how Gregg woke him up and asked him for help in the middle of the night, and how he wrote the last verse, the one that says, "I'm beyond the point of caring..." because according to him, he was. He broke the window to let them in to Capricorn Records' recording studio and recorded the demo that very night. You can read all about it on Wiki; it's a really good story on the birth of a great song that's been recorded and sung by just about everybody. Later on, Phil Walden of Capricorn Records gave Kim a contract for 5% of that song, which must be a pretty penny by now. We all move in tribes. Either it's our soul pod from past lives, meeting up here on Earth *again,* or it's something less existential that draws us to the same folks, over and over. There was a recording engineer at Capricorn named Sam Whiteside. Long after Sam died, Doug got together with his widow, Denise. It's only thanks to her calling me that we even knew Doug had the brain tumor that killed him. That connection went full circle.

In the car with his friend pawing at me, Doug was useless. First of all, he was coked up, as usual, and full of bonhomie and "the good old days," and reveries of times gone by. He wasn't really a sentimental guy, but he sure did think all those guys hung the moon.

He stayed friends with Mike Callahan, the original roadie for the Allmans, until he died. Mike rode his motorcycle up from Florida to visit Doug in hospice as he lay dying, in and out of a coma. "Hell," Mike told me, "I've seen him worse than this." A year or so later, Mike was dead, too.

The other thing was, Doug so idolized these guys that if one of them had said, "Hey, your old lady is hot. I'd like to fuck her," he would have said, "Thanks!"

I know because that actually happened. We went to see Gary Rossington from Lynyrd Skynyrd one day in some office building or hotel room. I don't know why for sure; Doug was probably taking him some coke. This was before the crash that killed half the band and injured the rest. Rossington said in later interviews that he was high too much of the time and had a bad car crash later that year thanks to Quaaludes. He was surely fucked up that day; he suggested Doug leave for a while and leave me with him. I think Doug was actually considering it when I got up and left.

And that's why I've never much cared for Southern Rock.

The Night of the Mexican Banditos

If there had been an Internet -- and believe me, the baby-daddy would have been on that in a New York second if it were available then -- we would have figured out where to have this baby from the comfort of his parents' Peachtree City, GA home. Since it hadn't been invented yet, the most expedient way to figure out where our baby should be born was to drive from country to country and see what each had to offer. Both of us carried the memories of the Sixties, and the draft numbers game, and the fear and anxiety of waiting for your number to be reached. If we had a boy, since only boys got drafted, we didn't want him to have to go through that, fighting or fleeing. Our gift, as we saw it, was to have our baby in a country where, if he was a boy, he could take refuge.

We were children of the 60's, revolutionary in our thinking, counter culture to some extent, both scarred in varying degrees by our experience of Vietnam. Neither of us had been to Vietnam, but we knew people who had and they usually came back pretty fucked up, when they came back at all. We had both been through the nerve wracking lottery of the draft. We had friends who said they were gay, friends who took about twelve hits of acid before they went in for their assessment (does "give me a rabbit and I'll fuck it" sound like someone you want in *your* Army???) We knew people who took so much speed they couldn't make the minimum weight, people who lied and pretended to be crazy, people who got married when they didn't want to. My first husband and all his friends taught in ghetto schools for draft deferments. Crazy people we knew went to dental school. Everybody we were friends with did whatever they could to stay out of the draft, and plenty of people left the country. It spoke to us when it came to having children. Would we ever want our sons to be drafted? No, no question. Even my father, a war hero, agreed. The only solution we could see was for our sons to be born in a country that would protect them from a US draft, should that ever come around again.

I know there are people reading this who think this is "unpatriotic," but I had talked it over with my dad. He was the original Boy Scout when it came to patriotism. He'd been in the Air Force, captured for lack of support from our own government, and held in Japanese prison camps in the Philippines He told me that no way would he want his sons or grandsons or anyone else he loved to serve in a war. The end. He had more right than anyone I ever met to say that.

It was 1975. If the Internet had been born, it certainly hadn't come to our house yet. In retrospect, there must have been an easier way to gather information than the method we used. What we wanted to know was: what nearby countries would grant our children, if born there, citizenship, or the benefit of protection should there be a U.S. draft? What country would allow us to live there and own land in our children's name(s)? We didn't know where to get this information except to get in our VW Bug and start looking for a place to land. Besides, we were both ready for a road trip. I was used to travel outside the US, and Doug was fearless when it came to that kind of adventure. He had worked for a bunch of bands and lived on the road, so a road trip to Mexico didn't present any problems for him, especially since I spoke Spanish.

My brother in-law Scotty, more accurately my brother-out-law, was a fifteen year old sociopath who had been in and out of juvenile detention since he mugged a woman and took her purse when he was eleven years old. He was nice enough to be with in a casual way, if he didn't get high on pills, his arch nemesis. My in-laws, slightly outside-the-law-ish themselves, begged us to take him with us, either to give them a breather, or to keep him out of jail for a little while. Now, forty-three years later, he has spent the majority of his life in jail. He's smart. He doesn't physically hurt people, but he has no qualms about stealing from his family, be it cash or identities. His parents might have thought a trip to Mexico would change his outlook.

Mexico turned out to be a strange adventure. I liked the fact that when we got tired, we'd just pull off the road and set up our tent and sleep. I was the map reader, and being pregnant, I was exceptionally quirky and particular with my directions. Our first ten miles in Mexico, on the highway, we saw a pickup truck, a big one like the good ole boys drive here in the South, plow right through a herd of goats, flinging goat bodies all over creation. From that very upsetting introduction, I decided that secondary roads would make for a more enjoyable journey. I got to pick our route, always trying to find the mythical lovely road that wandered along the coast. My idea -- and don't try to argue with a pregnant Virgo -- was to ride the scenic route through Mexico to Guatemala.

Even forty years ago, this was a stupid idea, but we didn't know any better. Our first afternoon of this meandering, using a Mexican map, the road abruptly ended at a four foot deep irrigation ditch about twenty feet wide (not on the map.) The people there said it would be about six hours before it was shallow enough to cross, and it was

267

flooded for most of the daylight hours, every day. To go back was at least fifty miles of crappy road.

Did you know that a VW bug is watertight, and that if you close up the windows and spin the back wheels, it will act as a little paddle boat and cross water? Doug wasn't sure the paddleboat idea would work, but he thought it probably would and anyway, it was worth a try. We rolled all the windows up tight, me driving, Doug and Scotty pushing. I gunned it; we motored right across to the other side, and off we went. That was one of Doug's greatest attributes: he was willing to try just about anything, and nothing much scared him. He and the material world were great allies, and he rarely met a machine he couldn't figure out, fix, or improve in some way

The next day we arrived to cross a big highway bridge (on the map) but all that was there was a bunch of dugout canoes with boards across them, since the bridge wasn't even started yet! It was there, on the map, a bridge that spanned a big lagoon and connected the highway. Only there was no bridge. Cars, trucks and even busses full of people were being ferried across by dugouts with boards across them. Some of the dugouts were very big, but you know what I mean? Handmade dugout canoes. We were game, since our other option was to drive back through Hell for a couple of hundred miles or so. We could swim, worst came to it, and the water was mostly pretty calm and shallow. As it turned out, it was fine.

So we crossed, laughing a little anxiously at the precarious arrangement. Having to wait on the shore for our turn on the dugouts put us hours behind where we wanted to be. Where it put us, as the sun was going down, was in the middle of jungle nowhere, in Guerrero State.

Guerrero State was well known to be a smuggler's state where lots of drugs left from the coast to go to the USA. What did that have to do with us? Because everyone had been so friendly, so far, we had been pitching our tent and sleeping wherever we wanted. As dark was settling in, we saw a small lane, mostly like a wagon track, headed off to the right into the bush. That looked promising. Pulling at least two hundred feet off the road, we began pitching our tent, a bargain from the Army Navy Store. Instead of little modern nylon tents that weigh a couple of pounds and set up in seconds, we had the Army's equivalent of a circus tent, a 10'x10' green canvas monster that set up in ten or fifteen minutes and weighed about thirty lbs. It was great to have, sturdy and roomy, but ponderous. Properly folded (another ten or fifteen minute job) it took up half the tiny back seat, with Scotty in the rest.

We were in mid-tent pitch, each on a corner, when we heard the dogs. That wasn't so worrisome: everyone so far had been so friendly and helpful that the last thing on our minds was trouble. They came on us suddenly, six or eight skinny dogs circling and growling, and then two men appeared, machetes in their hands. One was tall and rawboned and lanky, the other mean-looking and little and wiry. We couldn't stay there, they  said. Circling their legs were the dogs, hound dogs or mutts of some kind, growling and menacing. We had to come with them, they told us. They were very insistent, and they were standing very close to me, on either side. They invited us to their house, only it was no invitation; one of them was brandishing his machete pretty close to my throat. My brother-in-law, cool as could be, reached over and felt the edge of the machete. "Very sharp," he nodded to them approvingly, as if that were a good thing.

"Okay, then," said Doug, "Looks like we're going to their house." With them watching our every move, machetes at the ready, dogs circling, we began to undo the tent. I explained to them all along the way, being the only one who spoke Spanish, that we just had to pack our things up and we'd be happy to come with them, which is what Doug told me to say. He just kept muttering, "Agree with everything they say," so I did.

I was stunned and terrified, so I just did what Doug said, since he was thinking for all of us. Instead of the careful fold and pack we normally did with the tent, we stuffed it, all unfolded and bulky and unwieldy, into the back of the Bug as the two men impatiently watched. Scotty climbed in there with it. He was kind of leaning over the front seat, there was so little room. I wasn't even thinking, just gone into the zone, trusting that Doug had this.

There wasn't room for all of us in the car, especially with the tent taking nearly the whole back seat. Doug got in the driver seat, I climbed in onto the space between the seats, and the big guy squeezed in next to me. The little guy stood by the side with all the dogs circling his legs, barking or growling. It was a generally chaotic scene, with a lot of noise and the two men yelling and brandishing their machetes. The little bandito started walking ahead with the dogs, back down the track toward the road. There wasn't room to close the passenger door, and the big bandito was kind of hanging on, holding the door half closed with his right hand, hanging on to where there would have been an "oh-shit" strap with his left. Doug quietly whispered, "Hold on."

Doug had to back the car to get going in the direction we were instructed to go. He backed way up for a wide turn, then gunned the little car into a sharp left arc that slung the big bandito off into the bushes, cursing and yelling. I grabbed the door and slammed it shut and we were flying down the lane when we saw the second man in the glare of the headlights, standing at the edge of the track, machete raised over his head.

Doug jammed on the brakes as the little bandito brought the machete down, aiming for the windshield. Instead, it cut a dent across the hood, severing the ropes that secured our trunk of earthly possessions to the roof. The trunk stayed on, somehow, and we flew down that little dirt lane with barking and yelling behind us as the two men raced to catch us on foot. Once we made it out to the main road, we were obviously not going to get caught by those two and we kept driving fast in the night, not knowing what was ahead.

Every other night, we had just stopped our little VW beetle on the side of the road wherever we wanted, pitched our tent and gone to sleep. No one had ever bothered us in Mexico, a refreshing change from the regimented campground approach. Now we were having serious second thoughts about our la-di-da attitude.

It was an hour or so before we got to a village with shops on both sides of the highway and a big wide grassy median where horses were roaming free and grazing. We pulled off into the median; the two guys were going to sleep on the ground while I was *firmly* ordered to stay in the car to sleep. I was uncomfortable, hot and twisted up, but after the last adventure, Doug wanted to know I was safe. There was no way to get comfortable all crushed up in the car. Doug slept outside on the ground, where he could stretch out, at least, and that was where I wanted to be. He just flat out refused me that, and said no matter what, until we got out of whatever sinkhole we had fallen into, I had to stay in the car. And so I did.

We didn't have to bother about me. It was a teeny crossroad village full of transvestites, or cross-dressers, which my brother-in-law discovered when he crossed the road to get a soda at the fluorescent lit tienda/café. He had a time of it, getting back to the car and away from their touching admiration. They could barely keep their hands off him. It's amazing that when he got back to the car, he thought it was funny and wasn't much bothered by it. I guess a couple of rounds in juvie had toughened him up, since he'd been detained as much as free since he mugged that old woman at age eleven!

271

We were so glad to get going the next morning, driving south on the main road, headed to Guatemala. Thank God for main roads, and stores with signs and a little bit of order! In the early afternoon we stopped for a cold drink at a roadside place that had beer and Coke signs and horses tied up outside. We pulled off the road and walked in. The place was full of men and a few very heavily made up women. The women glared at me as they smiled seductively at Doug and Scotty. The men stared at us all. It was a freaking whorehouse or lap dance cantina or something. We got a drink, anyway, because I was the only nervous one. Doug and Scotty kind of liked it, or thought it was funny, anyway. We obviously were gringos down south, because we were not picking up on the signs very well! After that, we stayed on the main road, headed south.

Oatmeal in Mexico

When we stopped in Palenque, we were there to see the pyramids and relax in this sweet little traveler's hotel we found. It was friendly and cheap and full of people our age from all over the place. I made friends with the young guy who ran the place, so he brought me little treats from home. One time he brought me bread made of corn and beans that his mama had wrapped in leaves and baked for hours in hot ashes. It was just about unbelievably good, tasty and nourishing in an ancient, primal way.

Doug and I wanted to see the pyramids at dawn, see the Temple of the Dawn the way the ancient Mayans did, so one morning we drove up there around 5 a.m. and got in somehow, past the guard. It was pitch dark. We parked our van and I was just getting out when we heard a blood-curdling scream that seemed to reverberate through the jungle, surrounding us. It was the cry of the panther, or jaguar, guardian of Palenque. We got the message, jumped back in the van, and came back when the park was actually open, during daylight hours

Palenque was pretty much a hippie scene, too. Besides the pyramids, the place was known for mushrooms of the magic variety. It's very important when eating wild mushrooms that you know exactly what you are doing, because we saw some people who got deathly ill, but not deathly enough to actually die. They were so very sick that it taught me respect in a way just hearing or reading about it wouldn't.

About a week into our stay in Palenque, as we started planning the next push, Doug got a call that his sister, Sherry, had been hit by a car on the edge of the highway in Atlanta and killed. She was the star of the family, a high achiever who was head of neonatal pediatrics at a big hospital in Atlanta. She had gotten pregnant really young and married the baby-daddy who unfortunately didn't like to work much. As a result, instead of a good car she drove an old beater with no gas gauge. When it ran out of gas, she got out to put the hood up to stop someone and got run into and killed. It about broke Doug's heart, and his mother's, and everyone else's in the family. Sherry had been really close to Doug. He and brother Scotty got on a plane and went back to Georgia.

I would have gone back to GA too, but I had only met Sherry once, and we had all this stuff in Palenque. Looking back it seems odd that I didn't, but at the time it seemed like the smartest thing, for me to stay with the car and all our stuff. That left me pregnant in Mexico with a VW full of our belongings and an agenda. The clock was ticking; I had to find a place to have this baby, with or without Doug. We knew the fan belt needed changing, but Doug didn't have a chance before he and Scotty raced out of there to be with their family. I got out the *VW for the Complete Idiot* book and changed the fan belt in a record twelve hours, including time-outs for overwhelm and passing out from the intense concentration it required. For those who may not know, that's normally about a 20-30 minute job for someone who knows the drill. I thought I'd hit the road the next day and drive to San Cristobal de las Casas, about two days away across the mountains. Collette, a beautiful, plump blonde twenty-year-old from Florida I had met at the hotel said she wanted to go with me.

I wasn't smoking or anything, being pregnant, but Collette loved her smoke, and rum too, when it came down to it. Which it did on a pretty nightly basis. Collette loved a good time.

When she got in the car the next day, she told me she had a little weed with her, so I told her to put it under her seat, or maybe under her ass. When we pulled up to the first roadblock, she admitted it was about half a pound! That was enough to get us into some seriously hot water, with some serious consequences and probably some serious sex with Mexican guards in our immediate future. I hissed, "Don't move, whatever they say."

I told her under no conditions was she to get up. Back in those days, it would have been unthinkable to tell a woman to get up from her seat. Ah, those were the days, thank God. We chatted amiably with the Mexican military guys and they let us through with a great big sigh of relief on my part. I didn't want to have my baby in a Mexican jail, especially for someone else's fuck up!

Around dusk we stopped at a teeny little mountain town and got a room for the night. There was no lock on the door, but I was exhausted from driving mountain roads all day and thought I didn't care. We went out for some food at a little hole in the wall across the road and a bunch of young guys came in, all with their eyes on her. I was twenty seven and she was twenty and as I mentioned, blonde. They were all hanging around and I told them to go away, that I was her mother and she wasn't interested.

Half the night these guys moaned at the door, "Mama, Chica, Mama, Mama, Guapa." We pushed a chair against the door and tried to sleep. I slept with a big knife, which I was happy not to have to use.

Sleeping with a big knife was a habit I acquired when I was about sixteen years old. My father was away for months at a time, working in Hong Kong mostly, and things got mighty loose around our house when he was gone. As in, no rules. One night a friend of a friend was sleeping there, and he came up to my room. He was just passing through and had called me on his friend's recommendation, either for me or a free place to stay.

I pretended to be asleep as he made lewd suggestions of what he would like to do with or to me. I knew what was within arm's reach if he really tried anything, and I knew what I would do. My weaponry was limited to the corners of the base of the metal alarm clock, so after that I started sleeping with a big knife close by.

I held my knife tight. Collette looked at me absolutely incredulous. "What are you going to do with *that*?" indicating the knife. I admitted that I had no idea, but she was obviously calmed by my protective presence, or else she was stoned, or both, because she fell into her usual deep sleep all night as the lovesick ones circled our door. Late into the night they were outside our door moaning, "Mommy, I want to see your daughter." In Spanish, obviously.

Would I use it? Collette was excitedly appalled as she asked me.

I was absolutely sure I would.

We left early in the morning and made it to a nice, but cheap, hotel in San Cristobal by evening. The moaners had taken off some time in the night.

Collette had a knack for trouble: the next day, while I was reconnecting with old friends out by the chicken rotisserie, the warmest spot in town, she went off with with a man she had just met who invited her back to his house to get high. That night we all, meaning all these hippies staying in the hotel, paid for Collette's good time, or more accurately, her date's lack of one. She had a thing about not seeing the obvious, especially if it meant that looking at what was really happening would get in the way of getting high. After she smoked all this guy's pot and drank the better part of a bottle of rum, he made his move. She was absolutely indignant! (see what I mean?) He brought her back to the hotel, totally pissed off at her refusal, and went to talk to his buddies in the local policia. We didn't know any of this was going on, of course. *We* meaning everyone but Collette, who paid it no mind.

I want to make my position clear here: I no way thought Collette had to fuck this guy because she drank and smoked him dry, but I did feel it was manipulative and naive to do all that in the first place. Context and culture.

The guy was either police, or friends with the police. That evening we were sitting around in our room, Collette and I and a man I was friends with from before, and I went out to pee in the outhouse in the courtyard. Suddenly I heard noises and looked down. Eight pairs of shiny black shoes surrounded the outhouse, their toes visible from inside.

Oh no. Shiny black shoes are always a big red flag.

I came out -- because of course I couldn't just stay in there -- and was immediately surrounded. "Sus papeles," they demanded, as if everyone takes their passport to go for a pee.

"No," I responded. "Sus papeles de Ustedes." Pretty brave, huh? If I was going to get surrounded, threatened, interrogated, whatever these guys had in mind, I at least wanted to make sure they were authorized to do what they were going to do. The shoes should have been the give-away. There was the Chief of Police, the Magistrate of so and so, the Mayor, maybe. Anyway, there were eight high ranking government officials, and we were in some considerable shit if we got busted. That was for sure.

Two prayers: the first, that Collette not be smoking pot when I opened the hotel door, since nobody but me knew about this little drama taking place in the courtyard. Second:

that I not go to a Mexican jail and have this baby start out life in such totally inauspicious circumstances.

Bingo, Collette was still sitting on her bed where I had left her, in her frumpy pajamas with a blanket around her and her ample bottom planted on her bed, right over where her stash was hidden under her mattress. There was no pot smoke in the air, Gracias a Dios.

Amazingly, only one of the men had followed me to the room, while the others fanned out to terrorize the rest of the residents. He told our male friend to leave, which he happily did, then planted himself by the door, watching us. This guy didn't speak any English, so I said to Collette, "Whatever you do, don't get up. They won't move you, so don't move." Then I racked my brain for something to do, something that would turn this from a women's boudoir to an unappealing, maybe even revolting scene.

I remembered my friend Susan telling me how she had thwarted a rapist by sticking her finger down her throat and throwing up all over herself and him. It did the trick for her since it was obviously a turn off, and my biggest fear was going to jail and getting raped, with either possibility on its own equally terrifying. So I suggested something cheerier, and measurably less revolting. Turning to Colleen with a cheery smile, I grinned, "Let's have oatmeal!"

She stared at me like I had gone mad until I said, "What could be more unappealing?" and she got it right away.

Thank God for Coleman camping stoves, and countries where you bring *all* your stuff in from the car, into your hotel room. Right then and there, I made us a big old pot of oatmeal, this man watching us warily from the door the whole time. I think he probably wanted to bolt, especially when I offered him a big gloppy bowlful and then ate it myself when he refused. We loved that oatmeal. We squished it through our teeth, and slopped it around with our mouths full and open as he stood and stared.

"OOOOH, that was good. Want some more?"

By the time I had a second pot full on the stove, some of the other guys came to check in with their buddy. He said something to them in hurried low tones, and they all left. They just left. None too soon, either, since we had eaten that whole first pot and were going to have to start in on the second one. Down the hall, someone got busted, and it was surely Collette's fault for being such an airhead about her behavior.

The next day, Doug and his brother came back from the US. From there we planned to head south into Guatemala, only a few hours' drive away. Within an hour, I told Doug that his brother Scotty wasn't going with us. Even at fifteen, he was just too much of a degenerate for me to want to deal with, and it was my car. I was sorry their sister had died, of course, but it took about an hour with Scotty for him to say some low life rip-off kind of remark that got all over my last nerve.

My exact words, if I can remember clearly forty three years later, were "It's up to you if you want to come with me or stay with him, but he's not getting back in my car." Now that probably sounds incredibly harsh, leaving a fifteen-year-old kid in Mexico by himself, but he was a criminal even then, and all these years have done nothing but made him worse. He married and became a breeder, and his progeny criminal. So it was harsh, but it was all I could deal with. I had to find a place to have this baby.

I gratefully left Collette, the lovely blonde trouble magnet, at the hotel, and off we went to Guatemala. Scotty was fine, in case you are worried for him. Some other American traveling hippies took care of him and brought him to Guatemala in time for Christmas, which he celebrated by coming to our house for his presents and stealing all the money in my wallet.

Guatemala the first time around

When Doug and I got to the border of Mexico and Guatemala, which in those days was two guys standing by a farm gate, the Mexicans wanted money. I was celebrating having driven the entire length of Mexico without giving anyone a bribe (the mordita, or "little bite") and I was not about to start. The two border guards told us we needed to pay an exit tax of one hundred pesos. I gave them my one thousand watt smile, for which I was famous back then, and a look of total incomprehension. Try as they might to figure out a way to tell me I owed them an exit tax, I just got stupider, my Spanish worse and worse. "Disculpeme, no entiendo," (excuse me, I don't understand) became "no entiendo" (I don't understand) several times until I just stared at them, smiling. Since Doug didn't speak Spanish anyway, he didn't have much to add. And it worked: we didn't pay a dime, and we crossed into Guatemala. Of course, Doug got in the car with me.

Now I might handle it differently. Having just been in Mexico, and realizing how very little people like border guards earn, I'd probably give them their bribe, with thanks. Right now is 2018 and our maid, because we rented an

AirBnB house with maid services, earned something like two or three dollars a day and depended on our tips. The mordita. That is unfortunately the way people actually earn a living that can support them and their families, from what I saw and was told.

Guatemala's scenery is just gorgeous. The country has had some horrific human rights abuses: massacres and genocides and totally horrible shit. We didn't know anything about all that until years later. We were looking for a place to park for a while, to enjoy beautiful Lake Atitlan and for Doug to get his groove on at the local bars. And of course, a place to have this baby, as my pregnancy progressed.

We drove into Panajachel, a small town hippie mecca on the lake, and stopped to take in the scene and have a little lunch. There were traveling folks everywhere, from ragged looking backpackers to upscale, clean-cut travelers. After lunch we decided to explore a bit and see what was just outside town. We kept driving, to see where the road went. Around the lake the road ended about a kilometer past the little village of Santa Catarina, which consisted of a couple of tienditas (teeny stores) and an equally teeny jail on a village square.

Looking at the map today, I am astounded that Santa Catarina Palopo is less than four kilometers from the center of Panajachel. Really? That's just under two and a half miles! Back then, it was a really poor dirt road with lots of stones and ruts and it took about twenty minutes to get there from Panajachel. It may still be dirt as Google maps puts it at eleven minutes! The road stopped about a kilometer past the village, according to my obviously not very accurate memory, although now it seems to go on to the next village, San Antonio Palopo, which in those days, you had to walk to.

At the very end of the road in 1976, where the only thing to do was either turn around or continue on foot, there was a little adobe house up a steep footpath from the road. As we stopped to admire the view, someone in the family looked out, saw us there, and gave a friendly wave. I ran up the hill to ask the family there if they knew of any houses to rent. They said, "Yeah, this one."

In less than twenty minutes, they had packed up all their gear, including their huge hairy pig, and headed to stay with family in the village so we would give them twenty dollars a month rent, a fortune. We had a great view of Lake Atitlan and the smoking volcanoes on the far shore, and eventually, terrible fleas, legacy of the pig.

This was a basic adobe, with a bedroom on each end and a large main room in the center. The beds were exactly five foot six inches long, so Doug was just ok but I had to sleep a little curled. We had to go down to the lake, a precipitous walk about fifty yards down a rocky path, and carry our water up in buckets. We bathed in the lake, so all we needed was cooking and drinking water. Of course we did boil the hell out of it, even though the lake was fifteen hundred feet deep and *looked* clean. Now, according to Google maps, Santa Catarina Palopo boasts the Hotel Villa Santa Catarina, a three star hotel where you can stay for eighty six dollars a night. In 1976, you could have rented half the village for that amount of money.

We drove in to Panajachel every day or two to buy food and meet people. There were restaurants and bars there, and we ended up hanging out most at Veggie Bob's restaurant. He was a fellow New Yorker, dry and caustic, but nice. You know, a New Yorker. That's where I met Cindi, a seventeen-year-old American girl, traveling alone. She was a great seamstress who supported herself with her fine clothes-making skills. After we had known each other about three minutes I invited her to come live with us and she accepted.

For such a young girl, Cindi amazed me. She was grounded and focused, and traveling alone at seventeen. Even though I was ten years older, it didn't seem that way to me. I had the impression she was alone there by intention, but actually she had come to Guatemala with her older sister

Sandy and her friend Vivian, and when they wanted to go back to the States, Cindi didn't have the money to make the trip. Unlike Scotty, who didn't get to vote on being left in Mexico at fifteen, Cindi insisted she would be fine and would make her own way back. So they left, and I met her and she came to live with me. Now that she and I have found each other and are talking again, and in a minute you'll see how that came about, it seems we both felt the other was a form of our salvation. I gave her a place to live and whatever stability I could muster, and she was company, and fun, and inspiring to live with.

Doug and I had already inquired about having a baby in Guatemala. Even though it was so beautiful and fun, it was worse for having a baby there than Mexico. In Mexico in those days, having a baby in the country didn't get you jack. If you wanted to own property, it *still* had to be in a Mexican citizen's name. But Guatemala was worse. It was totally fine to *have* a baby there, but when we wanted to leave, we had to pay eight hundred dollars for an exit visa for the baby to leave with us. What??? We didn't have eight hundred dollars, so Doug was going to Belize to find out what the conditions for baby-having looked like there. Once Cindi settled in, Doug left on his Belize adventure. He went by bus so we had the car for going in and out of town to the market. Of course, it was my car. I had traded my friend Victor from St. Simons Island a pound of Mexican weed for it when I finally figured out I was staying with Doug.

Doug had this dream of building a wooden sailboat (which he eventually got to do, twice) and wanted to find out if there was a place where he could do it. It was weeks before he came back with his discovery of the Promised Land.

While he was gone, Cindi and I went to the market in Panajachel every other day and ate, *a lot*. That girl could eat as much as I could, and I was supposedly eating for two. She was a teenaged girl, strong and thin. We'd stuff our string bags with tortillas and beans, avocados and limes, papayas and bananas and coconuts, and make feasts for ourselves. Heaping bowls of fresh fruit salads, guacamole and tortillas and black beans were our staples. We'd eat at night sitting on straw mats on the floor of the living room, watching as the sun set right into the mouth of the middle volcano of the three volcanoes across the lake. Every night one of us would say to the other, "We are the richest people in the world right now," as we bit into our penny tacos. We spent nearly nothing and had the most magnificent view and lake access imaginable.

Between meals, which obviously we took seriously, and trips to town to buy all that food, we swam in the lake, carrying our buckets of drinking water back up the hill, and she sewed. She was actually able to teach me to make yoga pants and a vest, by hand. I was amazed. We bought cloth in town at the market and she helped me make Doug some pants as a surprise for when he got back, the pull on, drawstring kind we all wore back then. Ok, in case she's reading this, she mostly made them. I could, then and now, sew a simple seam, but Cindi was a clothes artiste. All her clothes were made with French seams, beautifully constructed. She sold her yoga pants in town for eight dollars a pair. How do I remember that?

One afternoon a couple of months ago, a woman came into the Trader Joe's where Rasta works now, in Idaho, looked at his nametag and, as she told me later, did a bit of a double-take. Should she talk to him? Should she just let it slide? Thankfully and gratefully, she went up to him and said, "I knew you from Guatemala." It was Cindi, forty three years later! What are the chances of that? Just when I thought I was going to have to lie about all this, she saved the day! She remembers! When Cindi reminded me she sold those hand-sewn, French-seamed yoga pants for eight dollars, I was able to remind her that back then, eight dollars was eight hundred avocados, por ejemplo.

284

Another memory Cindi rekindled for me was that we used the kitchen of a friend's restaurant to bake pot cookies to sell. Boy oh boy, those were simpler times! The restaurant was right in the middle of town, a nice old house with a big veranda around the front and sides. It was owned by a Guatemalan guy who loved having gringos around, loved the music and the culture and the fun. We had the kitchen to ourselves a couple of afternoons a week, either because they closed that day or he just didn't care. He was probably wealthy anyway and just had the restaurant for a lark, a way to meet people and hang out. I know that's where English John hung out, selling acid.

Our house was a bit simple for most people, especially people who have choices. No bathroom, no running water, and built into a super steep hillside. And then, there were the fleas. Unfortunately when the huge hairy pig went to town, he left fleas behind. At first it wasn't too bad, but with nothing else to occupy them, those fleas started having more fleas. We had a dilemma.

We covered the floors in pine boughs and wore long sleeves and sweatpants to bed, which was ok because it's chilly in the mountains. On every exposed bit of skin we rubbed pennyroyal oil and never got a flea bite again. Later I learned that pennyroyal is super contraindicated for pregnancy because it can actually bring on contractions, but thankfully I didn't have any problems.

When Doug came back after a couple of weeks he told me Belize was the answer to our search. He loved it there. Everyone spoke English, they made boats, and he had already met a guy who said we could stay at his house in Belize City. I was in love with Guatemala, and thought it would be wonderful to someday live right in Panajachel, in the heart of town, with running water and maybe even electricity, but for the moment, having a baby was a priority. I put it on the list; we were definitely coming back to Pana at some point.

Apparently a baby born in Belize could be a Belizean citizen, which also meant they could be British citizens, since Belize was a part of the Commonwealth, formerly known as British Honduras. Too bad, in retrospect, that neither Doug nor I got it together later on to get that British citizenship thing taken care of, but he was overwhelmingly lazy and distracted by minutia, and I was simply distracted and not very down to earth. Doug also told me Belize City was clean, which had become quite an obsession of mine, but he flat out lied about that.

He absolutely promised me I was going to love Belize. We had already been three months on this journey to find the place where our baby was going to be born, and he swore that Belize would be it.

"Is it clean?" I demanded.

"It's very clean, and the air is good. The water is clean. It's British, everyone speaks English, you're going to love it!"

"Do they have running water and electricity?" These were two commodities we were lacking at that moment, and I didn't fancy having a baby without them. I didn't know much about babies, but I knew they used up a good amount of water.

"Everyone has both. It is very clean, very advanced. The British have been there a long time, and they've taken care of all that. You'll really love it."

Doug could sell ice to the Eskimos, when he was still alive. Up until he died, I never stopped believing he was actually going to do what he said, even though experience should have long taught me that he almost never did. Belize was no exception. I hated it, but let me tell you first how we got there, because it wasn't a straight line.

We packed our Bug and left our wonderful but flea ridden little adobe and our amazing million dollar view of the lake and the volcanoes. I was not sad to leave Santa Catarina, which was a weird little village, albeit peaceful and colorful. I didn't spend much time there; if I went to town,

Panajachel, I took the car. Sometimes Cindi walked though, and every time, a big tom turkey chased her through town, much to the spirited amusement of the townspeople. They hadn't really seen that much of gringos yet, since in those days Sta. Cat. was just a teeny village with little to offer except as yet undeveloped access to the lake.

One night I did go in, with Doug or Cindi or both, to a fiesta. There were two bands playing on opposite sides of the small plaza, both highly amplified and playing at the same time! There was also the little jail, which was more of a cage on the square. Most of the people who ended up in there were men who got very exceedingly drunk. The drunkest I ever saw people get, to where they fell down face first and didn't get their hands out to block the fall, was in the mountains in Guatemala. Our smiling landlords were disappointed to see us go, since we paid them what was a lot of money in Sta. Catarina in those days. With Cindi in the back seat and our truck of worldly possessions tied firmly to the roof, we took off once more on this baby-having, home-finding expedition.

Earthquake in Guatemala

There were only two routes to get to Belize: one was through the jungle, through the Peten, and the other was through the mountains, the way we had come. We were headed to Belize, for sure, and we decided to take the jungle route. Now's the chance to get your maps out and trace the route. I only say that because that's what I just did, to refresh my memory of where we must have gone. Remember I said at the beginning to be like Lenny? He learned the whole world by mapping our travels. I'm still learning because when I looked at the map, I just could not figure out the next part of this story. Roads were bad, travel was slow, and somehow I made the entire circuit, from Panajachel to Belize to Yucatan to Panajachel and for the life of me, I couldn't figure out how. Thank God I got some help when I reconnected with Cindi, who remembered more than I did, or at least different parts of the story.

We could have gone through Guatemala City and stayed on bigger roads for a while, but we decided to just do the mountain route, since Guatemala City was at least as exhausting as small curvy roads. We had only been there once when we probably had to go for a visa issue or something similar. The main thing I remember is the guy whose body was missing from the chest down, wheeling himself around on a square of wood nailed to four casters, begging. I had not seen anyone in that condition before, even in India. It was hard to imagine how his body functioned with so much of it gone. There were a lot of very poor people and other beggars, but he definitely stood out as the primo hardship case, even though he was laughing and joking and fucking around with his pals. That just amazes me about people I've seen, how the ones with the least (materially) often seem to be having a great time anyway. I saw it in India, and definitely with this guy, that people who seemed to have so little can appear so happy in spite of it. I had no idea, really, who he was, but the condition of his physical body was mind boggling. And in spite of having a body only down to his chest (surely below his lungs?) he appeared healthy and happy. His black hair was glossy, he was paddling around with his hands, and he was laughing. *Laughing*. Note to self: remember this next time I'm having a "bad day."

The jungle route took us up through the mountains, from Panajachel to Solola to Chichicastenango, a beautiful and colorful mountain town known for skilled weavers. We stopped there for the night. Doug and I got a hotel room for a dollar or so, but Cindi, living as she did on the tightest of budgets, slept curled up in the car. Our hotel room, which was actually a room in someone's home, was only slightly more luxurious than the car, since the bed was really short and I had to sleep curled up anyway.

As we drove along, we pulled over sometimes, bought food or just walked around. There were processions and a fiesta or two where bands played and people wore costumes and some men fell down drunk. The biggest town we came to was Coban, after Santa Cruz del Quiche, Sacapulas, Uspantan and San Cristobal Verapaz. After Coban we started downhill, through Chisec and Sayaxche, La Libertad and

Flores. We were in the jungle, beautiful, hot and sweaty. The road was narrow, like an opening cut through impenetrable walls of green.

We had just come around a bend in the jungle road when to our right, emerging into a clearing, ten or fifteen men appeared, carrying a huge yellowish snake. It took all the men to carry him, and as we went by, that snake stared straight into my eyes. Of the few regrets I have, one has been that I didn't yell for Doug to STOP! And offer those men $200 for that snake and let him go. But I didn't. And then we were gone, with just the memory of the power of those eyes staring into mine. It was a really powerful moment, big snake medicine. It's one of the first things Cindi and I talked about after forty three years; it was huge for us both.

I might not have had $200 anyway, and certainly not to spare. It would have been my last $200, most likely, and as it turned out, it was needed later.

The trip to Belize City took about a week, with Cindi curled up in the car every night while Doug and I usually pitched the tent or found a cheap hotel room. Cindi and I were always looking for fruit, which was amazingly hard to get in the jungle. At one point someone gave or sold us raw cashews, which are poisonous. We didn't know that and we didn't know how to eat them anyway. Surely the person we got them from thought we knew what they were. I don't think anyone was trying to kill us; they didn't even know us!

We also bought plantains, thinking they were giant bananas. Cindi and I realized quickly what they were, with their starchy not good taste, but Doug insisted on eating one raw. I'm sure he paid a price for that, as he did for all his gustatory adventures.

After wandering through the amazing ruins at Tikal for a day or two, we were ready to get back on the road. We had seen the ruins in Palenque, where I met Colette and we drove through the mountains. Tikal was so much more primitive, and huge. I had this impression that the little bit that was cleared was just the tip of the iceberg, that the settled area of Tikal was enormously larger than we could explore. Recent scientific research proves that to be true. And of course, having seen the size of that snake, I wasn't eager to get out in the jungle, although I know from what I read that the entire area is now much more parklike and developed than it was then, in early 1976.

We crossed the border into Belize at San Ignacio. From there it was a pretty easy drive through the capital city, Belmopan, and into Belize City.

Doug had met two guys on his initial voyage of exploration: Arthur, a black Belize City guy about our age, and Natividad Verde, a Mayan boatbuilder from the village of Sarteneja, in the northern part of the country. It was to Arthur's house, actually his mother's house, that we headed first, right smack in the heart of Belize City.

Arthur's house was simple and very clean, so I was good with that as they welcomed us warmly and invited us to stay. I always found people in other countries to be so welcoming and hospitable. I try to be, but I can't really see inviting strangers into my house to have their baby there. Maybe Arthur's mom thought I was going to the hospital when the time came, or maybe she didn't get to vote, since he was the man of the house. I didn't get a chance to talk to her much. I was getting a bit germaphobic as the birth time got closer and I got nestier, but the floors were mopped and swept and we had clean beds. Cindi did a bunch of cleaning and sweeping there, too. There was electricity, which was one bare, bright bulb suspended from the ceiling. When you turned it off to go to sleep, the bugs went *wild*.

Somehow it happened that our car was broken into the very first night we were there, and everything Cindi owned was stolen. I don't know why her stuff was out in the car and ours wasn't. Maybe she was being loving and trusting, but in any case, she was devastated. This was a bad situation, as she was living so close to the bone anyway and trying to get enough money saved to go home. I mentioned that $200 being needed elsewhere, and eventually I lent it to Cindi so she could get home. Although I had forgotten about it, she was quick to assure me that she paid it back when we had our first forty-three-years-later phone call!

Besides that it obviously wasn't that safe, there was something else that bothered me. In spite of Doug's assurances that Belize was clean and modern and quite British, everyone went behind a little curtain to piss and shit in a bucket. It did have a lid, and a seat. In the morning, Arthur took the bucket and emptied it into the ditch in front of the house. It wasn't a dirt ditch, it was a paved waterway ditch, and every single house dumped their buckets into it every morning, and then I guess it all made its way to the sea.

Arthur was a nice enough guy and all, and he and his mom were very nice to put us up, but there was no fucking way in hell I was going to give birth in a city full of stinking raw sewage. I was just about five months pregnant by then. We still had some time before my due date, but I never gave going back to the States a thought. (Boy, you can bet I thought about it the second time around!) And so with a fond adieu, we headed north to catch some fresh air.

In the northern Belize town of Corozal, we left the car at an American lady's bungalow colony and caught a ride with a fisherman to Sarteneja, a long slow ride across the bay, to visit Natividad Verde and his family. It seemed like a nice village and we thought we'd come back there to have this baby, but first, Doug had to go back to the States and earn some money. I wasn't keen to stay there alone, and Cindi was trying to figure out how to get home, so our visit was short. Had I stayed long enough to experience the kitten-sized mosquitoes, I might have had second thoughts, but I was ok with coming back in a few weeks, getting a house and having a baby. It turned out to be a tad longer, which was par for the course with Doug.

There was work waiting for Doug, in Atlanta or New York, and he couldn't afford to say no to that. As a recording engineer, he made enough in a week or two for months of jungle living, so whenever work was offered, he jumped at it.

The fastest and cheapest way to get to the States from Sarteneja was through the brand new international airport in Cancun, so that's where we headed, driving up the coast, through Chetumal, Tulum and Isla Mujeres, having a bit of a walkabout before he took off. On Isla Mujeres we stayed at Reuben's campground where Reuben himself said we could stay for free if Cindi and I together gave him a massage. I think she was on the feet and I was on the head, or vice versa, when the sheet rose in a non-stop erection. We almost choked trying not to laugh, because we wanted that free campsite! And we got it!

At that moment, we were living pretty much moment to moment. Doug was going back to the US to earn money. Cindi wanted to go back to the US and had no money. I was pregnant, knowing or planning to eventually get back to Sarteneja with Doug and have our baby there. That accomplished a couple of things: our baby could be a dual national (remember our original goal? seems we barely did, either!) and Doug could build his much longed-for and dreamed-of sailboat.

At Reuben's we met Nan and Jerry, yogis and Californians like Cindi. Nan was a beauty with a yogini/dancer body who stopped watches. Literally. She put one on and it stopped. She had quite the energy field, and in the way of travelers on the road, we became instant friends. All it took was a conversation by our tents, or a meal together, and we were connected. Nan and Jerry and Doug and Cindi and I were hanging out, making plans, figuring the next steps. Even though Nan and Jerry had no plans at all to go to Guatemala, once I started telling them about Panajachel and how beautiful it was, they shifted. We made our plan: Doug would fly out of Cancun and the four of us

293

would head south together. We'd hang out in Tulum on the beach until he let me know when he was coming back.

Here's something I don't remember: how in the world did we all stay in touch? When I was in India on my honeymoon with Glenn, I called my parents once, collect. It cost $25 for three minutes, about the cost of a nice dinner out for the two of them (my parents) in those days. I had to go to a special government telephone office to place the call, and it took a long time to do it. I may have had to make a reservation the day before or a few hours before. I thought they would be so happy to hear my voice after a year, but for the next few years after I got back, every time that story came up, they would bitch up a storm about how much it cost! It always amazed me.

Here we were, just five years later, and we were able to stay more or less in touch from the Yucatan. That was amazing, how fast technology had advanced in those five years. Not to mention now, when every nomad in Outer Mongolia has a cell phone, if not a Facebook page!

Doug and I headed to Cancun to get him on a plane back to the States, planning to meet the others at a hotel in town in a couple of days. On the way to Isla Mujeres we had stopped there and made some friends we wanted to see again.

The city of Cancun was under construction and the guys we made friends with were the ones who were building the city. If you've been there, you probably know it as a strip of huge hotels along the beach, but before all that was there, or when there was maybe one small hotel, we stayed with the guys doing the building at the edge of the jungle. Once upon a time, it was all jungle.

These guys had hammocks strung in a small concrete block house with a single tap of running water and electricity in the form of a light bulb hanging from the ceiling. There were six guys living there, all super nice and friendly. Doug and I stayed there in hammocks with them for a night. The guy we made friends with first, Ismael, spoke perfect English and was an engineer on the project. His family lived in Merida. Later in our wanderings, we stayed at their house for a night, because I remember going into false labor there and drinking Kahlua to make it stop, which it did.

In late 1975, Cancun was in the planning phase; after the first couple of hotels, there was still jungle out along the length of the beach. "Downtown" was made up of concrete block houses for workers and a few simple beans and tortillas food stands with crates for seats. There was a lot of dust and rebar as concrete was poured and pounded to create a city to bring tourists to the area. The idea was too successful: the flavor and essence of the jungle and the heritage of Cancun was erased over the years, replaced by what is there now, essentially one long bar, dance floor and tanning booth. And Mexico's second largest airport.

Ismael wanted to buy the car. We knew that all along, so when Doug got on the plane, Ismael got the car. Cindi, Nan and Jerry showed up and together we got on the bus to Tulum. Some French people got on the bus and they were pretty lost or confused about their trip. I tried to explain to them in French, which just three years ago I had spoken fluently, but what I was trying to say came out one third French, one third Spanish and one third English. My brain circuitry was overloading, trying to keep all that straight.

Tulum beach was pretty isolated in those days. You could walk for a long time down the beach and never see another person. The water was perfect, the skies mostly sunny, I could live in a bikini and eat fresh fruit. What wasn't to love? I had no desire to go back to the USA, and everyone was having a good time. And then, alas, it got boring. I mean, seriously, how many walks on the beach and perfect sunny days and swims in the beautiful clear ocean do you need in a row?

I've never been much of a beach person, besides when I was a kid and my aunt and uncle had a house in the

Hamptons. That became my Uncle Sandy's house, Aunt Fran having died of a massive brain tumor while I was in Nepal. It's one thing to live in a nice house right on the beach, with comfy furniture to lounge on and indoor plumbing, and quite another to live in a tent, even though we had an outdoor shower we could use.

We were set up right next to a little snack shack. Even when nobody was there but me, I always felt safe because the guys who owned and lived there watched out for me. One morning they brought the most adorable little baby animal they found in the jungle, a taquesin, they called it. That must be a Mayan name since I can't find it in a Spanish dictionary. Those guys were always bringing fruit and treats in a super sweet and protective way. None of them ever tried to hit on me or be even borderline weird, and I felt safe camping near their shack. Maybe in some parts of Mexico the men were macho and hard, but the men I met in the Yucatan were gentle and very kind to me. Like the people in northern Belize, they were Mayan.

I got tired of waiting for Doug so I called his parents' house in Peachtree City, GA, knowing they'd know where he was, figuring I'd get a number at the studio in New York. He answered the phone! He'd been helping out at their store and hanging with them. A week had gone by; I'd figured he'd be winding things up and heading back. Instead, he told me Ted at Bearsville Studios outside Woodstock, NY had a project for him, which is where he'd been heading all along. He was headed up there "in a day or two" (driving) and he'd be headed south in another week or so. Fuck that. We were going to Guatemala. I told him to find me back in Panajachel, my way favorite place so far. I'd have stayed there this whole time if not for the required $800 to get the baby back out if he got born there. That bothered me for theological and ethical reasons, and besides, most of the time, we couldn't afford it.

Nan, Jerry, Cindi and I geared up for the twelve hour bus ride to Palenque, which was on the overland mountain route back to Guatemala. This is the educational part of my story: if you look at a map, and Google maps is a dandy place to go, you will see Panajachel, or Lago de Atitlan (same area) in the central Western part of Guatemala. To get there from Tulum, on the Yucatan, either you had to go through Belize and the jungle of Guatemala, which we had just done, or around on the high roads. We took the high road, aiming first for Palenque.

Palenque is where we stayed in the cool little hotel with the sweet manager who brought me bread his mama baked in a pit in the ground. We were delighted to see each other again, and he made all four of us feel totally welcome as he gave us the best rooms he had.

One of the best parts of putting this book together is getting back in touch with people I hadn't talked to for years. Cindi worked that out for me by talking to Rasta at work that day, and when we talked, of course Nan came up. I remembered her last name. Lo and behold, she was on Facebook, making reconnection so simple.

Nan and I talked. She filled me in on so much of this that I had gaps about, and one thing she totally remembered and will probably never forget is that when we took a break from the bus, there was nowhere to go pee except right out there on the side of the road. And she had on pants.

I had a great, multi colored long dress that I wore just about every day. I'm big on mono wardrobes, wearing the same thing over and over so I don't have to think about clothes. Nan was, too. She had on her handmade super cool burgundy floral harem pants, and she had to pee. While I could squat sort of inside my big skirt, she finally had to pull her pants down in front of God and everyone. It reminds me of when I had on jeans in the Philippines and had to pull them down to pee. Gratefully, it was just women in the enclosure and I had taken enough Quaaludes to not really

297

give a shit. It was more traumatic for Nan, obviously, because she brought it up when we talked. Ahhhh, travel memories.

Nan also reminds me that when we got to Palenque, Margaret Trudeau, wife of the Prime Minister of Canada, was also there, with some pomp and circumstance surrounding her visit. So I Googled it, and found it was true, just as Nan remembers.

Margaret Trudeau was definitely the wild child of Canadian politics and Palenque was probably lots of fun for her, if she could get away from those security guys!

At the hotel we met lots of travelers, including a couple of Germans who were headed to Houston, and were happy to give Cindi a ride that far. From there she had an easy bus ride or plane home. They were going to meander through Mexico, which suited her just fine. I actually got invited to Oaxaca, too, by one of the German guys who had just returned from Cuzco and gave me some beads. Dios Mio, he was so kind and cute and wanted me to go with him. What to do? I decided the best way to decide was to flip a coin. Heads I'd go to Oaxaca, tails I'd go to Panajachel. It came up heads. Seven times. Fuck that, I was going to Panajachel. I knew it all along.

Cindi and I had done quite a few miles and adventures together, and as sad as I was to see her go, I was also glad she had a good ride back to the States so she could go home. She was just seventeen, after all, and traveling around with no money was hard. Luckily I had the $200 to lend her, the money I had saved by not saving the snake. The last time I saw her, after we moved back to the States, was 1978 or so in Brooklyn, where she lived with her husband and her cute, fat little Buddha of a baby, Chelsea. Chelsea looked like a melted candle, she had so many chins and was so calm, like Cindi. Doug, two year old Rasta and I had driven down from Woodstock, NY in our VW bug to visit Cindi and meet her baby. I haven't seen her since, but I'm planning on it.

Nan and Jerry and I hopped the next thing smokin', which is often literally true when talking about Third World busses, and rode over to San Cristobal de las Casas, scene of Collette's nefarious air-headedness only months before. It was a short stay as we were headed to Panajachel and didn't want to dawdle. Joining up with a multinational group of travelers, we hired a truck to take us to the border, where we had tortillas and beans and beer. Well, everyone else had beer. I was pretty sober through my pregnancy. Nan remembers the guards at the border taking us to a dorm-like room to sleep, where they woke up their own children and made them get up to sell us their beds for the night.

In the morning, there was a bus through Huehuetenango and Solola to Panajachel. As we rolled through Solola, the town at the top of the hill above Panajachel, Nan was drawn by the beauty of the town and its market. Nobody in the group wanted to stop except her. She remembers someone telling her, "It'll be there tomorrow. You can come back then."

That turned out to not be true.

In Panajachel I ran into Doug's brother Scotty, who was still staying there, somehow. Talk about by hook or by crook! He acted so happy to see me. That was a funny thing about Scotty. He had, or acted like he had, totally no hard feelings about my having left him in Mexico. He had gotten to Guatemala just fine and always seemed glad to see me. Of course that didn't stop him from stealing from me whenever he got the chance. We had had him over for Christmas in our little adobe, and he got his presents and took whatever else was around, like my cash. But he was happy to see me.

Scotty and I had dinner. I wanted to have dinner with him and make sure he was ok because I did feel a little guilty about leaving him and wanted to make sure he was all right. Outside the restaurant I ran into Nan and Jerry, who were headed to the hotel room we had gotten right next door. It had a double bed for them and a single for me. Perfect.

In the middle of the night, at three in the morning, the room started jumping around and there was a huge roaring sound. I woke up and saw Nan and Jerry on the floor. "Hey you guys, cut it out," I yelled at them as shit fell off the shelves and bounced onto the floor.

"It's an earthquake!" they yelled back. "We've got to get out of here."

Along with everyone else in the hotel, we stumbled down the stairs, feeling our way in the darkness, and made our way out into the courtyard, which was big enough to be well out of the way of the two story building, should it fall down. Being from California, Nan and Jerry knew what to do. They'd been through earthquakes before; this was my first. After the initial shaking stopped, Jerry ran in and got us shoes and blankets, and we slept out in the courtyard. The biggest danger was walls collapsing in the aftershocks and after that, broken glass. Everyone stayed outside in the cold.

That was February 4, 1976, my mom's fifty-ninth birthday. Twenty thousand people were killed by that earthquake, most of them buried in their adobe houses, mostly south of Panajachel toward Guatemala City. My friends Jamie and Brad had their adobe house collapse on them somewhere south of Panajachel. They were both face down and Jamie had one arm free, behind her back. Brad was totally pinned. It took her four hours to dig them out, but she did, and they were basically ok, with the exception of cuts and bruises and the effects of the trauma. I could feel her panic when she reenacted it for me later, how she had to move forty pound adobe blocks off them with just one arm bent behind her back. She was such a cool girl, seemingly so calm, but years later when I ran into her again and actually stayed with her in Florida, the calm seemed to have abandoned her. She had become a used clothing hoarder, and there was almost no clear space in her whole three bedroom house that wasn't buried three or four foot deep in old clothes. I don't know if the experience of being buried in adobe that night had triggered her behavior, although it can't have helped. I really loved her and hope she is well, wherever she ended up. She did give birth to a baby girl in Pana and almost bled to death, but eventually she and the baby were ok and made it back to the States. Apparently they had the $800 for the baby's exit visa.

In Panajachel, right on Lake Atitlan, four people died when the beach opened up a huge fissure and swallowed their van. I saw that fissure a few days later walking down to the beach and it was really deep. There was no trace of them. But because of Lake Atitlan being so deep, it acted as a shock absorber for the towns around it and compared to other places we heard about later, the damage was minimal.

For a week I stayed in Pana, not because I wanted to, but because there was no way out. There was no transportation out. After the first night, when the earthquake measured 7.6, there was another, either the next night or the one after, also over 7 on the Richter scale. More people were killed, over twenty five thousand in all. The steeple of the church in Solola fell from its perch, killing all the people sleeping below, taking refuge outdoors. Houses definitely weren't safe, but the outdoors wasn't necessarily safe, either. The market Nan wanted to see was no more. It was completely destroyed.

There was no communication from Pana to the US. Doug and my family didn't know if I was ok or dead, but I couldn't do much about that. Roads were impassable with boulders and mudslides. There were no busses or cars moving in or out of town. I moved my things into Veggie Bob's house, but with so many aftershocks, all of us staying there took to sleeping out in the field next to the house, in case there was another big one. There were cracks in all the walls and no one trusted the houses not to fall on us.

I was far enough along in my pregnancy that the baby was moving. I'd lie on the ground and the baby would move and the ground would move. There was a fluidity and liquid quality to what had once seemed solid. The Earth, the foundation of our stability, was no longer still. She was moving, often. Most of the tremblors were small, but unnerving nonetheless.

Nan and Jerry were there, too, and a bunch of other people who hadn't been living at Bob's before. It was a warm, safe place where we shared food and stories for a week as we tried to piece our realities back together. We got food for a communal meal at night; like a big campout, we passed Nan's guitar around, singing and telling stories by the fire. The nights were chilly, but we kept each other warm.

Every night when we made the meal, Jerry volunteered to dice the chili peppers for whatever we were having. Every single time, he rubbed his eyes afterward. It became so regular, you could set a watch by it, which wouldn't do any good with Nan around. She could stop any make or model.

One day Nan and I walked and walked, talking to people in whatever language we had between us. We were as shocked as most of them, wanting to do something to help, but not knowing what to do. Nothing was organized and there was all this energy with no place to go.

The Casa de Pies was the most popular place for gringos, but the Guatemalan cooks were spooked to go back in and cook, so the owner asked me and Nan to help. Finally! We had something useful to do. We made rice and beans and salads and whatever was there, and after a little while the Guatemalan cooks noticed that we hadn't been killed yet so they came back, too.

The second morning, when the regular cooks were back, I was dishing up the beans and beating eggs, when they pulled a piece of meat out of the fridge that was *totally green*. I said (my Spanish was good) that there were some dogs who looked like they were starving; I'd give it to them. They looked at me like I was crazy, sliced it up and fried it for the steak and eggs breakfast. GAG! Another very good reason to be a vegetarian, especially when travelling.

As soon as I could, I got out of there with a guy named Rufus in his big old pickup truck, riding in the front with him and his best friend, with more hardy travelers in the truck bed stuffed with backpacks and sleeping bags. The road out was a wreck, and the going slow. There was devastation everywhere. It was about a week after the earthquake, and we were among the first to get out. I told Rufus about the gigantic army tent I had stashed with the snack shack guys in Tulum, that he could have it if he drove me there, and he did.

Nan and Jerry decided to stay and help with the recovery. There were so many reasons to leave: fear of disease from all the dead, fear of food shortages. But Nan was not to be dissuaded. When I told her all this, in her very yogic way, she told me, "That's ok, I'm used to fasting." She had a life transforming adventure there that is hers to tell, but I wanted out.

When we got to Tulum, Rufus and his pal (Buck?) and I stayed in the big tent for a few days. I gave them everything we had for camping, the tent and the stove and pots and pans and whatever was there, for my ride from Panajachel to the Cancun airport.

Coming back into the US, the Customs agent was very suspicious of me. I was all tan and breezy with my long hair and my long multicolored dress, coming from the Yucatan with my little bag of clothes, no story for him about how I supported myself (a mistake; I didn't know I needed a story) and a bottle of black Yucatan wild honey, which he opened and sniffed and got all over his nose. I told him he could keep it and he let me go. I mean, he had to let me go; I wasn't doing anything wrong. He was such an asshole to me, and I was an American citizen! In those days, that was rare.

Welcome to Planet Earth, Rasta

Doug and I couldn't have taken long on whatever he had going on in Georgia because next thing I knew, we were headed to Belize, for real this time with a VW van and Martine and little Jesse who was about four years old. We were dropping them off in Abbeville, Louisiana at Bobby Charles' house. Abbeville is a little town about twenty miles south of Lafayette, in the heart of Cajun country. Bobby, Robert Charles Guidry by birth, was on tour with Paul Butterfield and Martine's husband/Jesse's father DJ was tour manager. Martine was going to stay there at Bobby's until they got back.

Bobby wrote such classics as "See you Later Alligator," "Walking to New Orleans" and "But I Do." He never had big hits singing his own songs, but those three were all huge for Bill Haley and the Comets, Fats Domino and Clarence Frogman Henry, respectively.

When Bobby was just starting out, he tried to pitch Alligator to Fats Domino, his musical hero. But Fats didn't want a song about Alligators! Later, he invited Bobby to a show in New Orleans, and Bobby told him he didn't have any way to get there. "Well, you better start walking," was reportedly Fats' reply. And so "Walkin' to New Orleans" was born.

After a spell at Chess Records, where Leonard Chess was amazed and disconcerted to find that Bobby was white, having signed him on the phone and arranged a tour of black clubs, Bobby got busted in Nashville in 1971 and had to disappear. He ended up in upstate New York, in Woodstock. In those days, Woodstock was full to bursting with talented musicians, and Bobby got to know them all. He spent time at DJ and Martine's house, which was where I met him.

Bobby was dark, sexy, funny, charming and broody. I didn't know him well, but I always liked him. He was always friendly and fun and definitely up for a good time. One day I overheard him on the phone with one of his sons, down at the house in Abbeville.

"Son, I'm coming home tomorrow, and I want that place *clean!* I mean, not one seed!"

Woodstock didn't really work for Bobby. One thing was it was cold as hell compared to Abbeville, and lacked that je ne sais quoi of Louisiana, that slow drawlin' ease he made so famous in songs. He wrote some great songs that were theme songs for Woodstock, back in the day, like "Small Town Talk" and "I Must be in a Good Place Now."

When we got to his Louisiana place, way out in the bayou, I never saw more snakes in my life, except the zoo. Martine reminds me that the first day we got there, there was this tall, languid blonde beauty leaning against the fence that surrounded the pond.

"Aren't you worried about the snakes?" I asked her, since there were snakes crossing the driveway and hanging on the fence.

"Naw," she answered coolly. "Snakes don't bother me at all."

I stared at her in disbelief, this fashion model beautiful girl with an angel's face, in her teeny cut-off shorts and tank top, barefoot among the serpents. "You mean you like snakes?" I asked, incredulous.

"Yeah," she answered with a big sweet smile. "I like to shoot their fucking heads off."

Snakes crossed the driveway every time I looked. I was decidedly markedly pregnant, and I was hot all the time, especially considering it was spring and already hot and humid on the bayou. I remember waddling around in a long white skirt, sweating, and the guys said, go on out to the pond and have a swim; it'll cool you off.

When I went out there, there were snakes swimming back and forth across the pond. I counted four or five, and as I turned and ran back into the house, another one crossed the driveway! "Are you guys fucking kidding me? That pond is full of snakes!"

The "guys" were two of Bobby's sons. Their favorite pastime was running barefoot through the bayou, shooting snakes. They kept a gallon jug of Tabasco on the kitchen counter. They looked at me like, what a baby! and said, "Just grab the rope, swing out in the middle and let go. They'll swim away from you." Right, like that was *ever* going to happen.

A woman came over to visit with a baby who was about two weeks old, a teeny little thing. She looked at my obvious condition and asked me if I'd like to hold her baby. Figuring I was going have to know how to do this pretty soon, I said yes, but then I sat there stiff as a board, holding that baby like she was Lalique crystal until she started to cry. Oh no. I had never held a baby since my brother Will when I was eight years old, or to be perfectly honest, had a maternal instinct or desire. This scared the shit out of me. That night I told Doug I was really scared to go to a foreign country when I didn't know jack shit about taking care of a baby and he told me not to worry. He'd had two kids by then and knew how to take care of them.

Well, that part was true. He had them, but how much he ever took care of those two is highly questionable, judging by how much he took care of ours. But I didn't know that at the time. I didn't realize that everything he'd done with someone else, he'd do with me. I mistakenly thought I was so special. There's a cautionary message.

I asked Martine if she was sure she and Jesse would be ok there with all the snakes and the shooters, and since she thought they would be, we got on our way. I was on quite an expansion program and we needed to get settled soon as we moved through month number seven. I remember that white skirt. I felt like a walking pup tent.

On the way south, we decided to drive through Merida and see Ishmael and his family. He was done with his Cancun gig and living home again. In a restaurant in Merida, Doug and I met an American couple, our age or so, on vacation. They were blond, both of them, and friendly. It was the kind of situation so typical of travel, in those days and circumstances, where you'd just start talking to people at the next table because they looked like you and/or looked interesting. I still do it, but in those times, most gringo travelers did, too.

This cute blonde American girl/woman started flirting with Doug as we were having dinner. Mostly I ignored it since I thought the guy was her boyfriend or husband and he'd get it in check. She and Doug collided on some Planet where the other guy and I didn't exist. After a while I got disgusted listening to them flirting. I was feeling a bit like a cow, huge and ponderous, and she was this hot little coked-out baby who just would not let it rest. If it was a different situation, I'd have said, Geeze you two, get a room! Which is apparently what they did.

I felt like if I had to say something to get him to come back to the hotel with me, that was already fucked up and stupid, so I walked back to our hotel room and went to bed. Truth was, I didn't necessarily want him to come back to the hotel with me. I didn't want him to touch me, which was frustrating him and he was kind of irritating me. I was hot and huge and hormonal and cranky. However, I honestly didn't want him to go spend the night with some skinny little cokehead, but that's what he did. I didn't realize there weren't more options!

Doug never came back that night, and I'm sure I didn't sleep much. I was angry and hurt but there was this part of me that wondered if my non-caring, non-intimate attitude lately had brought this on. I was sort of relieved that at least now if I was bitchy, I had a good reason! I thought we'd probably have to deal with it, but neither of us knew thing one about having the kind of relationship where we talked through problems.

The next morning, he came back to the room as I was getting ready to go out for breakfast, get some coffee, get out of town. He told me since I left the night before without a word, he figured it was ok with me for him to go off with her.

Who's in the restaurant when we get there but her? I was all over my victim role, my martyr self. I wish I had just slugged them both, but as I've mentioned, that doesn't come to me naturally. She sat down next to him and put her hand on his leg. I thought of that line from "Coal Miner's Daughter," "Woman, if you want to keep that arm, I suggest you take it off my husband." But I didn't say it. I just glared until she removed her hand. It was obvious *they* were cool. They'd been up all night having fun. I was the one with the "bad vibes."

I couldn't just leave him though, and not for that. I was close to eight months pregnant, and I needed him for whatever support I could get, so we got back in the van and headed for Sarteneja.

It was a quiet trip. I didn't have much to say. I was angry and my eyes filled with tears when I tried to talk. Besides, really what was there to say? Behind the obvious was my lack of commitment to him, to a marriage. I knew that, inside, which was why I really couldn't get madder. So I had these hurt feelings, but they were incidental. That was an interesting interlude. We never talked about it again.

I rested a lot on the bed in the back of the van, which was my vantage point when we crossed over from Chetumal into Belize. I saw a road crew working, filling potholes. There was a guy with an extra-large serving spoon scooping hot tar out of a big can, like an institutional sized green bean can, and putting it in the holes. Yeah, I thought, I can deal with this level of technology. It's my preferred speed, right up my alley.

Doug's whole reason to go to Belize was to build a sailboat. It was as if our original intention of finding a safe haven for our children in times of war and the military draft had gone out the window. All he cared about, besides the aforementioned detour, was building a boat. As he said, if he took all the wood we burned all winter in Woodstock, which was a pile of it, he could build a boat. It wasn't the same wood, but eventually he did it.
He had met the boat builder, Natividad Verde, who had told him he'd build him a boat.

It took us all day to drive to Sarteneja on the road that barely was. We were lucky, because when some friends came to visit a few years later, they were stuck for three days in the jungle before the Mennonites came along with a tractor and hauled them out in exchange for twenty cases of beer. We didn't get stuck, amazingly, but took *hours* at five and ten miles per hour, climbing over rocks and avoiding gaping, crater-like holes.

Once we got to the village we rented a little house with a bedroom and a kitchen, a bath house and an outhouse, and we were all set for a modern birthing experience. Oh my word. This is one of those examples of my mom and dad just blithely accepting that I was going to Central America in a Volkswagen to have their first grandchild! Nobody said anything like, "Gee Sukoshi, that might be a little primitive and maybe even dangerous." Instead, they smiled and bid me a fond farewell. Or maybe they did say it, and I answered with my stock phrase of that time: "people have been having babies for thousands of years, so I'm sure it will be fine."

Of course my mom and I didn't ever have those nitty gritty talks about the actual birthing process. She had her children in hospitals, and I was so small at four pounds and some, she did tell me she thought she just had to shit when out I came. Now that's prophetic, eh?

Rasta's Birth

I could call this "birthing, Belizean style," only it *so* wasn't. For one thing, *no* Sarteneja woman went swimming the day she gave birth, especially in a bikini. (Perish the thought! I must've given them fits!) The closest I saw to it was Sarteneja women wading out in their dresses. They didn't even *have* bathing suits, or swim, much less when they were pregnant! Hardly anyone, including the fishermen who went out to sea, knew how to swim. Secondly, if a baby was late, as mine was, according to my US doc's forecast due date, the woman almost always went to the mainland to have the baby in the hospital. And third, as I found out well after the fact, nobody who knew any better used Nurse Gwen for their delivery. She was brutal.

Nobody in town told me about the Government Nurse, Nurse Gwen. As soon as I got there I had registered for her classes on prenatal care, and all the pregnant women were there getting their vitamins and their check-ups, but nobody told me not to let her deliver the baby! I had my natural childbirth book, Ina May Gaskins' Spiritual Midwifery, which I had read to tatters and found comforting and encouraging. But the Government Nurse totally pooh-poohed it, giving me instead a horrifying book on birth defects and possible catastrophic birthing disasters, with color pictures. That would have been a good clue, but I was pregnant for the first time, in an extremely foreign culture, and clueless. I didn't actually know I had a choice, and didn't know who or where to ask, since I saw all the pregnant ladies at her prenatal classes.

But first, the swimming: It was hot. Of course it was hot. It was mid-June in Belize and I was three weeks overdue. I remembered a story I read somewhere about a Rastafarian in Jamaica who liked to swim out as far as he could in the ocean, for the rush of seeing if he could make it back. It seemed like a sensible idea, which is a measure of what pregnancy and tropical heat can do.

I waded out as far as I could in the bay, and then I swam until I had a contraction. Just one. Then I swam back in, put my dress over my wet bikini, and walked the three blocks home to our rental house and went into labor around midnight.

Doug ran over to Gwen's house, very close to ours, to wake her up and tell her I was in labor. She arrived quickly with her assistant, who was a really sweet village woman. Both of them were black as night and had neon pink rollers in their hair, quite the vision. The Nurse kept belching and saying, all ladylike, "Oh pardon me, I took a loxative!" If I hadn't been in labor, it would have been funny.

I had issues of my own to deal with, this whole having a baby thing. It was hard work, worse than skiing, and that bitch Nurse really made it hard and dangerous. I'll spare you most of the details except to say I was torn by her fingers, not the birth. Rasta was born with a large hematoma on his head that took about three weeks to go down, and I was a mess. It was a horrifying and scary experience, when I was so prepared for this beautiful, gentle delivery I'd been reading

312

about. Instead of being born calm and quiet, Rasta was born stressed and screaming and pissed right in Doug's face as he came out. Another prophesy of birth. He was born at 6:25 am, as Venus was on the horizon. The Morningstar.

We put on the birth certificate that Rasta was born on June 15, 1976. It was Sunday, and it was Father's Day. Oh boy, thought I in a spasm of overachiever nonsense, what a great gift for our dads! By Tuesday I was able to walk to the village phone, which worked in good weather, and telephone both our families. I don't remember what mine said, but Doug's dad, Howard, said, "Rastus? What you name that baby Rastus for?"

Twenty seven years later, sitting around our backyard in Georgia having dinner with Rasta and his friend, Frank who are visiting from California, for some reason we get on the subject of birthdays. Out of the blue, or so it seemed, Frank told Rasta, "I hate to tell you this, Champ, but in June of 1976, the fifteenth was on a Tuesday, not Sunday." The worst of it was, he was right! No, the worst of it was, I felt like a total wreck hippy parent that didn't even know the day he was born! It was a Sunday, I'm pretty sure...

Anyway, we all lived, in spite of all the absolutely kooky stuff people were telling me about having a baby. It was like ninety degrees every day and they said if I didn't keep him in a wool hat and booties he would get a fresh cold and die. Whatever. I was sooooo glad when my very grounded and practical mother-in-law Peaches arrived. She had had four kids, none of them had gotten fresh colds and she taught me how to be a mom, something I had ignorantly thought was going to come naturally.

Doug had put out the word that he could fix anything mechanical, so outboard motors and radios began piling up on our porch. He got electricity running at the bar next door, a dubious achievement since it kept us up every night with the thump of reggae music. He was gone or working every day while I took walks and tried to figure out this baby thing.

313

He got lots of radios. People would drop them off and say, "No anda." It doesn't work. When he opened them up invariably a zillion cockroaches would pour out of them, and then they would anda. He learned very quickly to open them outside.

After that the women in the village told me they *never* had The Government Nurse deliver their babies. She was too rough! And they never offered that information because I never thought to ask, since I saw them all at the clinic all the time. That's how conversations generally went there. People would tell me anything I asked, but I had to know the right questions because useful information was rarely forthcoming. They did tell me crazy superstitious shit about raising a baby, and even though Rasta was my first, I knew not to listen.

A month or two later, when she was done with government mandated baby care for me, the Government Nurse confessed to me that she had never liked white people. Aye yi yi! That, as an example, would have been a useful piece of information before the fact.

I wanted out of that place. Just one person could have told me she was a brute. I could hardly wait for Nativ to finish Doug's boat so we could get on it and get the hell out of there. Besides, there were mosquitos like crazy, the bay was never clear, so God knew what you'd bump into swimming, and I was kind of claustrophobic. I didn't really think about what sailing around with Doug, a complete novice, and our brand new baby would be like. As it turned out, it was fun once in a while, but usually challenging and sometimes downright terrifying.

Meanwhile, I put Rasta in a Snugli that I had brought and walked and walked around the village every day. Everyone wanted to hold him because they had never seen a blue eyed baby before. "Mira sus ojos!" they would exclaim, one after another. "Look at his eyes!"

314

Peaches stayed for a couple of weeks and absolutely fell in love with the place. It was simple, people were friendly, and most of the village venerated her Douggie, because he had brought electricity. Granted, he brought it to a bar, but it was a start.

The local folks did funny stuff I had never seen; the kids would all come over with a big bag of fruit, and we'd eat it in the living room. They'd spit the seeds and throw the peels all over the floor, and then when we were done they'd get the broom and sweep it out. The girls loved to come over and carry baby Rasta around, which was great so I could get something done like cooking, or laundry, or get back to my yoga practice, which was so important to my sanity. By the time a girl was seven years old in that village, she was an old hand at babysitting. Unfortunately, by the time she was fifteen, in those days she was often a mother herself.

There was one awesome tradition around childbirth in the village. Well there were a few. For one, someone came and took all the sheets and stuff that had blood on them and washed them for me and brought them back spotless. She was a neighbor I hardly knew, but that was what women did for each other. The other really cool thing, which I didn't do, was that village women spent their baby's first month bonding with the baby in a hammock, just resting and nursing. Village women brought food, took care of their other children, and basically gave them the first month together.

When I finally got the okay to take a bucket bath so I wouldn't get an infection in my torn up parts, I grabbed the bucket in the bath house to pull it toward me and got my first scorpion sting in my hand. The little fucker was hiding just under the lip of the bucket. It was okay though, like a bad bee sting because it was a little one. They were the hurt-like-hell but not really poisonous brand of scorpion.

Later on, when we lived in Nativ's house, there were scorpions about four and five inches long that lived up in the

315

rafters under the tin roof, basking in the heat. Nativ had eleven or thirteen children so he couldn't afford to have those things fall down. He'd climb up in the rafters with a pair of scissors and cut their tails off before he killed them so if he missed and they fell, they couldn't do any harm.

I found a huge one, about five inches long, in the pocket of a raincoat I had hanging on the wall. They loved to get in shoes on the floor or clothes hanging on the wall. I cut off its tail and about a teaspoonful of poison came out. The big ones hurt like hell, I hear. Especially when you're a guy and you grab your pants off the wall and pull them on and get nailed in the cojones! I knew two guys that happened to and they both said yeah, pretty painful! But they didn't die or get sick besides swelling in the localized part.

The people in the village didn't know much about medicine. You might think they were all natural and traditional and primitive and close to the land, but it was rarely like that. They used Vicks Vaporub for almost everything, just like the dad with Windex in "My Big Fat Greek Wedding." One afternoon I heard a kid just wailing and screaming so of course I went in his house to see what was up. He had fallen off his bike and scraped the crap out of his leg, and his parents were diligently rubbing Vicks into the abrasions. Oy! I explained that Vicks was not for open cuts, and told them to wash his leg gently with warm water and soap and I'd be right back. I ran over to my house and got antibiotic cream and put that on. It was a great substitute for Vicks, since it worked and it didn't hurt. After that, people with all kinds of ailments started showing up at our house because we had a first aid kit. And because, truth be told, none of them liked that bossy Government Nurse either.

It may seem crazy that I just walked into those people's house, but it was more or less accepted. Earlier on, I'd tried to train Rasta to nurse and sleep on a schedule. I had a copy of Dr. Spock's Baby and Child Care, and he was all about having a schedule. One afternoon Rasta was crying in his bed and I was outside hanging up wash and trying to ignore him. A woman I'd never seen came in the yard.

"Mon, your baby is *crying*!"

"Yes, I know," I whingeingly started to explain, "I'm trying to get him on a schedule...." Whereupon she walked right past me into my house and picked up that poor baby and said, "Mon, your baby wants to *eat!*"

And that was the end of schedules.

Eventually the boat, which we christened the Kozma Wave, was ready to go. Rasta was a few months old and we'd go out on test runs, like across the bay to Corozol. On the very first trip, sitting in a café in Corozol, a man offered me $25,000 for Rasta, with his blond hair and blue eyes. I told him no, it was too hard to squeeze this one out, so I was going to keep him. That was one hell of a lot of money back then, and I think that man was serious, but he was perfectly nice about it.

It was quickly apparent that Doug didn't know what he was doing as a sailor and was probably going to get us killed. The first trip we took back from Corozol, a whole bunch of women and children from the village asked for a ride back to Sarteneja. After tacking back and forth in the bay for about four hours and getting nowhere, they were all crying and begging us to turn around and go with the wind and take them back to Corozol, which we did.

We had to. I looked down in the hold and there were women crying and pleading with me, "Please ask Senor Douglas to turn around and take us back to Corozol." they

317

were holding their children and looking terrified. It was the only thing to do.

Then we started off again, the first of the terrifying voyages that made me the anti-sailor I remain today. We got hung up in shallow water on some rocks and I had two week old Rasta in one arm, the tiller in the other, as Doug and our one remaining intrepid passenger, a Frenchwoman, pushed and rocked the boat until we got free of the rocks.

Shallow water, rocks and reefs, were a constant challenge to boats in Belize. It's why the native sailboats had such shallow drafts, so they would clear the reefs and not get hung up like regular sailboats did. These made the cabin areas extremely low, so you could only crawl around or sit below deck. This was definitely *not* yachting.

Doug went down to Belize City and got Arthur to come sail with us, and we took off down the length of Belize for a few months of beauty and trauma, through terrifying storms and tranquil, transparent seas.

Sometimes it's amazing to me we made it through, me and my two fabulous sons who are relatively unscathed and live productive lives. I left out some parts so I wouldn't look quite as insane as I surely was.

It was a cool adventure, living in the tropics, being on the sailboat, killing giant scorpions, moving to the jungle into fer-de-lance land and emptying tarantulas out of the teacups in the morning. I think I was in shock some of the time because if you asked me to do it again I would say *no way in hell!!!* At the time it was just the next thing that came along, as if there were no other choices or options.

Three years later I went back and did it again, giving birth to Pablo on the floor of Nativ's kitchen. It was way better than the first time, but not so great that I'd do it again.

Diapers in Paradise

When my friend Bernard, now with the Angels, told me that having my son Rasta on a sailboat was so romantic, or "romantique," he would have said, being French, I had to laugh in his face. It was only romantic in some fantasy sense. The thing that was the least romantic about it, next to holding a baby for eight hours below deck in a storm, was diapers.

Diapers to First World mommies and daddies are no big deal, and now, more than forty years later, they're probably no big deal in Central America, either. Just about everyone up here in North America uses paper ones and throws them away. In Belize in 1976, there were no paper ones, and in Guatemala, which is where this story takes place, a box of Pampers cost eight dollars. That was roughly the same price as eight hundred avocados or eighty freshly baked breads, four hundred mangoes, eight restaurant meals...well, you get my drift. And so we used cloth diapers, when we used diapers at all, and every port we sailed to my immediate search was for enough fresh water to rinse them well. I could wash with sea water, but especially for a tender baby bum, everything had to be rinsed well in fresh water to avoid rashes and harshness.

I'm sure Doug got the idea to go up the Rio Dulce (Sweet River) from the people we stayed with in Placencia as we sailed down the length of Belize with Arthur, Doug's buddy from Belize City whose house we stayed in when we first came to the country. When I Google Rio Dulce today, it's of course unrecognizable, with marinas and hotels and development that hadn't even been dreamed of when we were there more than forty years ago. At the headwater of the river, miles and miles upstream, was an ideal boat hideaway from storms, especially hurricanes, the bane of the Caribbean basin. With our teeny little putt-putt of an outboard motor, it took us all day to go upstream. Arthur rigged a shade for me and baby Rasta to lie under on the deck and watch the river go by. It was leisurely and lovely, a tropical river lined with huge trees that grew right down to the waterside. Eat your heart out, Disney World. This was the real deal, with swinging monkeys and an occasional break in the trees where women washed their clothes while children splashed and played.

When we got up the river, it opened into a big lake. To our right we saw a simple marina with a bar (of course) and restaurant and we headed over there. That's where we met Mark and Bonnie, who had lived there for several years, first on their trimaran, and then in a sweet little house they built right over the water. They had sailed around the world, *twice,* in trimarans, through hurricanes and typhoons. Doug was excited by that in equal proportion to my horrification. Like many people in the area, they had come up river to escape hurricane season out on the open waters, fallen in love with the place and stayed.

Mark knew a house we could have for free. Good God, someone should have paid us to stay there! It was a thatch hut in the jungle, accessible only by boat or a footpath that went through dense bush for about a mile to the nearest settlement. Living there was both terrifying and beautiful, with the balance tipping seriously toward terrifying when the sun went down and creatures crawled. We moved in, sleeping in hammocks with the lanterns burning on low to discourage scorpions and fer-de-lance, who lived in the area. Mark tried to put the make on me, telling me that he and Bonnie had an open relationship. Probably true, but the only way I was *ever* going to sleep with him was if Rasta and I got to go live in *their* house, which had real walls and a real kitchen and bathroom.

Call me cheap and sleazy, but we were out of money and living more or less like savages. In fact, after a couple of weeks, Arthur got a ride back to Belize City. It was all the jungle that city boy could take. He was a big help while he was around, but I was glad to see him go. He was getting kind of edgy and weird and watching me nurse Rasta a little too closely. I foolishly thought all native guys down there were used to that kind of deal, but maybe not. He helped himself to a bunch of Doug's tools when he left, but we never had any money to pay him so I suppose it all evened out.

My dad had carried those tools down on a plane when they came to visit and bitched up a storm when he heard Arthur stole them. Now my dad is dead, and Doug is dead, and for all I know, Arthur probably is, too. Makes me wonder how much any of this shit matters.

Doug got a job working for some old American guy, so he was gone with the boat from dawn to sundown. He wasn't making much money, but it was something. A couple of native women walked over to visit me once in a while, but mostly I was alone with Rasta, boiling the hell out of the water after straining out the wiggling things, picking grapefruit which grew all over our yard, and trying to keep us both from dying. I drank so much grapefruit juice I gave Rasta diarrhea, since I was still nursing. It was so good, so different from the ones we buy in stores, not sour at all, but I had to stop.

My mornings started by shaking the tarantulas out of the teacups so we could have tea. Once we had a rain of baby scorpions that fell from the thatched roof. There was the ongoing, constant awareness of the fer-de-lance, also known as a bushmaster, prevalent in the neighborhood. Four people had been bitten in the last year. Two had lived. I would have killed Doug for landing us there, but he was the only one who could get us out because I didn't know how to work the boat, and I am, as I've noted, attracted to the unusual.

We had to go to Guatemala City to get paperwork so we could move along. I remember that much, although why the boat would need paperwork from Guatemala was anyone's guess. Maybe Mark had convinced Doug he needed something to stay there, although I didn't want to stay there anyway.

Doug's mom had sent us $300, only she sent it as a US Postal Money Order, which was no good outside the US. She didn't realize that, since she'd never lived outside the US. So Doug gave it to the old American man he worked for. The old man told him he would deposit it in his bank account and if it cleared, give us the money in thirty days, which is about how long it took. *Of course* it was going to clear! It was a fucking U.S. Government Postal Money Order, but he wasn't taking any chances, nosiree Bob! He died on the 28th day, and naturally nothing had been written down about it, so we were out the three hundred dollars. It might not sound like so much today, but down there, all those years ago, it would have made a huge difference and probably gotten us home. We were desperate to get out of there. At least I was.

To get to Guatemala City we took the boat over to this crappy little collection of riverside shacks and caught a ride to the main road to take a bus, which you just waved down when it approached. We got a ride to the road in a pickup truck with a young man, his young wife and baby. The baby was drinking something bright orange from a bottle. I asked the mom what it was and she proudly exclaimed, "Fanta!" and pulled the bottle right out of her baby's mouth and offered it to Rasta.

I politely refused, telling her, "No thanks, he doesn't like orange." Besides, I'd like him to have his own teeth someday, but I didn't tell her that part.

We stayed in a nice old hotel in the city near the bus station. After a long bus ride, I was just damned if I was going to do all that *and* deal with diapers; I splurged and bought a box of Pampers. They turned out to be an excellent investment.

We were two or three days in the city, eating in restaurants or street food, trying to conserve money as best we could. When we finally had our affairs in order, we boarded a bus as old as the hills to take us back to the river. It was packed, but we found a couple of seats toward the back and settled in for the couple of hours' ride.

Doug started complaining of his stomach cramping. Let it be noted for the record, Doug was an eternal optimist when it came to culinary adventures on the road, and as a tender stomached Libra, he couldn't take it. This wasn't quite as severe as the time he indulged in tacos fried in black grease in a hubcap on my first ever visit to San Miguel de Allende that gave this book its name, although it was certainly explosive!

That time we were walking back to our hotel when we saw the woman frying tacos in a hubcap in the blackest nastiest looking grease, like what comes out when you change your engine oil. Doug walked toward her.

"You're not going to eat that, are you?" I asked him.

"Yeah, sure, it looks good."

"Doug," I told him, "that grease is black. No telling where it's been."

"Naw," he drawled in his charming Southern drawl. "It's fine. All the Mexicans eat it."

That would have been my opportunity to point out two things so obvious I let them slide. Number One: he wasn't Mexican. Number Two: there was nobody else eating it. He spent five days in bed shaking, freezing, boiling and shivering between mad dashes to the toilet while I took walks around town, checking in periodically to make sure he was still alive. This time on the bus was more cinematic.

As the bus would chug and churn up a hill, Doug's face would get super white and he'd start to sweat. Just as I would be about to yell to the driver that he had to stop, that my esposo was sick, we'd crest the hill and coast and somehow, stopping the grinding of the motor would relieve the urgency in his bowels.

"Doug, you have to let me have him stop!" I told him several times, but each time he refused. He said the bus was so old, if it stopped on the uphill, it probably wouldn't be able to make the hill. Maybe he was right; we never put it to the test.

We were in the back, sitting next to a little native girl of about ten who shyly studied us. "Please honey," I'm thinking, "don't get the idea all foreigners are like us!" Doug sweated and paled over one more hill and suddenly, desperately said, "Get me a diaper!"

I grabbed one and handed it to him, and he slid it somehow into his pants or under him and sitting there next to that poor little girl he unloaded the hugest pile of stinking wet poop I ever saw. Especially in one diaper.

The girl's eyes were like saucers. I was doubled over laughing, for which he never forgave me, and then he said, "Get me another one."

After he filled that one up, he managed to heave them both out the open window, right over a man sleeping there with his mouth hanging open. Thank God, they made it, intact.

I was helpless, laughing like mad and hanging on to Rasta and just not helpful at all. Men in the front of the bus started yelling, "Siento la mierda aqui," which means "I smell shit here." Hell, yeah!

Our stop was only about another couple of miles, which was a damn good thing. And of course, once off the bus, he was fine.

We got back to our hovel, threw all our shit on the boat and got the hell out of there. Especially having been in the city in a hotel, the contrast coming back was just insane. Somehow we got the boat back to Sarteneja, secured it for the duration, and headed back to Panajachel on our way back to the USA.

Panajachel, a rerun

With the boat pulled up and stored for the winter, and all our stuff more or less stowed away in it in Sarteneja, we headed back to the US, stopping first in Panajachel. This was way more my call than Doug's. He didn't care about socializing and didn't have much interest in people, unless it was work or coke or sex related. Sitting down to have a conversation with another human would have been way down on his list, unless it was one of those blathering coke and alcohol fuelled philosophical tirades that solved all the world's problems and evaporated by morning. That may sound harsh but when I read it to our son Pablo, now 39, he nodded and said, "Yeah, that's about how it was." Meanwhile, I was as social then as now, and I wanted to have conversations about something besides raising babies and cooking beans. This time I know we took the jungle route, because the border between Guatemala and Belize had just been reopened and it was big news.

326

In Sarteneja some guys had wanted to sell us Mayan artifacts stolen from the graves at Shipstern. There were little statues and carvings and a solid gold ax blade. They wanted $300 for the lot, and we didn't have it. Truth be told, I was a little nervous about smuggling that in, and from a graveyard, too.

Since we had lived in Panajachel before, we knew just where we wanted to stay, right in town in the house of Veggie Bob, who unfortunately would soon be known as Dead Bob due to some twist of fate, or maybe heart attack. There were four bedrooms in the house. Bob and his girlfriend lived in one, her two sons in another, and the other two were rented out. We were lucky enough to get one.

It was great to be back in town where we already knew people. Even though they might not be close friends yet, there were people we liked and could relate to, unlike the isolation of the jungle.

The first day in town, a few people from Bob's house piled in the car with us to ride through town down to the market and get supplies, fruits, veggies and tortillas, at least. As we were passing my old pal's restaurant, we saw English John on the porch and one of the guys in the back seat said, "Hey, stop. English John has acid and I want to get some."

Doug obligingly pulled over and John walked out to the car. He was expecting the order and gave our friend a hit of acid.

"How much do I owe you, mate?"

And John answered, "It's free."

Our guy said, "That's great, thanks!" and we started driving away.

John began running alongside the car yelling, "Man, it's free, it's free."

It's that Cockney accent. How were we supposed to know he meant three?

I played with baby Rasta all day, cooked and went to the market. In the early part of the day, a bunch of us, all from the USA, met down at the lake, on the beach. When the wind started picking up, as it did every afternoon, we went home, had lunch and took the traditional siesta.

Rasta was about five months old and the cutest, most agreeable baby. He was never fussy or sickly; he just nursed and slept and grew, like healthy babies do. I saw babies in Guatemala who were all shriveled and skinny, trying to nurse from gaunt, desiccated looking mothers. Rasta was a picture of health.

I was too, most of the time, but I had had a run-in from time to time with my ileocecal valve, which is what connects the small to large intestine in the lower right side of the abdomen and keeps matter moving in the right direction. On some people (me) it sometimes gets stuck, either open or closed. Nobody had ever told me what an easy fix it was, or how to fix it, which is to put your hands under it and pull up if its open and put your hands over it and push down, if it's stuck closed. Or maybe vice versa. Doesn't matter: since then, I push down then pull up, or vice versa, and it always corrects. I later learned to fix it from Rita, my body worker friend with a farm in PA. She knew more about the body than anyone else I'd ever met.

But this time, I didn't know what hit me. It was pre-dawn and I woke up screaming in pain. Doug ran and got Veggie Bob, and they bundled me and Rasta into Bob's van and drove up the mountain to the hospital in Solola. It's was a bad, twisty road back then. We passed a man carrying his wife to the hospital on a chair strapped to his back. Many people there are very poor. We hit a couple of really bad potholes because Bob was driving fast so I wouldn't die in his van, and he must have jarred that valve loose, because all of a sudden, it didn't hurt anymore.

I didn't want to just go home though. I wanted to find out what this was that could hurt so much. I had a lot more faith in that hospital than it warranted. They put me in a room alone on a table to wait for the doctor. It was freezing in there, so I asked Doug to find me a blanket and he found one folded up in the corner. When he opened it up, it was full of dried blood. Not drops of blood, but whole big dried up pools of blood, all crusted in the blanket. He folded it back up and we waited in the cold. When the doctor came in, he thought exploratory surgery was a good idea, since he didn't have a clue what had happened. I said, "I'll take my chances at home," and we decided to go back to Bob's.

Only Bob had already gone home. I was happy enough he had gotten me there, and I was really happy that I probably wasn't going to die that day. We got on the next public transport back down the mountain to Panajachel, a Suburban. Women holding babies got in the front with the driver. I think there were four of us with babies. Altogether, there were thirty two people in that vehicle, counting babies.

I used to talk about the way Guatemalans got on a bus as an example of how they weren't really thinkers. They would pile five, six, seven guys in one seat, all sitting on top of each other. Just the other day I found out from a travel blog that in Guatemala, bus tickets are sold by the seat, not per person. Those guys were traveling for close to nothing, and we were paying high dollar. Or high quetzal. Guess that makes us the not really smart ones!

For a week I treated myself with thick clay packs. Green clay was my one first aid kit in those days. I used it for cuts, sores, tooth abscesses. It was said to correct a breech birth! I'd mix up a batch of clay from the powder I carried and spread it across my abdomen about ½ inch thick. Within minutes it would be burning hot, pulling out the toxins. I started having black diarrhea that lasted about a week. I kept the clay packs up a few times a day, and after a while they didn't get so hot so fast, and then it was all over and I was ok again.

The English speaking doctor we knew in town came over to see me. He was so concerned that I was going to die at Bob's, because I was bona fide sick, but from what I'd seen in the hospital, I wasn't taking my chances with them. He wanted to take me to Guatemala City, but I didn't want any more to do with Guatemalan hospitals. He thought it might be appendicitis, which is also in the lower right quadrant, but it wasn't.

Sometime in all this, while I was lying around with clay on my belly, I met Johnny Starbuck. He should have his own book in my book, except we were never really together, like living together. We just got together sometimes in this crazy love affair that went on for years and years.

He remembers that we were sitting in a bar or restaurant down by the lake, and he was staring at me. As he romantically puts it, because he is a major romantic, he fell in love with me, staring at my eyes, and then, too late, realized, "Oh no, that's Doug's old lady!"

Johnny walked with a cane. He had fallen into a pyramid in Mexico and broken his neck and his hip. For about thirty years, nobody knew he had broken his neck,  which, given what I saw of the hospital at Solola, was probably a good thing. He gave himself ample tequila therapy, forcing himself to move his leg a little every day until he passed out, and after a couple of months, he could walk with a cane and went on to Guatemala, living on the lake and continuing his tequila therapy.

When I was a massage therapist years later, I saw the picture his friend Jason had taken of him lying in the hole in the bottom of the pyramid excavation. His neck was at an angle I instantly recognized as *wrong*, but everyone had always focused on his hip, including him. Around that time he went to a chiropractor for shoulder pain. Looking at his x-rays the doc said, "This probably goes back to when you broke your neck." Imagine hearing *that* for the first time

Oh my God, I had such a crush on him. He was so handsome and romantic. He worked for the Rolling Stones and gave me his staff t-shirt from the last tour he'd been on. I slept in it every day until someone stole it. He played with Rasta and threw him up and caught him, which may be where Rasta developed his love for heights and speed. He came to see me every day, and at night he prowled the town with Doug, looking for coke, while I snuggled with Rasta and went to sleep. We spent time together, just the two of us,  falling in ridiculous impossible love that had no consummation at all. It was so exciting and painful and compelling that way. Besides, I was with Doug, we were going back to the States, and Johnny needed to finish his healing and move on to the next adventure.

Finally it was time for all the fun and games to end. Doug needed to work. Johnny had an adventure up his sleeve, or in his roll bar, that I hope he'll write some time. We kissed goodbye and went our separate ways.

Woodstock in the late 70's

Once we left Central America and came back to the US, it was time to visit both sets of parents. After the way we'd been living, without electricity or running water, their houses were the Ritz. Everything was so easy! They had hot water from a tap, cold water you could drink without having to boil it first, indoor toilets and showers, electric lights, big kitchens with refrigerators full of good stuff, stoves you didn't have to light, TV's, comfy beds, washing machines and clothes dryers, paved roads, air conditioning, and at Doug's parents', beer from a keg in the corner of the kitchen. That was one of the things I had loved about Doug's family when I first met them, that they had this beer keg in the kitchen and sat around for hours, talking and drinking beer. I didn't drink beer or much of any other alcohol, but I had never seen a family do that, so I was in. I was always a sucker for a family that sat around and talked to each other.

Baby Rasta was a total hit. He was a great baby, cute and happy, smiling and laughing, just getting to that stage where he was more of a little person, less of a sleeping baby. We spent a few weeks with Doug's mom and dad in Peachtree City, GA, then drove our VW van to New York,

333

where we stayed with my mom and dad in Chappaqua. From there we moved on to Martine and DJ's house, in Woodstock, NY, a couple of hours away. I had lived with them in Atlanta when Jesse was a toddler, and now he was almost five years old.

Except for all the cigarette smoking, so popular in those days, life in the Martine and DJ household was wonderful. Martine, a very tidy and excellent French chef, didn't mind Rasta playing in the pots and pans, and set up an area just for him. Jesse loved to race him around in his little wheelie walker. They had all these talented friends who were either famous, or soon to be: John Sebastian of the Lovin' Spoonful and his gorgeous wife Catherine, actor Brad Dourif and Janice, his musician wife, singer/songwriter Eric Anderson and his girlfriend Zona, blues great Paul Butterfield and the guys from The Band. Woodstock was full of musicians, artists, photographers. DJ was in the music business, managing and promoting people as he had done for years, and Martine cooked amazing delicious meals for whoever was there, every night.

Doug got a job eventually at Bearsville Studios designing and building the first digital sound control module that synched all the analog equipment together for recording. This made it simple to control sixty-four tracks of audio for the first time. If he had been another kind of person, we would have been millionaires, but he didn't know how to finish things, explain things, or definitely market anything. He was a coke snorting engineer, a science savant. He knew the shit out of how things worked, but if he tried to explain it, he got so tangled up in the intricacies and details that I'd either fall asleep or leave the room. He read schematics for bedtime reading, a clue to his personality.

We moved around and stayed with different people. We had our VW van, but with baby Rasta and it being fall and chilly, we really liked being inside. Of course, it was a lot to ask, staying with other people, but mostly it was fun and

334

easy. Marsha and David, my friends from Brooklyn and Formentera, lived in a farmhouse out in Kerhonkson, about a half hour out of Woodstock across the Ashokan Reservoir. David got over having us there after a week or so and made it clear that we should find somewhere else to stay. He was a friend of Glenn's from Brooklyn College, and they were part of that whole Park Slope gang when I lived there with Glenn, before we got on the freighter. They were the first people I knew who moved out of NY to eastern PA, around Stroudsburg and the Delaware Water Gap where we used to all go visit them on their farm and smoke hash and pat the donkey who came with the place.

I knew Susan Towlson and Nicole Wills from Delaware Water Gap, from the health food store. Now they lived in Willow, a teeny bump on the road outside Woodstock. They rented rooms in a big old farmhouse that belonged to Alice Wise. We sometimes stayed there but we never got our own room or lived there. We were definitely drop-ins. Nicole's boyfriend Jim Collier, who played killer guitar and wrote songs like "Nightshift" was this gorgeous volatile sweetheart. He and Nicole performed together in the local clubs, singing great harmonies. Roly (Rowland) Salley who wrote Killing the Blues, was there with Alice. They were all well-known on the local scene, which I knew precious little about since I was usually busy being a mommy, and I hardly ever went out at night.

We moved around, staying here and there, sometimes back at Martine and DJ's, until finally, Doug and I figured we were staying in the area awhile and needed to find a house of our own. Around this time, Doug took off for somewhere, probably Belize to check on the boat, or maybe GA to check on his family, or maybe just down to New York City for a job. I went to a party at the neighbors' house, just down the road from Alice's. They told me about a cool house, "Uptown" it was called, right up the hill from them, and it was empty. I think the owner, Whitter, was at the party. He told me to go ahead and move in. "I'll get in touch soon and we can set up an agreement and sign a lease." He wanted $300 a month. Doable.

Whitter never got in touch. He had just bought this house, and he never got in touch all winter. I tried once or twice to call him, but I never heard back, so we just lived there and kept it warm and kept the water from freezing. It was a big old cold house with a wood stove, up a driveway so steep that even the six-wheel-drive snow plow guy couldn't get up it once winter set in. Susan left Alice's and moved in. When it got really cold Doug took off for Belize with his very adorable young friend, Woodstock native JP Paturel. Susan and I kept the home fires burning, best we could. JP had never been to Belize and he and Doug were just going to sail around and eat fish and be warm until the spring came. I'm sure to a guy who had spent all his twenty-something winters in Woodstock, that sounded mighty good.

I wasn't going back to Belize because Doug was a *terrible* sailor and I hated living on the boat. I was willing to put up with freezing cold and heating with wood rather than ride around in a sailboat with a baby, searching for fresh water and watching out for scorpions.

One cold, snowy afternoon Susan and I were trying to cut wood with this fucking gigantic chainsaw, the only one we had, when Jim and Nicole walked up the driveway and started laughing. Obviously, we weren't doing too great a job. Jim said, "Go inside, stay warm, I'll do this..." and cut us a huge pile of firewood that he and Nicole then stacked on the porch! They were pretty amazing. First of all, hearing them sing together was beautiful, and then they were beautiful to look at and always having a much more exciting life than I was. I remember them going out in a snowstorm to hear someone play music, sliding their old Volvo off the road and walking home through the snow. I was enthralled with them. She was so beautiful and so totally herself, and Jim was gorgeous and funny and kind.

I had met Nicole years before when Patrick and I lived in Delaware Water Gap and she lived on a farm nearby with Peter Coyote, way before he became famous and Buddhist. At that time, she seemed unapproachable. I would see her drifting into the Health Food Store where I worked, looking all manner of ethereal, while I was up to my arm pits in pizza dough and granola. I heard people did heroin up at that farm, which surely accounted for the way they floated through the world while I sweated through pizza and granola production in front of a scorching six foot tall pizza oven.

Now, in Woodstock, Nicole and I became friends. She inspired me with her singing and I was awed by her ability to harmonize, which she attributed to being deaf in one ear. It's true that if I hold one ear closed, I can get closer to harmonizing, but I'm still really bad at it. I learned two songs from her I still sing today, "Roly Poly, Daddy's Little Fatty," from Bob Wills, and "Put Your Sweet Lips a Little Closer to the Phone," from Jim Reeves.

If the snow plow guy with his six wheel drive vehicle couldn't make it up the driveway, we sure couldn't. We had an old Volkswagen hood that we'd drag down the hill and stash at the bottom of the drive. Then we'd get in the car we left parked down there on the edge of the road and go to town. Susan usually kept a pair of decent boots in the car so she'd look less country when we got to town, but I didn't even bother. Carrying Rasta was what I could manage. We'd do our rounds, drive to the bottom of the driveway, pile Rasta and all our groceries on the VW hood and drag it up that long hill home. I bought one bottle of wine at a time, believe you me. I loved when men were coming over.
They could drag a lot more. It was almost a full time job to

live in that house; it took so much wood to keep it warm, which was exactly Doug's point about building a boat.

Whitter finally surfaced in the spring, telling me I owed him for the last eight or nine months of rent, but I just laughed. I didn't have that kind of money, or much of any other kind, either. We re-negotiated. It was a good summer house, but really tough in the cold.

Doug also surfaced in the spring when he came back to work at Bearsville Studios. I'm not sure how I was supposed to support baby Rasta and myself, but thankfully Bernard, my old friend from Ibiza who had taken lots of acid to practice dying, was now living in Colombia. He started sending me magazines with coke in them under another name, and that was how we made it through the winter. I'd take this absolutely pure coke to people I knew did it all the time, but they didn't even know it was good! They were so used to coke that was cut with speed or baby laxative that gave it a burn or made you run for the bathroom. When they tried this smooth pure high, they couldn't recognize it. But it sustained us for the winter until Doug came back and we made up and he went back to work at the studio.

That was the winter I was hanging out with Paul Butterfield. I had met him several times over dinners at Martine and DJ's. He was funny, handsome, smart and of course already a famous musician. When I was in college I had taken acid and sat on the roof of my friend's apartment in Roxbury, a suburb of Boston, banging a tambourine, probably annoying what were fabulously tolerant neighbors, listening to "Paul Butterfield, East West." Now I was sleeping with the great man himself! (He'd laugh, for sure.)

The first night we went down to the Bear Cafe to meet Martine and DJ, Albert Grossman, Paul's manager and friend, head of Bearsville Records, owner of the Bear, and bona fide Godfather of the whole area, was sitting in the entranceway. He was talking to Martine when we arrived, Paul and I with baby Rasta on my hip.

Albert looked at me and my baby. It might have been the first time I was in there, and certainly the first time with Paul. He gave Paul the quintessentially Albert quizzical look, like, "What's up *here?*"

Without missing a beat, Paul shot back, "Slow night in Detroit."

Martine says the looks on my face and Albert's were enough to knock her off her bar stool, laughing. I had actually met Paul years earlier, when Patrick and I were living with Lonnie and Maj on their farm in New Jersey. We were out in Newton, in the still very rural western part of the state, and we got a call from DJ that Paul was going to be playing in Paramus, NJ with Stevie Wonder, a double bill. Did we want to go? Where does a bear shit, exactly?

That night we piled into whatever car we took and headed to Paramus. It took us about two hours to get there, what with country roads and all, even though New Jersey is a teeny small state. It was probably around eight or nine when we got there, and Stevie was on or just going on. DJ took us back to the (shared) dressing room and pulled out a huge joint of absolutely blow your cells out weed. We'd been smoking that gentle Pennsylvania homegrown for months and this was some serious shit. Sort of like the hyper-engineered weed these days.

We all sat around talking and smoking this joint, listening to Stevie from backstage, like we had the radio on. Stooooooopid, right, to miss that show!? That's what getting stoned can do. It was at least 11 pm, maybe later, when Stevie finished his set and it was time for Paul to go on. He and DJ and the band left to go set things up, Lonnie, Maj and Patrick left to see Paul's show, and I could not move. I mean *could not!* I was just too stoned to move, even though I watched them go. I probably said, "I'll be there in a minute," or something because they just left me there, sitting in a comfortable chair, all by myself.

339

All the white people left the dressing room and it started to fill with black people, all Stevie's people, who kind of did a double-take at this white chick sitting right on the entrance chair waiting for her spaceship to come collect her. They'd just look, hmmph, and go into the room and talk. Suddenly there was silence. Stevie had entered the space.

He came in and stopped right smack dab in front of me. For those of you who have lived in a space pod, Stevie is completely blind. I looked up and there he was, weaving and bobbing in that way he has, reading the energy. It was so intense. Apparently I wasn't a threat because he moved on after a minute or so, but all that energy was all it took! I shot out of my seat and went to find my friends and watch Paul's show. I don't remember a bit of it, but I'll never forget the

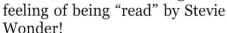

feeling of being "read" by Stevie Wonder!

Paul and I had fun times and fun dates. When I read about him now, it's all how he was such a drug addict and degenerate, but that was not what I experienced. He did drink a lot, well, a lot more than me, but nothing else. Beer, tequila and cigarettes. I guess either the reports are off (although he is reported to have died of an overdose) or I just didn't realize what was going on.

Woodstock had a wonderful macrobiotic restaurant for a little while, and I went there with Paul and Brad Dourif one night for dinner. Paul was a traditional macrobiotic's nightmare. Breakfast was fried hotdogs and Miller High Life and dinner was often steak and tequila and Miller High Life, all of it punctuated with Pall Malls, smoked with abandon throughout meals or whenever the mood struck.

They rolled with the macrobiotic food just fine. It was grains and vegetables, all tasty and well prepared. That was the night Paul wrote the song about me, "Millet Eatin' Mama," while we waited for our dinner. It was all about gruel and granola, and then they asked for coffee. They were sorry, the waiter said, but they didn't have coffee. Perhaps they would like a cup of bancha tea. Ok, right, they were being agreeable.

For anyone who doesn't know about macrobiotics, it's about balancing yin and yang, so the idea with the diet is to eat the most balanced foods, not try to balance foods on the extremes, like red meat on one end of the spectrum, and sugar and alcohol on the other. I'll pose the possibility that people who eat steak but drink tequila with it are creating a balance of sorts, but it's not the calm kind of balance macrobiotics are looking for. All that to say, there was no sugar. None on the table, and probably none in the whole restaurant.

When the bancha tea came, which is a twig tea that probably tasted like twigs to the guys, they reached for the container with brown powder on the table and  heaped in the salty sesame condiment, thinking it was brown sugar. I just laughed. This was a familiar world to me. I had been so strictly macrobiotic in Paris, Morocco, all the time I was with Patrick. I could have been more educational about it, but I knew they weren't going there again. It definitely wasn't their kind of food. In fact, it wasn't most of Woodstock's kind of food because the restaurant only lasted a few months, even though it was really good.

For someone who worked at Bearsville Studios, Doug didn't make it sound very glamorous. There were lot of big names who came through to record, and I remember meeting all the Stones one time when they were there for a week. As far as Doug was concerned, his job was to make people sound better. He told me once, "They're all screechers."

I mostly stayed home, cooked, made bread, grew gardens and played with Rasta. Susan worked at different restaurants as a cook. She made an omelette for Albert Grossman one time and he was not pleased with it, because it was browned, and a proper French omelette is never browned. According to Susan, "Albert went home and got his omelette pan, came back, showed me how he wanted it done and then stood over my shoulder while I practiced making eggs. He kept asking me to throw them in the trash 'til I got it right, a proper French omelette." She looked at me in total disgust, "Albert Grossman would eat dog shit with croutons on it, and he's got the nerve to complain that his omelette is a little browned!" Albert was the head of Bearsville Studios and everything else in the area. If there was a Godfather, he was the man.

One of Susan's jobs was cooking for the different bands that stayed at the "barn" at Bearsville Studios. Obviously it was a barn that was nicely fixed up for all sorts of bands, including the Stones. Susan would go over there in the afternoon and prepare a feast of delicious food, and leave it for the band when they finished recording. The next day when she went back, the food would still be sitting there, untouched. Cocaine.

Doug, a great lover of cocaine anyway, often didn't get home from work until dawn, or past dawn. Everyone was doing coke. Susan reminds me of this terrible little event: she and I both had female dogs. Her dog, Raven, had one beautiful adorable puppy named Wally. My slut of a dog, Lily, who was the second stupidest dog I ever had after Buck the Malamute, had twelve puppies when she gave birth. I think I gave her, and those puppies, back. She was a terrible dog who went to the neighbors' and stole groceries as they were unloading their car, things like that.

Wally went down to the main road, all the way down the hill, and got hit by a car and killed. All the dogs were down there that day, but unfortunately it was Wally's time. The kids came up screaming, and Doug buried him in a corner of the yard where the ground was soft.

The next morning, I had to go wake Doug up from his coma of sleep to rebury the dog, 'cause the other dogs were digging him up. Nicole's son Jeremiah was with us then, Martine's son Jesse might have been there, and all the kids were screaming with horror, "They're digging up Wally! They're digging up Wally!" Poor Doug got up after just being asleep about two hours and started digging and probably throwing up too, but he was the kind of man not given to complaining. If you could get him there, he'd do the job.

When winter started coming around again, I rented a little cabin, just for a few months. I couldn't face the cold at Whitter's again. That house was about impossible to heat, even when we closed off as many rooms as we could. Jim and Nicole had just moved out of the cabin: there was a huge old potbellied stove in the living room, and Nicole had left a beaver's tail in the rafters of the front porch. She collected animal parts, wings and tails and the like. Rasta was over a year old; Doug was headed back to Belize for the winter again, and Johnny Starbuck, friend from Panajachel, called. He was on tour with Dave Mason and they had a Christmas break. He wanted to come to Woodstock and spend the week with me and baby Rasta. I was thrilled.

Johnny and I had stayed in touch, but hadn't seen each other before this. He was flying in to New York on his band break and would take the bus up to Kingston, where I went to pick him up. When I did, it was snowing, and first things first, he needed a pair of boots.

We went into Woodstock to the boot and shoe store, a narrow little place, and who was there but Paul Butterfield.

Paul was known all over the world for his Chicago blues, but in Woodstock he could wander around with relative impunity, like all the other famous people. It was obvious he wanted to know who this guy was I was with. Paul was a cool guy, funny as shit and obviously a great musician, but I knew Johnny was only there for a short time and I really didn't want to share that time. Still and all, I leaned over to Johnny and whispered, "Hey, you want to meet Paul Butterfield?"

"Shit, yeah!" He knew all about Paul, and they hit it off right from the get. It was a beautiful thing, too, because years later, when Johnny was living in the Chateau Marmont, the L.A. hotel where John Belushi died, trying to kill himself slowly with vodka and coke and whatever else, Paul saved his life. He saw his name on the guest register, called him up, invited him to his room on the pretext of listening to his latest recording, and kept him there for three days until Johnny came down enough to get right enough to quit killing himself. It's a terrible shame Paul wasn't able to do the same for himself. He was only forty four when he died in 1987.

One time a woman came to Woodstock telling everyone she was a powerful witch. Paul heard about it, that all these people were afraid of her and didn't want to piss her off, so he made a point of finding out where she was going to be and showing up. Walking up to her as she held forth on her powers -- and this story is straight from his mouth -- he told her, "I'm gonna make you itch, witch." He wasn't afraid of witches and curses and shit he thought was just nonsense. But then, he drank a lot, was Irish, and played the blues. Or is that all one thing?

Johnny and Rasta and I slept up in the loft and heated that little cabin with that big old wood stove. It got hot as hell in there. After Johnny left, I sat in the kitchen every day and wrote my first book, a handwritten manual for life on the road called Footloose and Free, still unpublished, while Rasta played on the floor with his toys or took naps. It wasn't bad living alone. I still had that big stupid dog Lilly, so I hadn't returned her yet, and it was kind of magical in the little cabin, even after Johnny went back on tour.

He'd call me at night from wherever he was, and we'd fall asleep still on the phone until one of us woke up and hung up. That was when you used to pay for long distance calls by the minute. Ouch. It had to cost him a bundle.

At one point he invited me and Rasta to travel with him on Dave Mason's tour. It was February, so of course Doug was still in Belize. Why not??? Martine and Jesse drove us to an airfield in New York to get on the private jet they had for the tour. I was lookin' really good, I thought, and as we were driving, with the sun streaming in the window at just the right angle, little Jesse piped up from the back seat, "Gee Sukoshi, you have a moustache!" I still think about that when I want to laugh at a vain moment.

We flew to Boston where they did a show, and then it snowed so hard we had to go by limo to Springfield for the next show because the plane couldn't fly. I was moderately disappointed because I had never been in a private jet before, and it was great to be so deluxe. But we had to switch to cars, with all the snow.

We were traveling in three limos in a row, and at one point on the Mass Pike we stopped at a convenience store or gas station. Dave Mason was in the car in front of ours and I saw him get out of his limo and go inside. Suddenly, our door opened and he handed Rasta a little toy rabbit he had bought. It was known for years as Dave Mason Rabbit until it fell apart. Dave and his beautiful girlfriend were so polite and considerate of everyone on the tour; I was touched and impressed by that. She could have been a prima donna, since it was her boyfriend's tour, but instead she was always getting stuff for people and making sure they were comfortable.

I loved Dave Mason's music, but mostly I sat backstage and nursed Rasta or talked to people because up near the music was no place for a baby. It was too loud. After a week, I was happy to go home to my little cabin, exhausted. I know guys on the road don't generally travel with babies, so that may have had a lot to do with it, but I was so tired from living in a different room every night and packing and unpacking and moving every day. Johnny stayed on the tour for months, calling me from here and there, but that did it for me as far as the romance of life on the road was concerned.

When spring came, Doug came home and we moved back to Whitter's house with Susan. According to my journal, on May 22, 1978, I woke up and it was snowing. There were a couple of inches of white fluffy snow on the sweet young tree buds, and I began to cry. Oh please, no more winter! Doug came in to console me, things took their course, and Pablo was conceived. I knew it the second it happened. Doug and I had our problems and we didn't know how to resolve  them, but we had just conceived our second child together. For better or for worse, we were staying together. I sat in a room at my parents' house in Chappaqua and wrote a letter to Johnny. I told him I'd always love him but I was pregnant and I was staying with Doug. I even used Carly Simon's lyrics: "What did you need to know, don't you know I'll always be your girl...." I said he was a romantic, but I was just as bad. For years, he was in my life like that. Even if I was with someone else, I was always his girl, or wanted to be. Geeze.

Woodstock to Belize to Georgia:
Welcome to Planet Earth Pablo

Summer in Willow and Woodstock was great. For one thing, it was finally warm after a typically brutal Northern winter. We lay out in the pale Northern sun, trying to get tan but at least getting hot. One summer day I was hanging out with Nicole. She had on a tight sexy little sundress and espadrille heels. She looked super-hot, as in sexy, not sweaty. I was probably in a bikini, or some lumpy hippy dress and Earth shoes.

"How do I look?" she asked.

"You look great, but those clothes don't look all that comfortable," was what I told her.

With a look of loving scorn, Nicole told me, "You don't dress like this to be comfortable!"

I never really did get that memo. Years ago I decided to wear clothes I could sleep in, and most of the time, I still do.

There were dinner parties and daytime garden and swimming parties, swimming in the Esopus River, trips to see our friend Rita in PA, fresh food from everyone's garden and carrot juices and smoothies at Sunfrost Farms. But as it always does in that part of the country, in the Catskill Mountains of New York, signs of winter begin to show as early as late September, when that frost gets on the pumpkin and it's once again time to get out of Dodge. Of course, the official start of winter in Woodstock back then was when the people at Sunfrost lined their roadside with jack-o-lanterns glowing on Halloween night and left for the Yucatan to dive all winter. Good idea.

We got an early start, heading south in early September, 1978, to Georgia and Western North Carolina, via Rita and Bill Goodwin's farm in the Poconos. Rita was really Susan and Marsha's friend more than mine, but I adored and pretty much idolized her. She was a brilliant body worker, doing massage and energy work way before it got trendy, way before anyone else I knew was doing it. She had studied shiatsu in New York with the great Japanese Masters and worked on celebrity musicians and movie stars. All the while she was this earthy little buzz saw of a woman. Her big farmhouse was always impeccably neat; meals from her huge organic garden were delicious, and she  seemed to get everything done with minimal effort and fuss.

Her husband Bill began his career as a jazz drummer playing with Charles Lloyd. In 1974 and for the next forty years, Bill played in the Phil Woods Quartet. In the jazz world, he was very well known. One time I went to a summer party at their farm where everyone famous in the New York jazz world was taking turns jamming on the porch. Keith Jarrett was there playing the piano, and I think Jack deJohnette was there taking turns with Bill on the drums. Bob Dorough was surely there, since he was a neighbor, close friend and inventive musician. I didn't know anything at all about jazz even though toward the end of my college "career"

348

I was hanging around in Greenwich Village for a spell with Charles Lloyd and his wife, who took me under their protective wings as best they could. I had no idea at the time that Charles had just been named "Jazz Artist of the Year" for 1967. When I look back at myself in those days, I seem so precariously perched between Earth and eternity. I didn't *particularly* want to die, most of the time, but I wasn't very connected to living, either. Lots of wonderful, brilliant people were kind to me and helped me through, for which I don't even know how to thank them except to say it here.

But here I was, pregnant again. One thing I was emphatic about: I was *never* going to have another baby in Sarteneja. We hear a lot about "the N word," and usually it means something else, but there's the other N word: never. It's almost a guarantee.

Susan travelled with us down to Georgia, following along in her own old VW bug with her trusty dog Raven by her side. That's the time we decided to take a new route we'd never tried, and came through the mountains in eastern Tennessee and western North Carolina on "the Tail of the Dragon," a curvy twisty road prized by bikers. By the time we got to the bottom, we were green. In North Carolina we visited Michele and Robert Boone at their old wooden farmhouse in the mountains outside Hayesville. Michele was a midwife assistant, working with a local doctor, Dr. Jim, and his band of intrepid midwives who performed home births. I was banking on that, a nice sweet home birth back in the USA after a few warm months in Belize. Michele told me I could stay with them and have the baby when the time came, which would be the beginning of March, best anyone could figure.

We had a plan for this trip to Belize. We were going to be in business, sort of. In Sarteneja in those days, the fisherman all used canvas sails sewn by their wives on treadle sewing machines. There were multiple disadvantages to this, mainly due to the weight of the canvas. When it got

349

wet, it could pull a boat right over, since it weighed a ton. It took a long time to dry, and for that reason was prone to mildew and rot. And for the women to sew it was a huge effort. Pregnant women were cautioned not to sew anything heavy with those treadle machines because of the risk of miscarriage, and of course they had to use treadle machines because there was no electricity in the village. What everyone needed, sailors and sewers alike, was lighter, durable material that would hold up for sails, shed water and dry quickly.

Dacron was the answer. Lo and behold, that was one of the main products of the company my dad worked for, DHJ Industries. Only problem was, if we just carried it down to Belize, the import tax would be huge. So I lied when I said earlier that I only ever smuggled hashish and Buddhas. Doug and I became Dacron smugglers.

Visiting Peaches and Howard again, we got our travel gear together there in Peachtree City. We bought a truck with a camper shell and built two huge three hundred yard rolls of Dacron into the bed. It was kind of lumpy sleeping, but it was doable. We were off, Doug driving and me amusing Rasta, who was just over two years old, with a healthy two year old boy's curiosity and energy. Thankfully, we didn't pick up Scotty this time as he was incarcerated.

When we crossed into Mexico, at the immigration station, we all went inside to show our passports while they searched the truck outside. I must have closed my eyes for about one second and Rasta was gone. Jesus y Maria!!!!! I had recently seen "Midnight Express," which had just come out, so I was paranoid as hell about foreign countries and borders. I became frantic. My baby had been stolen!!!!!! A very long minute or two later, he came walking out of the back office holding the hand of a giant guard who had taken him in and given him his very first lollipop. This was so fucked up in a couple directions, first being, who takes somebody's child away????? (Not to mention giving him sugar, which I was *never* going to do.) But this was Mexico, and that guy was the law. It occurred to me it might be imprudent to scream at him for taking my child away without asking, especially since he was three times my size and well-armed, so I gave an insincere smile and took Rasta's hand. Here I was so worried we'd get caught smuggling cloth, I had no idea how freaked out I could be in those minutes before Rasta reappeared, all smiles. I breathed again.

We made it to Sarteneja, sleeping on our lumpy bed at night, choosing to sweat in the heat rather than open a window to the swarms of mosquitoes beating against the light. The people in the village were thrilled to buy Dacron from us. We charged them a really fair price. If we'd been legit and paid the tariff we would have had to double or triple it, but we'd gotten the Dacron super cheap, and all we wanted was to make enough money to live on for the next couple of months. At the Sarteneja level, cooking for ourselves and living in our camper, this was pretty low budget. Tortillas, avocados and coconuts were pennies apiece. Lobster tails, for the big splurge dinners, were about fifty cents each from the fishermen when they first came in, before they took their catch down to the co-op to be weighed and frozen.

I hated Sarteneja: The mosquitos. The fact that we couldn't get out of there without the boat. That there were no other foreigners there to hang out with and talk to. It's not that I was elitist or anything, but village women had such simple lives. There wasn't much philosophy involved, not much thinking or awareness of anything happening in the "outside world." Not much awareness that there was an outside world. Honestly, after you've birthed and nursed and raised ten kids, I get how you might not be much into anything very complicated. It was a village somewhat short on philosophers, except the babbling old rum drunks.

Rasta had a plastic wind-up choo-choo train. It was pretty cool. You wound it up with a big plastic key that stuck out the side, and it chugged around in a circle, making choo-choo sounds. The coolest part was that it was clear plastic, so all the gears inside that made it move were visible. The first day we brought it out, people started gathering in the yard to watch it. Pretty soon half the village was there watching this plastic train. They had never seen anything like it. The fishermen looked so delighted, watching the gears go round and round.

They had never seen a stroller. I had brought a really light umbrella stroller, and the kids all wanted rides in it. Then they wanted to push each other in it. Pretty soon it was a wreck from jamming over the rocky ground at top speed with a too heavy kid in it. There was no way I was going to make them stop having all that fun.

The little girls liked to have tea parties. They got metal can lids out of the trash piles to use for plates. I was particularly fond of one little girl, Isela. She had never had a doll, so I made her one, a simple cloth doll with yarn hair and button eyes and pieces of cloth tied on for a dress and a shawl. She seemed to love her, and two days later, I saw her with the doll, all dirty and messed up. She must have liked her better that way.

Our medicine chest and our "cosmetics" were a source of some awe. At the time we were big fans of Rachel Perry lip balm, which came in flavors like coconut and pineapple. We had little tins of it in the camper, probably just a few of them, but Estere, a young teenage girl, was crazy about it. She ate at least one full tin, loving the fruity greasiness of it. Doug wanted her to stop, so he filled a tin of mandarin orange, one of her favorites, with Tiger Balm. She never stole another bit of it.

They stole everything small they could. They took Rasta's matchbox cars and our Rachel Perry lip balm. I don't remember missing money, but we didn't have much cash and that would have been serious. As it was, these were just kids wanting things they had never seen or heard of before.

There were stories in the village where you knew life was really hard. The woman behind us had birthed *seventeen* children, nine of whom had lived. She was very poor and her husband was not helpful. I can't remember if he was an abuser, or just a drunk. She was lost and crazy-looking, but who the hell wouldn't be? Combine seventeen cases of postpartum-depression with grief with poor nutrition with poverty and it was a sad case indeed.

Other women dealt with abusive husbands, most of whom drank rum. The rum was very cheap and tasted like gasoline. You could buy a bottle for about a dollar. As our friend Agnes would say, "That first glass is so hard to get down." In the hands of a mean drunk, a machete, the all-purpose do-everything tool, became a weapon. I heard of women beaten with the flat of it. I also heard of machete murders and choppings, but that was a whole 'nother category that didn't happen in our village, that I knew of.

Since I didn't want to stay in Sarteneja with the relentless mosquitos and limited conversation, we sailed down to Caye Caulker where we had stayed when Rasta was a little baby and our parents came to visit. Back then we had rented the biggest three bedroom house on the island, so that our parents could be really comfortable. Unfortunately, it was summer, the breeze quit blowing, and the "sand flies" were out. Even though the house was totally screened, those little bastards squeezed through the openings and stung us all night long. On the third morning, my father, Bert, announced we were moving to San Pedro, fourteen miles or a couple of hours' sail north. San Pedro is much nicer, and is now quite the tourist destination. Then it was a sleepy little village with just a few houses. I sure do wish we had bought one, or talked my dad into buying one, but we didn't have the money and that was definitely not his style.

When the parents were visiting, we got a nice second floor place to stay. No mosquitos. It was both my parents, Peaches, Doug, Rasta and me. I loved being in San Pedro in a nice place with a shower and electricity and fans and real beds, but once the parents left, we were back to basic living. That was back in the summer of 1976, when Rasta was just a couple of months old.

This time, in the fall of 1978, we rented a little place in Caye Caulker from an American woman who was married to a Belizean and had a little boy Rasta's age named Simi. They played together most days as I tried to keep him covered from the sun and unbitten by the tropical bugs who loved his soft pale skin. Mine, too.

Doug left me alone quite a bit. He always had something going on somewhere else. Agnes had driven down with us from Georgia, supposedly to be my assistant, Rasta's babysitter, and company for me. Truth be told, once she got a taste of cheap rum and native boys, or native rum and cheap boys, sometimes I didn't see her for days. I was moving into feeling quite pregnant, feeling very alone, and I was afraid. My experience of birthing with Rasta had been so traumatic; I didn't want to do that again, no way.

One night Rasta and I walked over to a local woman's house to have dinner. There were a couple of women in the village who made a big dinner every night and for a very nominal fee you could eat fish and rice and veggies, usually cooked with fresh grated coconut and very tasty. We were sitting out on her second story porch with five or six other tourists and of course we all started talking to each other, since we were all at the same big picnic table.

The woman across from me looked very familiar. It took a minute to realize she was Sandy, Louie's old girlfriend we had traveled with in Japan. She looked gorgeous, with her signature long flowing red hair and her lithe dancer's body. She told me she was working as a nude model for a guy named Mr. Tie, a performance artist in New York. She went to the East Village with him, got naked, and he tied her up in men's neckties. Of all the things I have forgotten, this is one that really stuck with me.

On the way home, holding little Rasta's hand, I began to cry. I felt so alone, and afraid of the birth coming up. He looked up at me and said, "Don't worry Mama, I'll take care of you." He was two years old. He still called me Mama then, before he started calling me Sukoshi. He was the only one there for me.

At some point we went back to Sarteneja, with Agnes, too. I was due in the beginning of March, if I counted right. We had time. I went to the town phone and called Michele in North Carolina, but she didn't answer. The phone just rang and rang. That was weird, since back then just about everybody had an answering machine. Little did I know that Michele had emptied out her woodstove, left the ashes in the wrong place, and her house had burned to the ground.

But no matter, because unlike his brother, who came late, Pablo decided to get born early and get it over with. It was a funny night. Doug and Agnes had gone over to Corozol Town to call his mother -- the Sarteneja village phone hadn't worked in days. If it was windy or too wet, the phone just didn't work. Our new sailing friends English Geoffrey and his girlfriend Bobbi, a half-German half-Aboriginal Australian, were at our place for dinner, along with Sam, a long lanky Belizean, and Claudia, his German girlfriend. It was a veritable UN.

Bobbi made a delicious chicken curry. The guys had been amusing Rasta, who finally fell asleep in his hammock. The *second* he did, my water broke, all over the place. Oh shit. I was still thinking we had time to go back to the States! Guess not. I sent Claudia and Sam and Geoffrey out for diapers, baby clothes, and a midwife, while Bobbi stayed to help me. I had to poop. No two ways about it, and the outhouse was too far away and out of the question. I had Bobbi help me down to the water, between two boats, because I could barely walk on my own. She was a nervous wreck, "Are you sure it's not the baby?"

"Bobbi, I think I know the difference between taking a shit and having a baby," I told her, not remembering at the time that my own mother didn't when I arrived.

When we got back inside and I started having contractions, she looked at me so worriedly. "Oh my God, I hope it's not the curry!"

Just as I was reassuring her that this had started months ago, way before the curry, Geoff showed up with the cutest, teeniest little Mayan midwife. She was wearing a white nurse dress because she was just walking home from delivering her three hundred fiftieth baby! She had never delivered a gringa's baby before so she was kind of excited by the prospect. She told me to rest; she was going home to get her birthing kit refreshed and she'd come back in a couple hours.

It rapidly became obvious we didn't have a couple hours. Someone went to fetch her, and she came in with her birthing kit: three cotton balls, a piece of string, and a washcloth for mopping her brow. Good thing we had scissors. And boiling water. And sheets and towels.

Sam and Claudia were over in a corner making out. I told them to get out; they were distracting me. Soon I had to tell Bobbi that if she didn't stop saying, "Oh my" every breath I took, she was going to have to get out, too. She promised to pull herself together.

It was about 11:20 p.m. when I gave my first little wimpy half-hearted push. "I wish someone else could do this," I told the room. There were no takers. Geoffrey held my hand and looked into my eyes, and then I closed them and pushed one big huge push and there was Pablo, all blue and silent. 11:25 pm, February 11, 1979, my parent's wedding anniversary. Bobbi uttered a huge, "Oh my!"

"Is it a boy or a girl?" I asked. The midwife said, "Shhhh," and I realized I didn't care. She stroked his spine gently, and then he began to breathe and turned all pink. It was the birth I had dreamed of, except for the hard work pushing part. No tearing, no screaming, nothing like before.

The next morning when Rasta woke up, he popped his head over the edge of his hammock and looked down at us on the bed, which was a mattress on the floor. "Look who showed up last night!" I showed him his baby brother. He gave a maniacal grin and climbed down to check him out.

We were snuggling on the mattress on the floor with Pablo when I heard the family talking on the other side of the wall we had in common: "How come the gringa has her baby in one hour and our daughter has been waiting in the hospital for a month?"

I had an opinion on that. I thought it might just be because I ate natural healthy food instead of living on white bread and canned margarine and out-of- date Bama peanut butter and jelly. I also thought my activity level -- walking and swimming and doing yoga instead of sitting around packing on the pounds with junk food -- might have something to do with it. But hey, what do I know? I'm not a doctor. Lots of the village women and young girls went over to the hospital in Corozol Town to have their babies in the hospital.

Later that afternoon, Doug and Agnes came back. She couldn't look me in the eye, so I figured they had been up to something she didn't feel too good about, which she later confirmed for me, maybe at Doug's memorial! I didn't care much at the moment. I had just had a baby and I was suddenly twice as busy, with both Rasta and Pablo to look after. Geoffrey and Sam had come by earlier and gotten Rasta to go play with a new toy boat they bought him, figuring I needed a break. And the midwife came twice a day.

357

This was a really cool part of birthing in the village. I don't remember the Government Nurse coming to see Rasta at home more than once, but until Pablo's umbilical cord fell off, the midwife came every day, twice a day. It took eleven days! Every day she gave him a bath and massaged him with the local coconut oil. Then she massaged my back and shoulders. I was ready to get out the super glue and keep that thing on there! And the cost of all this, for you folks who wonder such things? We bought her a raincoat with matching umbrella and rain boots. She was so stoked!!! Honestly, that's all she wanted. She was sixty-six years old and the sweetest woman. I loved watching her with Pablo.

The funny thing was that Pablo had colic. And I don't mean "funny" like fall down laughing, because for several hours every evening he would scream in pain. You'd think, or I'd think, given the gentleness of his birth, he'd be all ok, and that Rasta, who had the rough birth, would have had colic. But I think it came from all my worry during this pregnancy. The first time, I didn't know what to worry about, so I didn't.

The good news was Peaches was coming soon to help me out. Doug had first called her to say we were coming back, but the village phone started working so he called again after he came back and found out Pablo was already born. Communications were an ordeal back then, for sure. In any case, Peaches was coming, which was great.

My own mother, Gaham, had never been much help in the child birthing, child rearing department. All three of us kids had nannies and au pairs from the time we were born. She was *not* a down-to-earth mom like Peaches, who basically taught me everything I knew about raising my kids. I was so happy and relieved that she was coming. Bobbi and Agnes were supposed to be helping me, but basically they drank rum most of the time. Even though they were both sweet as could be they definitely were not the nanny help I needed. Even during the birthing process, I spent nearly as much energy calming Bobbi down as I did having the baby.

Afterward she did tell me that Pablo's birth, the ease, speed and quiet of it, erased all the fear she'd had about birthing ever since she was a little girl and witnessed her brother's birth, so I was glad to have been of service.

Peaches had just been there for a day or two when John Berry and Larry somebody showed up in a box truck. They had been bringing twenty-two cases of beer, but after three days stuck in the mud on the road to Sarteneja, they had agreed to the Mennonites' terms and paid them twenty cases for a pull out with their tractor. There was about a case left. Larry handed me a bag of weed and asked me if I could bake it into a cake. I was pretty unschooled in the world of edibles, but I melted the butter, crumbled in the weed and made a decent enough cake for someone who didn't have an oven.

When it was cool, Larry broke off a nice big chunk and gave it to Rasta, who gobbled it down before I could stop him. Larry sneered at me, "Well I knew *you* wouldn't give him any!" As if that made me an uptight mom, that I didn't give my two-year-old weed. Peaches and I looked at each other like, *Now What?* She wisely told me, "Well, there's nothing we can do about it now, so we'll just have to keep an eye on him."

Nothing much happened. I got kind of a headache from watching him so intently and his (Rasta's) eyes got more sparkly than usual. That was really it.

I didn't care for Larry. He was a hard ass drug smuggler and obviously an asshole. If I was mad at a Mexican Customs and Immigration officer giving Rasta a lollipop, imagine the smoke coming out of my ears at this jerk-off. But he was Doug's big buddy, probably someone Doug needed to make money with, so I kept myself and the kids as far away from him as possible. In Texas, Larry had macaws that had ripped his girlfriend's earrings from her ears. She was really pretty, except for the scars around her ears, but obviously dumb as a stump because she was still with him.

After Larry and John left, when Pablo was about a month old, my old friend Lenny and his girlfriend Jeanne came from California. Lenny was Glenn's best friend, and one of mine. He's the greatest guy, light-hearted and fun. For the next thirty-five years, Lenny continued to be really close friends with both me and Glenn, even though Glenn wouldn't talk to me or allow me in his presence. When we met up in New York, Lenny stayed first at Glenn's for a few nights, then got together with me. It couldn't overlap. Glenn was always pissed at him for staying friends with me, which made Lenny laugh, which surely pissed Glenn off more!

Jeanne Brown, Lenny's great love and wondrous goddess woman, helped me organize my stuff; we were going back to the States. Winter was over, and Doug needed to earn some money. We all left Sarteneja, Lenny and Jeanne to continue their Belizean vacation before going back to California, and us back to Georgia.

It was May, 1979. Pablo was almost four months old. Rasta was nearly three years. Doug and I decided to settle in Blairsville, GA because we had friends there, actually people he did coke business with. We were staying with them when my parents came for a visit and bought a funky little old farmhouse on twenty acres for $27,000. Bert was retiring soon and wanted to be around his grandsons. Gaham was horrified at the thought of moving to a small town in the South, because she had grown up in one in Alabama, and knew just what it was like. The idea was Doug and the kids and I would live in the little old farmhouse, which we did, and Gaham and Bert would build some exalted structure up the hill from us, which they never did.

We moved into our house, which was wonderfully cool and shady in the summer and freezing ass cold in the winter. Doug's family came up often. His father shot our only black snake, because it was a snake. I yelled at him for it, but of course it was too late.

We tore all the old wallpaper off and realized we'd just removed our insulation, four or five layers of it. This was the old house where Mike Thevis, DJ's pornographer boss in Atlanta, had hidden out from the FBI years before. We found bags of weed all dried out between the layers of wallpaper. Once we peeled all that wallpaper off, we could see daylight through the boards! Insulate and cover as we might, that little house stayed freezing cold in the winter until my dad, who owned it, burned it down after a particularly horrible renter trashed it beyond repair when I moved away. Especially after prison camp, he hated things that smelled really bad.

And so ended the 70's, me stoking the woodstove in a freezing-ass house with a baby and a toddler to keep warm, while Doug spent all the time he could up North in Woodstock, hanging with my old friends. This doesn't sound like me, does it? No, I didn't think so either.

Afterward and Acknowledgements

Writing this book really started forty years ago telling Rasta and Pablo stories. They were my most enthusiastic audience, my cheering section, my support team. They still are.

Writing is mostly a solitary process but bringing it to publication is not. Clare Newbury, my editor, held my hand from the time we met to her final edit. I am grateful for both her editing skills and her total lack of judgment about my life. Just when I'd think about quitting, an email from Clare would arrive with corrected copy and enthusiastic support. She passed away unexpectedly recently and I will deeply miss her help and friendship.

Johnny Starbuck, living in Mexico now, agreed to read for me after some hesitation. I believe he didn't want to get bored and/or find out this was a piece of shit and have to be the one to tell me! Instead, he sent me a note halfway in: "I never knew you were this interesting!" He is the most prolific reader I have ever known, so I take it as a great compliment.

Chuck Rogers painted the cover and created my great logo woman. We've been friends nearly forty years, and it was always going to be him that did my book cover. He may not have known that, but I did. He made Doug taller and thinner, which he would appreciate, and me look kinda hot, I think.

My friends from these days: Susan, Martine, Cindi, Nan have all filled in with memories I'd lost as well as giving love and support.

Pablo has been absolutely invaluable in formatting this book. Some people think having a template makes it a piece of cake. I am so not one of them. Thank God he's got all this together and was able and willing to help.

Thanks to my parents for raising me, much to their bemused consternation, and trying their level best to foster what was unique and fun in me. They did drive me crazy, but no more than I did them. Their love and acceptance made my life of adventure and freedom possible.

Thanks to all the great memoir writers who have had the courage to tell their stories. Because of them, I have begun to tell mine. I hope because I have, you will tell yours.

In the end, re-membering all these stories showed me again that love never goes away. It changes, people go off into their own Universes, and then in the moment of reconnection, it is just the same, the connection is there, and the story picks up right where it left off.

Pictures

About the Author

After years as a traveler, meditator, mom, phone conversationalist, yoga teacher, cook, singer, guitar player, entertainer, writer, massage therapist, Reiki Master and TAT Professional, Sukoshi moved to a small town in the North Carolina mountains where she lives with her faithful sidekick, Mimi, writing what she remembers and making up the rest.